Elbridge Henry Goss

The Melrose memorial : the annals of Melrose, county of Middlesex, Massachusetts, in the great rebellion of 1861-65

Elbridge Henry Goss

The Melrose memorial : the annals of Melrose, county of Middlesex, Massachusetts, in the great rebellion of 1861-65

ISBN/EAN: 9783337208226

Printed in Europe, USA, Canada, Australia, Japan

Cover: Foto ©ninafisch / pixelio.de

More available books at **www.hansebooks.com**

THE
MELROSE MEMORIAL

THE

ANNALS OF MELROSE

COUNTY OF MIDDLESEX, MASSACHUSETTS

IN THE

GREAT REBELLION OF 1861–65

BY ELBRIDGE H. GOSS

PRIVATELY PRINTED BY SUBSCRIPTION
1868

TO THE

BOYS IN BLUE,

WHO WENT FORTH TO BATTLE,

FROM

MELROSE,

THIS VOLUME IS RESPECTFULLY INSCRIBED.

PREFACE.

It has been the aim of the writer of the following pages to gather such facts and incidents pertaining to the action of our town, and of its citizens, in the late Rebellion, as may be interesting to us and to those who shall occupy our places hereafter. With what interest would any of us read a similar collection of facts concerning the action of our native town in the Revolutionary war, or the war of 1812; the sacrifices it made, the heroes it furnished, and the martyrs to justice and liberty then offered upon their country's altar.

Soldiers' monuments are appropriate memorials; and it is well that the memory of our dead heroes should be thus embalmed. May scores of monumental piles be yet reared throughout the length and breadth of the land, reminding us and future generations of their bravery, of their virtues, and of their patriotism. And where such monument has or has not been raised, it would be a desirable fact, and an interesting matter of history, if each town, or city, would have a published record of the items of its individual action in the late war. Future generations would turn the leaves of such annals with pleasure and gratitude.

Two years and a half had passed away after the close of the great contest between Right and Wrong, before the task of gathering the material for this volume was commenced. Had it been undertaken sooner, or begun and continued during the progress of the war, the labor would have been easier, and, probably, some facts which have been forgotten, and the whirl of time has confused, might have been recorded. Undoubtedly many interesting incidents, which were not minuted at the time of their occurrence, have passed away never to be recalled.

Words of encouragement have ever been given by all my fellow-citizens whenever mention was made of this undertaking; and when information has been sought it has been very readily given. My thanks are due to the Selectmen of the town, past and present, to many of our Soldiers, and to Adjutant-General Cunningham and his gentlemanly clerks, for information given and favors granted.

The well-known historian, Mr. Benson J. Lossing, author of the deservedly popular "Pictorial Field Book of the Revolution," "Pictorial Field Book of the War of 1812," "Pictorial History of the Civil War," "Washington's Home," and many other useful historical works, says, in a letter to me:

"I am glad you have undertaken the work you mention. These local histories will form the solid and reliable materials for the use of future historians, and cannot be too minutely given. They will be of immense value. I hope you will make thorough work. Give the name of every man who took up arms for his country, with brief biographies of the leading ones. You will thus leave an enduring legacy of honor to their posterities."

Believing that something of this kind was due to our town and to those who went forth to fight our battles, this work has been accomplished during moments of limited leisure, and is now submitted to my fellow-citizens with the hope that its faults and deficiencies, — and no one knows better than the writer that they are many, — may be kindly overlooked, and with the wish that some abler pen than mine had been prompted to perform the task.

E. H. G.

MELROSE, Sept. 18th, 1868.

CONTENTS.

		Page.
I.	Index to Names of Melrose Citizens	xi.
II.	Index to Regiments and Batteries	xxvii.
III.	Index to Battles and Engagements	xxviii.

I.

1861. Opening of the Rebellion. — Call for Three Months' Troops. — The Sixth Massachusetts Regiment. — Governor Andrew's Address. — Our Three Months' Men in the Fourth and Fifth Regiments. — The Massachusetts Troops.   1

II.

1861 continued. Call for Three Years' Men. — Our First Town Meeting. — Votes passed. — Enlistments. — Our Men in the Thirteenth Massachusetts Regiment. — Second Regiment. — Twelfth Regiment.   12

III.

1861 continued. Call for more Troops. — Our Men in the Sixteenth Regiment. — Seventeenth Regiment. — Eighteenth. — Twentieth. — Twenty-Second. — Twenty-Third. — Twenty-Fourth. — Twenty-Sixth. — Thirtieth. — Thirty-Second. — Ninety-Ninth New York Regiment. — Second Battery. — Third Battery. — Fourth Battery. — Fifth Battery. — First Cavalry Regiment. — Number of Men furnished in 1861.   20

IV.

1862. Third Call for Troops. — War Meeting. — Town Meeting. — Action taken and Votes passed. — Our Men in the Eleventh Regiment. — Thirty-Third. — Thirty-Eighth. — Thirty-Ninth. — First Heavy Artillery. — Ninth Battery. — Thirteenth Battery. — Second Cavalry. — Third Cavalry.   37

V.

1862 continued. Call for Nine Months' Men. — War Meetings. — Town Meeting. — Action taken and Votes passed. — Our Men in the Fifth Regiment. — Forty-Second. — Forty-Third. — Forty-Fourth. — Forty-Fifth. — Forty-Eighth. — Fiftieth. — Number of Men furnished in 1862.   54

VI.

1863. Conscription Act. — Another Call for Troops. — Town Meeting. — Our Recruiting Committee. — Our Men in the Fifteenth Regiment. — Fifty-Fourth. — Fifty-Sixth. — Fifty-Ninth. — Third Heavy Artillery. — Fourth. — Number of Men furnished in 1863. 71

VII.

1864–5. Town Meetings. — Votes passed. — Injunction. — Recruiting Fund Meetings. — Citizens' Subscription. 82

VIII.

1864. Call for One Hundred Days' Men. — Our Men in Fifth Regiment. — Sixth. — Eighth. — Sixtieth. — Ninety Days' Men. — Seventh Unattached Company. — One Year's Men. — Sixty-First Regiment. 93

IX.

1861–5. Navy. — Non-residents credited to Melrose. — Our Men in Naval Service. 99

X.

The Draft of 1863. — Names of the Drafted. — Draft Celebration. — Draft of 1864. — Names of the Drafted. — Substitutes for Enrolled Men. — Representative Recruits. 109

XI.

1861–5. Whole number of Men furnished. — Our Surplus. — Quotas. 123

XII.

1861–5. Relief of Soldiers and their Families. — State Aid. — Subscriptions by Citizens and Churches. — Various methods taken for showing our good will. 130

XIII.

Our "Roll of Honor." — Obituary Notices. — George J. Morse. — George T. Martin. — Henry F. Fuller. — Martin Greene. — William H. Macey. — Sidney R. Morse, 2d. — William F. Barry. — John P. Shelton. — Thomas H. Stevens. — Edmund W. Davis. — Jonas G. Brown. — Benjamin Lynde. — Nathan H. Brand. — Richard Lever. — Augustus Green. — Albert W. Crocker. — James R. Howard. — Francis Peabody. — George E. Richardson. — Benjamin F. Wide. — John E. Sullivan. — George W. Lynde. — William F. Krantz. 137

XIV.

In Rebel Prisons. — Forty-Second Regiment. — Archibald Boyle. — Henry H. Jones. — George E. Richardson. — Albert W. Crocker. — William H. Eastman. — Edmund W. Davis. — George W. Batcheider. — John L. Chambers. — Benjamin F. York. — Frederick W. Krantz. — George W. Elliot. — John E. Quinn. — Henry Stone. — Andersonville.   185

XV.

Close of the Rebellion. — Fall of Richmond. — Death of President Lincoln. — Funeral Ceremonies. — Rev. Henry Baker's Address.   205

XVI.

Miscellaneous. — Cost of the War to Town. — To Citizens. — List of Town Officers. — Valuation. — Table of Debt. — Table of Bounties. — Of Men. — Destruction of Rebel Blockade Runner. — Farragut's Naval Victory at Mobile. — Incidents. — Articles Exchanged.   229

XVII.

List of Commissioned Officers. — Alphabetical Roll of Melrose Soldiers. — Melrose Men on other Quotas.   241

APPENDIX.

A. Certificate of a Non-resident Recruit   277
B. Form for Payment of Bounty   277
C. Certificate of Consent to the Enlistment of a Minor   278
D. List of Citizens liable to Draft in 1863   279
E. Exemption Certificates   285
F. Exemption — Substitute for Enrolled Man   287
G. Receipt and Certificate — Representative Recruit   289
H. Instructions to Enrolling Officer   290
I. Discharge Papers   291
J. Town Action Nov. 3, 1868   292

I.

INDEX

TO THE

NAMES OF MELROSE CITIZENS.

———•———

SOLDIERS IN SMALL CAPITALS.

A.

PAGE.
Abbott, Benjamin F., M. D. 90, 222
Adams, John Q. 89, 283
Alden, David A. 118, 279
Allen, John L. 87, 114, 279
Allen, William H. 86, 279
ANDERSON, JOHN H. L. 96, 118, 244, 279
ANDERSON, LEONARD B. 62, 244
ANDREWS, EDWIN A. 32, 244
Andrews, John L. 89
Astle, Abel, M. D. 90
Astle, James 89, 113, 279
Atwood, Joel 89
Atwood, Sullivan C. 90, 279
Avery, Ephraim 222
Avery, John Q. A. 283

B.

Babb, Walter 56, 83, 89, 113, 279
Bacon, George A. 40, 56
Baker, Rev. Henry 211, 212, 214
Baldwin, John 86, 283
Banfield, Addison W. 56, 279
Barker, Josiah H. 91
Barker, Samuel 89, 283
BARNARD, JOHN M. JR. 59, 244

INDEX.

	PAGE.
Barnes, Rev. William S.	211, 212, 213, 225
Barrett, Artemas	88, 120, 222, 225
Barrett, Augustus	86, 283
BARRETT, CHARLES	59, 244
BARRETT, CHARLES L.	59, 244
BARRETT, DAVID A.	272
Barrett, Henry W.	112, 279
Barrett, Jonathan	88, 113, 279
Barrett, James A.	87, 279
BARRON, ELLIOT F.	66, 244
BARRON, HENRY	27, 244
BARRY, ROYAL P.	63, 90, 244, 278
BARRY, WILLIAM F.	15, 43, 139, 149, 244
Bartlett, George W.	88, 283
Bartlett, Nathaniel J.	86, 112, 279
BATCHELDER, GEORGE W.	9, 27, 31, 187, 242, 244
Batchelder, Peter	89
Beckett, James M.	87, 222
Biathrow, Franklin	279
Bickford, Ira H.	86, 283
BICKFORD, NELSON W.	40, 47, 244
Biffin, James	118, 279
Bigelow, Liberty	88
Bird, Henry S.	283
Bishop, Daniel H.	279
Blaisdell, Charles H.	87, 114, 279
Blake, John	222
Blanchard, Samuel D.	92
BOARDMAN, CHARLES	59, 88, 244
Boardman, George F.	88, 224, 283
Boardman, William W.	283
BODWELL, HENRY A.	28, 100, 244
BOGLE, ARCHIBALD	23, 35, 70, 80, 187, 189, 241, 244
Bowker, Charles F.	90
Bowker, Joel	87
Bowker, Joseph C.	91
Brackett, Gilbert A.	279
Bradford, Erastus F.	87, 283
BRAND, NATHAN H.	40, 50, 140, 246
Brooks, Augustus	91, 283
Brown, Benjamin	283

INDEX.

	PAGE.
Brown, George E.	90, 279
Brown, Increase H. Jr.	283
Brown, John	283
BROWN, JONAS G.	66, 139, 159, 246
Brown, Laroy	279
Brown, Oren	113, 279
Bryant, Dexter	122, 279
Bryant, Hon. Napoleon B.	13, 40, 43, 56, 73, 86, 283
BRYANT, THOMAS O.	59, 246
BUFFUM, ADELBERT A.	29, 246
Buffum, C. Edgar	87
Buffum, Carlon	91, 283
Bugbee, Francis	222
Bugbee, Samuel S.	87, 283
Burgess, William B.	13, 42, 43, 73, 82, 89, 132, 223, 224, 278
Burnham, George P.	223
BURNHAM, OLIVER R.	94, 246
BURNHAM, PASCHAL E.	59, 91, 246
Buttrick, John P.	91
BUTTRICK, JOHN W.	58, 88, 246

C.

Chadbourne, Thomas W.	89, 225
CHAMBERS, JOHN L.	195, 272
CHANDLER, ROSWELL W.	35, 246
Chapin, Calvin N.	90, 283
CHAPIN, JOSEPH A.	51, 246, 277, 278
Chase, Daniel G.	283
Chase, Daniel L.	113, 280
CHASE, EDE K.	58, 246
Chase, Sanford W.	280
CHEEVER, AUGUSTUS L.	76, 114, 246, 280
CHIPMAN, GEORGE A.	63, 89, 94, 243, 246
Chute, Robert J.	87
CLARK, FREDERIC F.	59, 248
Clark, Colonel John H.	13, 39, 43, 55, 73, 82, 83, 87, 116, 118, 132, 224, 278
Clark, William	90, 118, 283
Cleaveland, Nathan S.	283
Close, Emery	91
Cobb, Elisha W.	40, 41, 283
Cobb, John W.	88, 283

xiv   INDEX.

	PAGE.
Coburn, Lewis G.	88, 131, 283
Coburn, Lucius	280
Cochran, Jonathan	222, 223
Cochran, Nelson	56, 88, 222, 225
Coffin, Galen	283
Collins, Walter R.	89
Connell, James	283
Conway, Daniel	91, 283
Conway, John Jr.	88
Coolidge, Charles G.	283
Coolidge, Rev. J. A.	223
Cook, William	113, 280
Cooper, Rev. James	14, 223
CORSON, FREDERIC U.	59, 248
Corson, George G.	280
Cowhey, Thomas	91
COX, JAMES P.	66, 248
CROCKER, JOHN H.	15, 114, 132, 248, 280
CROCKER, JOSEPH C.	62, 248
CROCKETT, ALBERT W.	24, 140, 171, 187, 248
CROCKETT, GEORGE F.	33, 171, 248
Crosby, Anthony	40, 41, 87
Crowley, Jeremiah	86, 283
Curriea, Charles M.	283
Currier, James C.	224
CURRIER, JOHN H.	22, 248
Curtis, Samuel	283
CUTTING, WILLIAM H. JR.	63, 248

D.

Dame, Frank O.	86
Daniels, J. B.	90
Davie, George	283
DAVIS, CHARLES L.	202, 272
DAVIS, EDMUND W.	27, 114, 140, 187, 201, 248, 280
DAVIS, JAMES L.	59, 98, 202, 248
DAVIS, JOHN E.	59, 202, 248
DAVIS, LOAMI G.	46, 77, 202, 248
DAWES, AMBROSE	15, 40, 157, 248
DAWES, RICHARD C.	62, 250
Dearborn, Samuel O.	56, 89, 223

	PAGE
Dennis, Rev. J. S.	223
DESHON, FRANCIS	40, 48, 250
DIX, JOSEPH O.	66, 250
Dodge, James W.	113, 280
Donalavy, William	112, 118, 280
DOUBLE, EDMUND B.	60, 250
Dow, Milo	283
DRAYTON, J. SPENCER	80, 241, 250
Dyer, John A.	283
DYER, N. MAYO	15, 70, 80, 100, 228, 231, 236, 243, 250

E.

EARL, WILLIAM H.	49, 104, 250
EASTMAN, WILLIAM H.	32, 187, 194, 250
Edgerly, Obadiah S.	87, 283
Edgerly, Peter	88, 283
Edmands, Bradford	114
Edmonds, Artemas B.	280
ELLIOT, GEORGE W.	187, 272
ELLIS, JACOB M.	32, 243, 250
Ellis, Martin	89
Ellis, P. Russell	88
Emerson, George	86, 222, 225
Emerson, George 2d.	40, 41, 120, 225, 283, 287
Emerson, George W.	40, 41, 56, 112, 280
Emerson, Isaac	222
Emerson, Isaac Jr.	40, 41, 43, 56, 73, 82, 85, 133, 222, 224, 225, 283
EMERSON, JAMES G.	60, 98, 250
EMERSON, JAMES W.	41, 48, 250
EMERSON, JOSEPH S.	98, 114, 250, 280
Emerson, R. Watson	40, 41, 56, 86, 280
Emery, Joshua Jr.	114, 280
Esty, Charles F.	12
EVANS, THOMAS C.	40, 63, 250

F.

Fairbanks, David	39, 122, 224
Fairbanks, John W.	40, 41, 43
Fairbanks, Joseph A.	86, 112, 280
FARGO, CHARLES O.	77, 250, 280
Farnsworth, George W.	118, 280

xvi   INDEX.

	PAGE.
Farnsworth, William J.	222, 223
FARRELL, MICHAEL	66, 250
Ferdinand, Jasper F.	91
Fernald James H.	280
Fessenden, George F.	283
Finnegan, Dennis	91, 280
Finnegan, Edward	114, 280
Finnegan, William	91, 280
Fennerty, Thomas	280
FISHER, GEORGE W.	22, 91, 252
Fletcher, George M.	13, 43, 73, 82, 86, 133, 222, 223, 224, 225, 278
Flint, Rufus H.	222, 223
Forsythe, George R.	88
FOSS, JAMES T.	63, 252
Foster, Daniel W.	85, 283
Fountain, Francis	90
Freeman, Leander T.	113, 280
Freeman, Thomas	91
French, Alonzo	280
FULLER, GEORGE P.	66, 252
FULLER, HENRY F.	22, 139, 143, 252
Fuller, Lorin L.	223
FULLER, WILLIAM A.	104, 114, 118, 243, 252, 280
Fuller, William E.	82, 83, 222, 223, 224
Furneaux, Charles	88, 280

G.

GALLAGHER, RICHARD	32, 252
Gardner, Elbridge	41, 43, 88, 222, 223
Gateley, John	91, 283
Gilman, G. W.	90
Gilman, Tristram	283
Gilmore, William M.	90, 280
Gooch, Hon. Daniel W.	44, 56, 85, 131, 223, 283, 292
Gooch, Mrs. Daniel W.	134
Goodwin, Joseph	113, 118, 280
Gordon, Curtis S.	113. 280
Gordon, William F.	112, 280
Goss, Allen C.	56, 87, 283
Goss, Elbridge H.	40, 41, 88, 113, 155, 176, 280, 292
Gould, Albert A.	91, 283

INDEX.   xvii

                                                           PAGE.
Gould, Levi S.   . 56, 85, 86, 225, 280
Greeley, William P.   283
Green, Aaron   92, 223, 224, 225
GREEN, AUGUSTUS   . 28, 140, 169, 252
Green, Elbridge   90, 222, 223, 225
Greene, Benjamin F.   . 87, 280
Greene, Joseph H.   . 86
GREENE, MARTIN   . 18, 139, 252
GROVER, ANDREW J.   . 28, 76, 252, 280
GROVER, GEORGE W. JR.   . 77, 114, 252, 280
GROVER, JOHN C.   . 25, 252
GROVER, WILLIAM W.   . 94, 252
Grundy, William   . 280

                      H.

Haley, Reuben T.   . 92, 284
Hamblet, James Jr.   . 284
HAMMOND, GEORGE   . 77, 104, 114, 254, 280
HARE, ANDREW   . 65, 254
HART, ABNER B.   . 62, 254
Hart, George   . 86, 284
HARVEY, FRANKLIN   104, 254
Hawkins, John   . 280
Hawkins, Thomas   119, 284
HAYNES, JOSEPH W.   . 25, 254
Hayward, Daniel E.   . 280
Hayward, Jabez G.   90, 284
Harris Augustine   . 280
Heald, S. W.   . 86
Heath, George W.   39, 40, 120, 131, 284
Hemmenway, George   . 89, 284
Hemmenway, William   . 280
Henderson, John H. B.   . 114, 134, 280
HETON, JOHN   . 60, 254
Hicks, Walter   . 284
Higgins, John S.   . 87, 131
Hill, David   . 284
Hill, William L.   . 280
Hodges, James D.   . 284
Hoeffner, Lewis G.   . 284
Holbrook, Joseph   119, 223, 284
        c

INDEX.

	PAGE
Hollahan, Lawrence	280
HOLLIS, HENRY P.	52, 254
Holmes, Philip B.	56, 131
Hopkins, James S.	280
Horn, James	284
Houghton, Samuel S.	85
HOWARD, AVERY B.	33, 254
Howard, Caleb	89, 222, 223, 224
Howard, Caleb G.	280
HOWARD, JAMES R.	40, 48, 140, 173, 254
Howard, Nathaniel	92
Howard, Otis	280
HOWE, FRANCIS E.	32, 254, 280
Howes, Jonathan C.	112, 280
Howes, Solomon L.	91
Hudson, Jarvis P.	87, 118, 284
Hurley, John	91
HYDE, GEORGE S.	60, 254

I.

Ingalls, Rev. John C.	136, 223
INGALLS, SAMUEL, M. D.	243, 254
IRESON, ALONZO D.	60, 254
IRESON, DAVID A.	59, 254
Irvine, Fayette J.	281
Isburgh, Charles H.	40, 43, 55, 73, 83, 86, 133, 225, 284

J.

JACKSON, JACOB F.	21, 256
JACKSON, WILLIAM H.	49, 256
JACKSON, WILLIAM P.	15, 256, 281
Jefferson, Daniel	87, 284
Jenkins, Osmore	91
Jones, Asa H.	89
JONES, CHARLES S.	40, 49, 256
JONES, HENRY H.	14, 187, 256
JONES, J. WESLEY	36, 70, 80, 242
JUDKINS, ROLAND C.	59, 256
JUNKINS, EDWIN W.	64, 256

K.

Kastner, Charles	131
Keating, Thomas	281
Keith, Charles E.	89, 113, 281

INDEX.

	PAGE.
Kelley, Farnsworth	284
KENDALL, EDWARD W.	22, 175, 243, 256
Kendall, Samuel E.	284
Kent, Elisha V.	284
Keyes, Silas	281
KILBY, THEOPHILUS	15, 256
KING, GEORGE L.	15, 256
Kimball, Thomas J.	88, 284
Kirmes, Christopher	89, 284
Knight, Edwin F.	281
Knights, Edward R.	87, 222, 224, 281
Knowles, Theodore L.	40, 41, 113, 281
KRANTZ, FREDERICK W.	46, 187, 203, 256
KRANTZ, WILLIAM F.	140, 272

L.

Lane, Addison	90, 284
Lamkin, Guy	223
Lamson, William A.	92, 284
Larrabee, Charles	87
Leavitt, Rufus	87, 284
LEEDS, SAMUEL	21, 258
LEIGHTON, WILLIAM F.	3, 258
Leonard, Henry A.	87, 281
LEVER, RICHARD	74, 140, 258
Linikin, Benjamin	223
Little, Edmund B.	90, 284
LITTLEFIELD, CUSHING W.	29, 258
Littlefield, Walter Jr.	86, 223, 284
Littlehale, Henry A.	281
Locke, Simeon	86
Long, Thomas A.	85, 87
Lord, Samuel	281
Loring, Martin B.	91, 284
Lunt, George G.	281
LYALL, DAVID S.	96, 258, 281
LYMAN, HENRY H.	66, 258
Lynch, John B.	281
Lynde, Alonzo V.	86, 284
Lynde, Alvin	90
LYNDE, AMOS W.	60, 97, 258

INDEX.

	PAGE.
LYNDE, BENJAMIN	41, 48, 140, 161, 258
Lynde, Charles A.	281
LYNDE, CHARLES B.	60, 258
Lynde, Charles P.	90
Lynde, Daniel A.	281
Lynde, George	91
LYNDE, GEORGE W.	23, 141, 161, 183, 243, 258
Lynde, James O.	120, 281
Lynde, Leonard	88, 281
LYNDE, SHERMAN	35, 260
Lynde, William O.	87, 284

M.

MACEY, JAMES	18, 260
MACEY, JOHN S.	23, 104, 175, 260
MACEY, WILLIAM H.	139, 272
Macomber, George, M.D.	87
Magoon, Sylvanus	119, 281
Mansfield, George A.	86, 225, 284
Marcey, J. T.	91
MARSHALL, JAMES	64, 260
MARSHALL, SAMUEL	60, 260
MARTIN, CHARLES H.	202, 272
MARTIN, GEORGE T.	47, 70, 78, 138, 179, 202, 242, 260
Martin, Jeremiah	88, 222
MARTIN, JEREMIAH JR.	105, 202, 260
MARTIN, WILLIAM H.	41, 48, 202, 260
MCALLISTER, DANIEL W.	28, 260
MCALLISTER, GEORGE H.	66, 260
McCafferty, Michael A.	56, 281
McCoubry, Thomas	284
MCDONALD, ANGUS	26, 260
McIntire, Joseph	88, 284
MCKAY, GURDON	9, 26, 35, 69, 243, 260
MCLAUGHLIN, FRANK M.	105, 260
MCLAUGHLIN, GEORGE W.	64, 260, 278
McLaughlin, Hiram	278
MCLAUGHLIN, HIRAM JR.	95, 260
McLenathan, Charles	281
MCMAHAN, PHILIP	24, 260
McNish, Wickham C.	85

INDEX.   xxi

	PAGE.
Mendum, Josiah P.	56, 88
Merrick, Theodore B.	225, 281
Messenger, Charles A.	89, 284
Messenger, Frank A.	40, 56, 86, 284
MITCHELL, GEORGE	105, 260
Moore, Edward	91
Morcomb, Henry P.	281
MORRISON, CHARLES H.	28, 47, 260
MORRISON, SETH	9, 260
Morse, Andrew J.	131, 132, 209
MORSE, GEORGE J.	16, 76, 80, 138, 162, 236, 242, 260
MORSE, SIDNEY B. 2d.	17, 139, 145, 162, 262
Morse, William	114, 281
Morse, William F.	86, 113, 281
Morton, Daniel O.	88, 284
Mosely, Randolph L.	281
Munn, Lawrence K.	90, 281
MUNN, THOMAS J.	16, 262
Munroe, Rev. William H.	158, 223
Murphy, Walter	91
Murray, John	281

N.

Nash, Gilbert	225
Nevens, Edward P.	223, 225
Newhall, Edward B.	88, 119, 281
Newhall, George	87, 222, 224, 284
Newhall, Henry B.	56, 88, 281
Newhall, John	284
NICHOLS, GEORGE G.	78, 97, 242, 262
NICHOLS, SMITH W. JR.	36, 70, 80, 105, 107, 243, 262
Norris, Henry A.	42, 43, 56, 86, 223
Norton, Daniel Jr.	56, 85, 284
Norton, John R.	281
Noyes, George N.	87, 223, 225
NOYES, GEORGE O.	41, 48, 262
Noyes, Moses A.	90

P.

PAGE, MOSES S.	95, 113, 262, 281, 291
Paine, John T.	223
Parker, Edward	281

INDEX.

	PAGE.
Parker, Moses, M. D.	40, 56, 87, 223, 225, 284
Parsons, Rev. Wilson R.	223
Patterson, Alonso	89, 118, 281
Paul, William F.	118, 281
PEABODY, FRANCIS	23, 28, 140, 175, 262
PEABODY, TORREY	28, 262
PEABODY, TORREY JR.	25, 262
Peck, Oren H.	86, 114, 281
Pemberton Calvin	284
PEMBERTON, LEWIS E.	98, 264
Perkins, Albert P.	87, 284
Perkins, Horatio N.	88
PERKINS, JAMES F.	70, 80, 107, 243, 264, 292
PERKINS, JOHN JR.	64, 118, 264, 284
Phinney, Erastus O., M.D.	223, 225
Phinney, Stephen J.	222
Phippen, German S.	223
Pierce, Ansel B.	91, 281
Pierce, Robert W.	88, 281
Pierce, William L.	90
PIKE, JACOB F.	49, 264
PILLING, JAMES L.	97, 264
Pollock, George W.	88, 281
Poole, William F.	89, 126, 131, 220, 284
Porter, Lucius L. D.	113, 281
PRATT, DANIEL S.	35, 264
Pratt, Dexter	90, 281
PRATT, HENRY W.	96, 264
PRENTICE, CHARLES	67, 264
Prentice, Rev. George	281
PRESCOTT, HORACE	40, 51, 264
PRINCE, ALBERT G.	25, 264

Q.

Quimby, Rev. George W.	43, 44
QUINN, JOHN E.	31, 172, 187, 264
QUINN, JOHN H.	31, 264
QUINN, PATRICK	96, 264
Quinn, Thomas	282

R.

Rankin, Frederick W. A. Jr.	88, 113, 282
Richards, Aaron H.	282

INDEX. xxiii

	PAGE.
RICHARDSON, GEORGE E.	41, 49, 140, 177, 187, 264
Richardson, Hiram D.	90
RICHARDSON, JOHN P.	23, 264
Richardson, Lewis H.	90, 113, 282
RICHARDSON, WILLIAM H.	77, 266, 282
Richmond, Rev. John B.	225
Ripley, Augustus	118, 282
Roach, Benjamin	90
Robbins, Charles	112, 282
Robbins, Charles G.	285
ROBERTS, CHARLES H.	62, 266
Roberts, John K.	285
Roberts, Joseph L.	282
Robinson, Henry	91, 223
Robinson, Henry J.	91
Robinson, Luther	225
Robinson, Samuel A.	118, 282
Robson, John	89
Rowe, Ai	91
ROWELL, STEPHEN P.	26, 65, 266
Russell, Daniel	40, 41, 122, 285, 289

S.

Sales, Ephraim	285
Sanford, Joseph B.	225, 282
Sargent, George	90
Sargent, George B.	89
Sargent, George C.	87
Sargent, Wingate P.	85, 224, 285
SASSARD, AUGUSTUS	16, 266
Sears, Elisha F.	85, 282
SEAVEY, LEONARD C.	33, 266
Selee, Rev. Nathan P.	90, 225
Sessions, Rev. Alexander J.	223
Severance, Sargent F.	87, 285
Severy, Solomon	89, 285
Sewall, John S.	56, 88, 285
Sewall, Hon. Samuel E.	85, 131, 225, 292
Sewall, Stinson	224
SHANNON, MARTIN	29, 266
SHELTON, ALBERT F.	16, 113, 266, 282

INDEX.

	PAGE.
SHELTON. CHARLES W.	17, 150, 152, 266
Shelton, John	87, 223
SHELTON, JOHN P.	17, 40, 139, 154, 266
Shelton, Richard H.	113, 282
Shelton, Stephen	71, 88, 225, 290
Shelton, Stephen W.	55, 56, 73, 83, 113, 133, 153, 158, 282
SHELTON, THOMAS	39, 67, 96, 266
Shepard, Charles H.	222
Shepard, Thomas	285
Simonds, Charles H.	223, 285
SIMONDS, JOSEPH F.	17, 53, 236, 242, 266
SIMONDS, JOSEPH R.	24, 35, 70, 80, 144, 225, 242, 266
SIMONDS, JOSEPH W.	61, 96, 266
SKINNER, CHARLES E.	34, 266
Skinner, Glover	282
SLOCOMB, HENRY W.	30, 268
Slocum, Asa	222
SMALL, EDWARD A.	70, 80, 108, 243, 268
Small, James	90
Small, James M.	282
Smith, John	88, 224
Smith, Rufus	39, 40, 44, 55, 56, 73, 83, 85, 133, 225, 282
SMITH, THOMAS	9, 33, 268
SMITH, WAYLAND R.	61, 268
Snow, Joel	56, 91, 225
Southwick, E. B.	91
SPAULDING, HENRY H.	95, 268, 285
Spinney, William K.	282
Sprague, Alfred W.	89, 285
Sprague, Henry	222, 223
SPRAGUE, SAMUEL JR.	19, 268
Stantial, George C.	89, 282
STANTIAL, THOMAS B.	34, 268, 282
Steele, Azel E.	90
STEBBINS, THADDEUS S.	50, 268
STEVENS, CHARLES H.	34, 243, 268
STEVENS, THOMAS H.	21, 139, 268
Stevens, Edgar M.	86, 285
Stevens, Rev. Henry A.	213, 214, 282
STILPHEN, JOHN E.	33, 141, 181, 268
Stone, Calvin	90

INDEX. XXV

	PAGE.
Stone, George F.	55, 86, 282
STONE, HENRY	49, 76, 187, 268
Stone, William H.	86, 113, 282
Stratton, William D.	90, 282
Sturtevant, James S.	90
Summers, Samuel F.	89
SUMNER, STEPHEN	58, 268
Sutton, Joseph P. B.	282
SWEETSER, THOMAS T.	60, 268

T.

TAINTER, GEORGE A.	17, 268, 282
Talbot, Rev. Josiah W.	223
Tay, Aaron	282
Taylor, Fernando C.	56, 87, 118, 285
Taylor, Franklin	222
Taylor, Shubael L.	222, 223
Taylor, Marcus C.	282
Taylor, William	282
Terwillager, Lyell T.	89, 118, 285
THOMPSON, JOHN	114, 118, 272, 282
Thresher, James M.	222
Tourtellot, Samuel M.	89, 282
TOWER, BENJAMIN	41, 48, 268
Tower, John W.	88, 282
Towner, Levi C.	282
Trask, Albert	282
Trott, Andrew P.	86, 113, 282
Trowbridge, Henry E.	225, 285
TUCKER, WILLIAM L.	41, 50, 268
Turner, Henry	285
TYLER, WILLIAM N.	95, 268

U.

Underwood, Benjamin	89
Upham, Albert	282
Upham, Asa	223
Upham, Benjamin R.	285
Upham, Charles F.	91, 282
UPHAM, CHARLES H.	60, 270
Upham, Freeman	222

UPHAM, HENRY W.	97, 270
Upham, Joshua	223
Upham, Orne	285
Upham, Osgood W.	112, 282, 286
Upham, Sylvanus	88, 282
Upham, Timothy	118, 282

V.

Varney, Cyrus	285
Vaughn, William W.	90, 282
Vial, John	223
Vinton, Aaron Jr.	285
VINTON, EDWIN A.	60, 96, 270
VINTON, GRAY	96, 270, 285

W.

Waitt, Charles A.	113, 282
WAITT, JOHN R.	95, 270
Walker, Benjamin R.	91
Warren, Ralph	86, 285
Warren, William	282
Watson, Frank	282
WELLS, CHARLES A.	45, 270
Wells, William H.	89, 282
Wentworth, Oliver T.	92
West, John	285
Westgate, Joseph E.	87
Wheeler, Gardner	86, 118, 285
Wheeler, George G.	86, 285
Wheeler, Robert	92, 285
White, Alverse L.	85
WHITE, CHARLES L.	40, 45, 270
White, George E.	223
WHITNEY, EDWARD H.	17, 270
Whowell, John	285
Whyte, Oliver	86, 285
WILDE, BENJAMIN F.	60, 141, 270
Wilde, Joseph D.	85, 282
Wilcox, Daniel W.	43, 120, 282
Wilkinson, William N.	222
Woodward, David R.	119, 285

	PAGE.
Woodward, George	91, 282
WYMAN, GEORGE W.	95, 272
WYMAN, WESTON	95, 272
WYMAN, WILLIAM	9, 30, 272, 282

Y.

YORK, BENJAMIN F.	79, 187, 202, 272
YORK, JOSIAH R.	60, 98, 202, 272
YORK, WILLIAM B.	60, 98, 202, 272
Young, Isaiah A.	56, 89, 285

II.

INDEX TO REGIMENTS AND BATTERIES.

Second Regiment, Infantry	18
Fourth " "	9
Fifth " "	8, 58, 94
Sixth " "	94
Eighth " "	95
Eleventh " "	45
Twelfth " "	19
Thirteenth " "	14
Fifteenth " "	74
Sixteenth " "	21
Seventeenth " "	22
Eighteenth " "	25
Twentieth " "	26
Twenty-Second Regiment, Infantry	26
Twenty-Third " "	29
Twenty-Fourth " "	29
Twenty-Sixth " "	30
Thirtieth " "	30
Thirty-Second " "	31
Thirty-Third " "	46
Thirty-Eighth " "	46
Thirty-Ninth " "	49
Forty-Second " "	58
Forty-Third " "	61
Forty-Fourth " "	61

INDEX.

	PAGE.
Forty-Fifth Regiment, Infantry	63
Forty-Eighth " "	65
Fiftieth " "	65
Fifty-Fourth " "	78
Fifty-Sixth " "	79
Fifty-Ninth " "	74
Sixtieth " "	97
Sixty-First " "	98
Seventh Unattached Co., Infantry	97
First Heavy Artillery Regiment	45
Third " " "	76
Fourth " " "	78
Second Light Battery	32
Third " "	33
Fourth " "	33
Fifth " "	34
Ninth " "	50
Thirteenth " "	51
First Cavalry Regiment	34
Second " "	51
Third " "	53
Fifth " "	243
Ninety-Ninth New York Regiment, Infantry	31

III.

INDEX TO BATTLES AND ENGAGEMENTS MENTIONED IN THE TEXT.

Fort Sumter, April 12, 1861	1
Attack at Baltimore, April 19, 1861	8, 145
Big Bethel, June 10, 1861	68
First Bull Run, July 21, 1861	9, 143
Forts St. Philip and Jackson, April 18-23, 1862	38, 104, 107
Fair Oaks, May 31, June 1, 1862	21
Gaines' Farm, June 27, 1862	27, 201
Baton Rouge, Aug. 5, 1862	68, 181
Cedar Mountain, Aug. 9, 1862	18, 68, 139
Thoroughfare Gap, Aug. 28, 1862	151
Groveton, Aug. 29, 1862	146, 150, 162
Second Bull Run, Aug. 30, 1862	16, 25, 28, 146, 151, 155, 163

INDEX.   xxix

	PAGE.
Chantilly, Sept. 1, 1862	146, 150, 162
South Mountain, Sept. 14, 1862	152
Antietam, Sept. 17, 1862	15, 16, 17, 19, 68, 139, 149, 152, 154, 160
Little Washington, Nov. 3, 1862	29
Fredericksburg, Dec. 13, 1862	169, 239
Kinston, Dec. 14, 1862	63, 64
Galveston, Jan. 1, 1863	58, 60, 196
Sabine Pass, Jan. 21, 1863	195
Blount's Mills, April 9, 1863	184
Bisland, April 13, 1863	174, 179
Chancellorsville, May 2-5, 1863	169
Port Hudson, May 27—July 9, 1863, 46, 48, 159, 161, 164, 174, 179, 181, 194	
Gettysburg, July 1, 2, 3, 1863	15, 16, 45, 46, 51, 132, 169, 187, 203
Batchelder's Creek, Feb. 1, 1864	25, 171
Olustee, Feb. 20, 1864	189
Red River Expedition, March 7 — May 20, 1864	53, 181, 199
Mansfield, or Sabine Cross Roads, April 8, 1864	199
Wilderness, May 5, 6, 1864	76, 165, 166
Spottsylvania, May 10-12, 1864	74, 76, 138, 140, 162, 166
Bethesda Church, June 2, 3, 1864	28, 140, 169
Cool Arbor, June 1-3, 1864	187
Mine Explosion, July 30, 1864	79
Mobile Bay, Aug. 5, 1864,	100, 102, 231
Deep Bottom, Aug. 15, 1864	30
Opequan, Sept. 19, 1864	53
Cedar Creek, Oct. 19, 1864	48, 49, 177
Fort Fisher, First Attack, Dec. 24, 25, 1864	104, 105, 106, 108
Fort Fisher, Second Attack, Jan. 13, 14, 15, 1865	104, 106, 108

I.

1861.

By our altars, pure and free ;
By our laws' deep-rooted tree ;
By the past's dread memory ;
  By our Washington —

By our common kindred tongue,
By our hopes — bright, buoyant, young,
By the tie of country strong ;
  We will still be one.
                    Samuel Gilman.

The first gun that spat its iron insult at Fort Sumter, smote every loyal American full in the face.
                    Oliver Wendell Holmes.

On the twelfth of April, 1861, the bloody hand of Treason was lifted against our Nationality, by the bombardment of "Fort Sumter," at Charleston, South Carolina. The "Stars and Stripes," which had hitherto waved aloft so gloriously, and so triumphantly, were now lowered at the impious behests of Slavery, and were trailing in the dust. Great was the surprise, intense the interest, and mighty the indignation which the telegraphic announcement of the fact created throughout the length and breadth of our land. By this infamous act every loyal heart was insulted ; and, at the reception of the news, every such heart was thrilled and stirred to its inmost recesses.

By the insolent assertion of Jefferson Davis, on the 18th of February, 1861, — when the Confederate Government was instituted at Montgomery, Ala., two weeks previous to the inauguration of President Lincoln,[1] — by the firing upon the "Star of the West" when on its errand of mercy, three months before the assault on "Fort Sumter," — by the boast of the Confederate Secretary of War, L. P. Walker, on the day of the bombardment,[2] — by the treasonable and rebellious utterances of the Southern press,[3] — by the seizure of arsenals, forts and other public property, to the amount of many millions of dollars, — by all these acts it became painfully evident that Slavery had determined to break up this Government, or commence a devastating civil war.

"The treasonable menaces, the Ordinances of Secession, the acts of violence and incipient war, which followed the choice of Presidential Electors in 1860, and culminated into flagrant rebellion upon the accession of Abraham Lincoln to the Presidency, had attracted the anxious observation of mankind. Never in the history of civilization had interests so manifold, so transcendent, been involved or threatened by the internal disputes of any nation or people. The industry of thirty millions of

---

[1] "The day of compromise is past, and those who now resist us shall smell Southern gunpowder and feel Southern steel."

[2] "No man can tell when the war this day commenced will end; but I will prophecy that the flag which now flaunts the breeze here, will float over the dome of the old Capitol at Washington before the first of May. Let them try Southern chivalry and test the extent of Southern resources, and it may float eventually over Faneuil Hall in Boston."

[3] The Richmond Whig, with others, reiterated the threats of the Secession leaders, saying, "From the mountain tops and valleys to the shore of the sea, there is one wild shout of firm resolve to capture Washington City at all and every human effort."

human beings, bond and free, the peace, happiness and welfare of every household of our continental Republic, the business of the busiest and richest people under the sun, the strength of Republican Government, the validity of Democratic ideas expressed in civil institutions, the success of Liberty, seemed trembling in the balance, where, poised against each other, were the struggling hope of continued peace, and the dismal presage of civil war. With the fortunes of the American Union were involved, by reason of the intimate complexity of all human relations in the social and political organization of modern times, the prosperity, if not the fate of many nations."[1]

By the attack upon the heroic band of patriots under Major Anderson, at "Fort Sumter," all hope of a peaceful settlement of the issue was extinguished; and, by its fall the mighty energy of the North was aroused.

> "Like some old organ peal,
> Solemn and grand,
> The anthem of Freedom
> Sweeps through the land."

One purpose seemed to spring into existence instantly, and animate every heart — a determination to maintain our national existence at any and all sacrifices. "Heart throbbed to heart, lip spoke to lip, with a oneness of feeling that seemed like a Divine inspiration."

On the instant we saw a "noble and puissant nation rousing herself like a strong man from sleep, and shaking her invincible locks." And, when on the 15th of April, Abraham Lincoln, President of the United States, issued

---

[1] Oration at the Dedication of the "Ladd and Whitney Monument," by Gov. Andrew, at Lowell, June 17, 1865.

his Proclamation,[1] convening an extra session of Congress, and calling upon the States for seventy-five thousand troops to defend the capital and public property, the response was truly wonderful and glorious.

"The plough, the loom, the counting-house, the bar, the pulpit, all the avocations of ordinary life were abandoned; men of all conditions and circumstances flew to arms in response to the call of the nation's Chief Magistrate."[2]

Munificent offers of money were made to the Government by city corporations, banking institutions and private citizens all over the land. The whole loyal North responded in the spirit of "Our Country's Call," by William Cullen Bryant.

> Lay down the axe, fling by the spade :
> Leave in its track the toiling plough ;
> The rifle and the bayonet-blade
> For arms like yours were fitter now ;
> And let the hands that ply the pen
> Quit the light task, and learn to wield
> The horseman's crooked brand, and rein
> The charger on the battle-field.

And, thanks to the foresight, thoughtfulness and energy of Governor Andrew, Massachusetts was ready at once to send forward her regiments to defend the flag and save Washington.

The first call upon Massachusetts for troops was by a telegram from Senator Wilson, April 15th, requesting twenty companies of militia to be sent immediately to Washington, and there mustered into service. Official

---

[1] This Proclamation was received by the Confederate conclave assembled at Montgomery, Ala., with "derisive laughter."

[2] History of the Old Sixth Regiment of Massachusetts Volunteers during its three Campaigns ; by John W. Hanson, chaplain.

requisition from the Secretary of War came later in the day. Governor Andrew at once issued his orders to the commanders of the Third, Fourth, Fifth, Sixth, and Eighth Regiments. On the 17th the Sixth Regiment was on its way, and on and before nine o'clock of the next Sunday, the 21st, — six days only after the call was made, — the Governor was enabled to say that "the whole number of regiments demanded from Massachusetts were already either in Washington, or in Fortress Monroe, or on their way to the defence of the capital." And Edward Everett, speaking at Roxbury a few days later, said: "Wide as the summons has gone forth, it has been obeyed with an alacrity and unanimity that knew no parallel in our history; and the volunteers of Massachusetts have been the first in the field."

To show with what willing obedience and cheerfulness our troops entered the service, it will be necessary only to specify a few facts connected with the Sixth Regiment, which was the "first to offer its services; first to reach its State's capital; first to reach the nation's capital; first to inflict suffering on traitors; first to attest its sincerity with its blood."

The official call was as follows:

COMMONWEALTH OF MASSACHUSETTS,
ADJUTANT GENERAL'S OFFICE, BOSTON, APRIL 15, 1861.

Col. Jones: —

Sir, — I am directed by his Excellency the Commander-in-Chief, to order you to muster your regiment on Boston Common, forthwith, in compliance with a requisition made by the President of the United States. The troops are to go to Washington.

By order of his Excellency the Commander-in Chief.

WILLIAM SCHOULER, *Adjutant General.*

Telegrams and expresses flew to all parts of the command, notifying members of the regiment, which were scattered over four different counties, — Middlesex, Essex, Suffolk, and Worcester, — and in thirty or more cities and towns. Some of the officers, Colonel Jones among them, rode all night in this duty.

> "Up the hill-side, down the glen,
> Rouse the sleeping citizen :
> Summon out the might of men!"

"The 'Middlesex villages and farms' then heard the pounding of hoofs and the alarum cry of danger, as in the olden time they had listened to the midnight ride of Paul Revere."

Most of the men assembled on Boston Common early on the morning of the 16th; the rest within a few hours after. Captain John H. Dike,[1] of the Stoneham Company, was aroused by a messenger at two o'clock on the morning of the 16th, and the order given him. After reading it, he said, "Tell the Adjutant General that I shall be at the State House with my full command, by eleven o'clock." Captain Dike was there, with his company at the appointed hour.

Captain Harrison W. Pratt, of Worcester, received the order to join the Sixth Regiment, with his company, late in the afternoon of the 16th, and was in Boston with his full command on the morning of the 17th.

The Major of the Sixth — Benjamin F. Watson, of Lawrence — had but two hours' notice; but he locked the

---

[1] Severely wounded in the thigh during the passage of the "Sixth" through Baltimore.

door of his law office, leaving a large docket to look out for itself, and important business interests, and for four months saw and knew nothing of them.

A member of one of the companies, living at Concord, said, "when the order came for me to join my company, sir, I was ploughing in the same field in Concord where my grandfather was ploughing when the British fired on the Massachusetts men at Lexington. He did not wait a minute; and I did not, sir."

Many other interesting instances might be mentioned, not only of this, but of all the regiments that then went forth, where lucrative positions and professional pursuits were given up and abandoned cheerfully by our citizens in order that they might go forth and defend their beloved country.

The Sixth Regiment left Boston on the 17th, previous to which it was drawn up in front of the State House, to receive the regimental colors, and Governor Andrew's parting words.

Soldiers, summoned suddenly, without a moment for preparation, we have done all that lay in the power of men to do, — all that rested in the power of your State Government to do, — to prepare the citizen soldiers of Massachusetts for this service. We shall follow you with our benedictions, our benefactions, and prayers. Those whom you leave behind you we shall cherish in our heart of hearts. You carry with you our utmost faith and confidence. We know that you never will return until you can bring the assurances that the utmost duty has been performed, which brave and patriotic men can accomplish.

This flag, sir, take and bear with you. It will be an emblem on which all eyes will rest, reminding you always of that which you are bound to hold most dear.

In reply, Col. Jones said:—

Your Excellency, you have given to me this flag, which is the emblem of all that stands before you. It represents my whole command; and, so help me God, I will never disgrace it.

Two days later,—on the ever memorable 19th of April, —the telegraph flashed the news over the land that the Sixth Massachusetts Regiment was fighting its way through the streets of Baltimore; that four men had been killed and many more wounded. Still deeper was the shock! More intense the feeling! Massachusetts men the first martyrs to this terrible Rebellion! Massachusetts blood the first to flow, and on this anniversary of Concord's opening scene in days of yore! The excitement increased; business was neglected; our Country's wrongs and our Country's danger was the most important and all absorbing topic of conversation.

Like all the cities and towns throughout the loyal North, Melrose realized the excitement and felt the danger as thoroughly as any of them; but being a small town, and having no military organizations, there was no immediate stir in our streets,—no sound of fife and drum,—nor the hurry and bustle consequent upon the gathering of military companies, that was experienced in larger communities; yet its citizens were aroused, and we had several patriotic young men that at once buckled on the armor and moved to the scene of conflict.

Our neighboring town, South Reading,—now Wakefield—possessed a militia company, commanded by Captain John W. Locke, and which belonged to the Fifth Massachusetts Regiment, Colonel Samuel C. Lawrence; and into this company — B — most of our men that went into the field at this time enlisted.

They were as follows :

Batchelder, George W.,[1]
McKay, Gurdon,[2]
Smith, Thomas,[3]
Wyman, William.[4]

The Fifth Regiment performed its duties well, and was in the first "Battle of Bull Run," July 21, 1861,[5] and sustained itself in this fiery ordeal with great credit. It returned to Massachusetts immediately after this battle, and was mustered out of the service on the 31st of July. None of our men were wounded.

In the Fourth Regiment, Colonel Abner B. Packard, Melrose had one man, in Co. F, viz :

Morrison, Seth.

This Regiment was stationed at "Fortress Monroe" during its three months' service. It returned to Massachusetts, and was mustered out July 22d, 1861.

The whole number of troops sent forward by Massachusetts, under this demand for three months' men, was three thousand seven hundred and thirty-six (3,736).[6] They were in five different regiments; and of these regiments it has been well said by Adjutant General Schouler, in his Report to the Governor, for 1861 : —

---

[1] Afterwards re-enlisted in the Twenty-Second Regiment, see chap. III.
[2] Afterwards commissioned 2d Lieutenant in the Twenty-Second Regiment, see chap. III.
[3] Afterwards re-enlisted in the Fourth Battery, see chap. III.
[4] Afterwards re-enlisted in the Twenty-Fourth Regiment, see chap. III.
[5] Union loss in this battle in killed, wounded and missing, 2,992. Rebels lost about 2,500.
[6] Of this number old Middlesex County bore off the palm, sending 882 privates and 57 commissioned officers.

10   THE MELROSE MEMORIAL.

They were the first to respond to the call of the President; first to march through Baltimore to the defence of the capital; the first to shed their blood for the maintenance of our government; the first to open the new route to Washington by the way of Annapolis; the first to land on the soil of Virginia and hold possession of the most important fortress in the Union; the first to make the voyage of the Potomac and approach the Federal city by water, as they had been the first to reach it by land. They upheld the good name of the State during their entire term of service, as well by their good conduct and gentlemanly bearing, as by their courage and devotion to duty in the hour of peril. They proved the sterling worth of our volunteer militia. Their record is one which will ever redound to the honor of Massachusetts, and will be prized among her richest historic treasures. These men have added new splendor to our revolutionary annals; and the brave sons who were shot down in the streets of Baltimore on the 19th of April, have rendered doubly sacred the day when the greensward of Lexington Common was drenched with the blood of their fathers.

Governor Andrew closes his address to the extra session of the Legislature, which was convened on the 14th of May, in the following words: —

But how shall I record the great and sublime uprising of the people, devoting themselves, their lives, their all? No creative art has ever woven into song a story more tender in its pathos, or more stirring to the martial blood, than the scenes just enacted, passing before our eyes in the villages and towns of our dear old Commonwealth. Henceforth be silent, ye cavillers at New England thrift, economy, and peaceful toil! Henceforth let no one dare accuse our Northern sky, our icy winters, or our granite hills! "Oh, what a glorious morning!" was the exulting cry of Samuel Adams, as he, excluded from royal grace, heard the sharp musketry, which, on the dawn of the 19th of April, 1775, announced the beginning of the war of Independence. The yeomanry who in 1775, on Lexington Common, and on the banks of Concord River, first made that day immortal in our annals, have found their lineal representatives in the historic regiment, which, on the 19th of April, 1861, in the streets of Baltimore, baptized our flag anew in heroic blood, when Massachusetts marched once more " in the sacred cause of liberty and the rights of mankind."

II.

1861.

THREE YEARS' MEN.

Northmen, come out!
Forth unto battle with storm and shout!
Freedom calls you once again,
To flag and fort and tented plain;
Then come with drum and trump and song,
And raise the war-cry wild and strong:
Northmen, come out!

Charles Godfrey Leland.

Then, in the name of God, and all these rights,
Advance your standards, draw your willing swords.

Richard III.

On the 3d of May, 1861, President Lincoln issued his second call for troops, which was for volunteers to serve for a period of three years, unless sooner discharged; and on the same day our Selectmen issued a warrant, calling a Town Meeting, to take place at "Concert Hall," on the evening of May 6th. A very large and enthusiastic meeting was accordingly held, at which Mr. Charles F. Esty was chosen Moderator, and the following votes were unanimously passed.

That the Town of Melrose appropriate the sum of three thousand dollars ($3,000) for the relief of the families of the citizens of Melrose, now absent in the service of the United States, or who may hereafter volunteer into the service of the United States, or the State of Massachusetts. Also to aid volunteers of the town in their equipment, and to give such relief in the premises as the exigencies and necessities of each case may require.

Also that above all other appropriations the sum of fifteen dollars per month be paid to those persons having families, and the sum of ten dollars per month to those who are single men, during their time of service in the war now pending.

It was also voted, that the Town Treasurer be authorized to borrow such sums of money as might be wanted from time to time to cover the appropriations then made; and that the Selectmen — Colonel John H. Clark, and Messrs. William B. Burgess and George M. Fletcher, — constitute a Committee to superintend the disbursements of the money thus appropriated.

A stirring and patriotic speech was made by the Hon. N. B. Bryant, ex-Speaker of the House of Representatives of New Hampshire, then a resident of Melrose.

As Melrose raised no whole company for any regiment, our men, as they enlisted, selected the regiment or battery in which they preferred to serve; consequently they were much scattered, and entered many different organizations before the war was ended.

Our earliest enlistments were in the Second, Twelfth and Thirteenth Massachusetts Regiments of Infantry, mostly in the latter regiment, which was commanded by Colonel Samuel H. Leonard, of Boston.

The nucleus of the Thirteenth Regiment was the Fourth Battalion of Rifles, into which our men enlisted when the President issued his call for seventy-five thousand (75,000) troops, or immediately after the assault upon the Sixth Regiment in Baltimore, April 19th, and which was ordered to Fort Independence. As no more troops for a short term were wanted, the Battalion was recruited to a three years' regiment. On a Sunday evening, just before the regiment left for Washington, the fourteen soldiers belonging to Melrose met in the Baptist Church, when the pastor, Rev. James Cooper, presented to each one a Testament, accompanied by an address and prayer. On a flyleaf of each Testament was written, besides the name, the words "God and our Country."

The roll of our men who enlisted in the Thirteenth Regiment at this time, — and later as recruits, — with items of their military history, is as follows:

THIRTEENTH REGIMENT.[1]

Co. A.

CORPORAL.

JONES, HENRY H.

Promoted Corporal April 1, 1863; taken prisoner at "Bat-

---

[1] The Thirteenth Regiment Massachusetts Volunteer Militia was recruited at Fort Independence, Boston Harbor, and left the State for the seat of war July 30, 1861. It was in arduous and faithful service for three years. Most of the stirring scenes in which the "Army of the Potomac" participated were experienced by the Thirteenth. It was in many sharp skirmishes, such as Bolivar, Dam No. 5, etc., and in the following battles: Second Bull Run, South Mountain, Antietam, Fredericksburg, Mine Run, Chancellorsville, Gettysburg, Wilderness, Spottsylvania, North Anna River, Laurel Hill, Cool Arbor,* and Siege of Petersburg.

---

* This battle is given in Adjutant General Schouler's Reports as both Cold Harbor and Coal Harbor; but Mr. Benson J. Lossing, in his History of the Civil War, calls it Cool Arbor, and gives the following note: "Cool Arbor derived its name from a tavern, at a delightful place of summer resort in the woods, for the Richmond people, even so early as the time of the Revolution. The derivation of the name determines its orthography. It has been erroneously spelled Coal Harbor and Cold Harbor."

tle of Gettysburg," July 1, 1863;[1] exchanged May 1, 1864; mustered out of the service with the regiment, Aug. 1, 1864.

PRIVATES.

BARRY, WILLIAM F.[2]

Killed at "Battle of Antietam," Sept. 17, 1862.[3]

CROCKER, JOHN H.

Discharged Dec. 30, 1862, for disability.

DAWES, AMBROSE.[4]

Wounded in head at "Battle of Antietam," Sept. 17, 1862; mustered out with the regiment, Aug. 1, 1864.

DYER, N. MAYO.

Discharged April 15, 1862, to enter the navy.[5]

JACKSON, WILLIAM P.[6]

Discharged Jan. 22, 1863, for disability.

KILBY, THEOPHILUS.

Discharged July 20, 1862, for disability.

KING, GEORGE L.

Mustered out with the regiment, Aug. 1, 1864.

---

[1] For sketch of prison experience, see chap. XIV.

[2] Enlisted July 28, 1862, and joined the regiment Aug. 18, while on the Rapid Ann River, Va.

[3] For obituary notice, see "Roll of Honor."

National loss, at this battle, 12,469; 2,010 killed, 9,416 wounded, and 1,043 missing. Rebel loss about 21,500 in killed, wounded and prisoners.

[4] Enlisted Aug. 7, 1862, and joined the regiment Sept. 9, at Mechanicsville, Md.

[5] For items of naval history, see chap. IX.

[6] Enlisted July 28, 1862, and joined the regiment Aug. 18, on the Rapid Ann River, Va.

MORSE, GEORGE J.

Wounded in hand at "Second Bull Run Battle," July 30, 1862; discharged March 2, 1863, to become 2d Lieutenant in Second Regiment, U. S. Colored Troops, in "Department of the Gulf."[1]

MUNN, THOMAS J.

Taken prisoner at "Second Bull Run Battle," July 30, 1862; paroled on the field of battle;[2] exchanged in September 1862; taken prisoner at "Battle of Gettysburg," July 1, 1863, but left in Gettysburg because wounded in thigh and leg; transferred to Veteran Reserve Corps,[3] May 1, 1864; mustered out July 16, 1864.

SASSARD, AUGUSTUS.

Discharged Nov. 14, 1862, for disability.

SHELTON, ALBERT F.

Wounded in right arm and side at "Battle of Antietam," Sept. 17th 1862; discharged Dec. 23, 1862.

---

[1] Wounded at Siege of Port Hudson, July 5, 1863; resigned July 20, 1863; re-entered the service in the Fifty-Ninth Massachusetts Regiment, see chap. VI.

[2] Held seven days before being paroled; all the food he had during five days of that time was one half pint of corn meal.

[3] The Veteran Reserve Corps was organized April 28, 1863, and consisted of men in the service who had been disabled by wounds or disease, and who had been discharged on account of wounds or other disability resulting from military service, but afterwards re-enlisted. Over 60,000 men entered this Corps, and May 31, 1865, it consisted of 762 commissioned officers and 29,852 enlisted men. It escorted thousands of prisoners, convalescents, recruits and conscripts, held important military lines and positions, aided in the enrolment and draft, or guarded depots of public property.

SHELTON, CHARLES W.[1]

Wounded in face at " Battle of Antietam," Sept. 17, 1862 ; detailed for duty in Adjutant General's Office at Washington, D. C., Dec. 10, 1862 ; transferred as Sergeant to the general service of the U. S. Army, Dec. 1, 1863 ; discharged April 1, 1864.

SHELTON, JOHN P.[2]

Killed at "Battle of Antietam," Sept. 17, 1862.[3]

SIMONDS, JOSEPH F.

Discharged July 5, 1862, for disability.[4]

TAINTER, GEORGE A.

Wounded in right arm at " Battle of Antietam," Sept. 17, 1862; discharged Feb. 14, 1863.

Co. D.

SERGEANT.

WHITNEY, EDWARD H.

Promoted Corporal Nov. 1, 1863; Sergeant Nov. 19, 1863; mustered out with regiment, Aug. 1, 1864.

CORPORAL.

MORSE, SIDNEY B. 2d.

Promoted Right General Guide, with rank of Corporal, July 5, 1862; died at Finley Hospital, Washington, D. C., Sept. 16, 1862, of typhoid fever.[5]

---

[1] Enlisted July 28, 1862, and joined the regiment Aug. 18, on the Rapid Ann River, Va.

[2] Enlisted Aug. 7, 1862, and joined the regiment Sept. 9, at Mechanicsville, Md.

[3] For obituary notice, see " Roll of Honor."

[4] Re-enlisted in the Third Cavalry Regiment, see chap. IV.

[5] For obituary notice, see " Roll of Honor."

Co. E.

PRIVATE.

MACEY, JAMES.

Mustered out with the regiment, Aug. 1, 1864.

We had but one man in each of the Second and Twelfth Regiments, as follows:

SECOND REGIMENT.[1]

Co. G.

PRIVATE.

GREENE, MARTIN.

Wounded in thigh and arm at "Battle of Cedar Mountain,"[2] Aug. 9, 1862; was left at Culpepper, Va., Aug. 17, 1862, in the evacuation of that place, where he undoubtedly died.

---

[1] The Second Massachusetts Regiment was the first loyal three years regiment raised for the United States service, and was mustered in May 11, 1861, and left the State July 8, 1861, under Colonel George H. Gordon. Its experience was arduous and varied, and has been well told by its talented historian and faithful chaplain, Rev. A. H. Quint, D. D. in his "Record of the Second Regiment." The following are the principal battles in which it was engaged: Jackson, Fort Royal, Winchester, Cedar Mountain, Antietam, Fredericksburg, Chancellorsville, Gettysburg, Resaca, Kenesaw Mountain, Peach Tree Creek, Atlanta, Raleigh, and Averysborough.

[2] Called by the Confederates "Battle of Cedar Run," and "Battle of Southwest Mountain." Nationals lost 2,000 killed and wounded, Confederates about the same.

TWELFTH REGIMENT.[1]

Co. A.

CORPORAL.

SPRAGUE, SAMUEL, JR.

Promoted Corporal May 23, 1862; severely wounded in ankle at "Battle of Antietam," Sept. 17, 1862; discharged June 24, 1863.

---

[1] The Twelfth Massachusetts was raised by Fletcher Webster, who, on the day after our boys were shot down in the streets of Baltimore, published the following notice in the Boston papers:

FELLOW-CITIZENS: I have been assured by the Executive Department that the State will accept at once an additional regiment of infantry. I therefore propose to meet to-morrow at ten o'clock in front of the Merchants Exchange, State Street, such of my fellow-citizens as will join in raising this new regiment. The muster-roll will be ready to be signed then and there.

Respectfully,   FLETCHER WEBSTER.

The meeting was held accordingly, Sunday, April 21, the regiment speedily raised and stationed at Fort Warren, Boston Harbor. It left the State July 23, 1861, and was commanded by Colonel Webster until he was killed, at Second Bull Run Battle, Aug. 30, 1862. It was in the following engagements: Second Bull Run, Antietam, Fredericksburg, Chancellorsville, Gettysburg, Wilderness, Spottsylvania, North Anna River, Cool Arbor, and Petersburg.

III.

1861.

THREE YEARS' MEN.

Oh, Star-Spangled Banner! the Flag of our pride!
Though trampled by traitors and basely defied,
Fling out to the glad winds your Red, White, and Blue,
For the heart of the North-land is beating for you!
And her strong arm is nerving to strike with a will
Till the foe and his boastings are humbled and still!
Here's welcome to wounding and combat and scars
And the glory of death — for the Stripes and the Stars!
* * * * * * * * * *
Oh, God of our fathers! this Banner must shine
Where battle is hottest, in warfare divine!
The cannon has thundered, the bugle has blown,—
We fear not the summons — we fight not alone!
Oh, lead us, till wide from the Gulf to the Sea
The land shall be sacred to Freedom and Thee!
With love, for oppression; with blessing, for scars—
One Country — one Banner — the Stripes and the Stars!

Edna Dean Proctor.

Other calls for volunteers to serve for three years, or during the war, were made by the President in the month of July,[1] — 1861,— and our citizens continued to enlist during that and the succeeding months of that year, in the various infantry and cavalry regiments then forming and

---
[1] The total number of men called for in the May and July Proclamations was 582,748; the number obtained was 714,231.

recruiting. Melrose was represented in the following organizations.

SIXTEENTH REGIMENT.[1]

Co. A.

PRIVATE.

STEVENS, THOMAS H.

Died at Boston, March 26, 1863, of chronic diarrhœa.

Co. C.

SERGEANT.

LEEDS, SAMUEL.

Wounded in shoulder at "Battle of Fair Oaks," June 1, 1862;[2] promoted corporal Jan. 10, 1863; re-enlisted Dec. 24, 1863;[3] transferred to 11th Battalion July 11, 1864; promoted Sergeant Nov. 1, 1864; Color-Sergeant soon after; mustered out, by reason of the close of the war, July 14, 1865.

Co. F.

PRIVATE.

JACKSON, JACOB F.

Discharged Nov. 17, 1861, for disability.

---

[1] The Sixteenth Massachusetts left the State Aug. 17, 1861. The lamented Arthur B. Fuller, — killed at the "Battle of Fredericksburg," Dec. 12, 1862, — was its first chaplain. The following are its principal battles: Fair Oaks, Glendale, Malvern Hill, Kettle Run, Chantilly, Fredericksburg, Chancellorsville, Gettysburg, Locust Grove, Wilderness, Spottsylvania, North Anna River, Cool Arbor, and Siege of Petersburg.

[2] Union loss, 890 killed, 3,627 wounded and 1,222 missing. Total 5,730. Confederate loss 5,897.

[3] All veteran soldiers enlisting, or re-enlisting were paid a United States bounty, — in addition to the State and Town bounties, — of $400.

SEVENTEENTH REGIMENT.[1]

Co. A.

PRIVATES.

CURRIER, JOHN H.

Discharged Aug. 26, 1862, for disability.

FISHER, GEORGE W.

Discharged June 23, 1863, for disability.

FULLER, HENRY F.

Died Oct. 6, 1861, at Baltimore, Md., of typhoid fever.[2]

KENDALL, EDWARD W.[3]

Mustered out at expiration of service, Aug. 3, 1864; commissioned 1st Lieutenant, by brevet, Sept. 2, 1864.

---

[1] The Seventeenth Massachusetts was recruited at "Camp Schouler," Lynnfield, and left the State Aug. 23, 1861. It was stationed near Baltimore, Md., for several months, and then sent to New Berne, N. C., and served the rest of its time in the "Department of North Carolina." It was in the battles of Kinston, Goldsboro', Winton, Batchelder's Creek, Weldon, and Wise's Forks. Concerning the good material and personal bearing of the Seventeenth Regiment, in which Melrose was well represented, we have the following testimony of Colonel John Quincy Adams, one of Governor Andrew's personal staff, who was sent into the "Department of North Carolina," in September 1862, to examine and report on the condition of our soldiers. He thus speaks: — "I examined every musket personally, and almost every equipment, and can say, with perfect satisfaction, that their condition, in almost every case, was admirable. The arms, particularly, were as bright as when they were issued. The regiment was then drilled by Lieutenant Colonel Fellows in various evolutions, concluding with the drill as skirmishers, in all which the men showed careful and faithful training and most commendable proficiency."

[2] For obituary sketch, see "Roll of Honor,"

[3] Enlisted July 28, 1862; joined the regiment at New Berne, N. C.

LYNDE, GEORGE W.

Mustered out at expiration of service, Aug. 3, 1864; commissioned 2d Lieutenant, by brevet, Dec. 31, 1864.[1]

MACEY, JOHN S.[2]

Discharged Nov. 11, 1862, for disability.[3]

PEABODY, FRANCIS.[4]

Re-enlisted Jan. 4, 1864; appointed Orderly for Brigadier General I. N. Palmer, Feb. 15, 1864; transferred to new organization July 16, 1864; died at New Berne, N. C., Oct. 3, 1864, of yellow fever.[5]

Co. D.

PRIVATE.

RICHARDSON, JOHN P.

Re-enlisted Jan. 5, 1864; transferred to new organization July 16, 1864; mustered out of service, by reason of close of war, July 11, 1865.

Co. I.

LIEUTENANT.

BOGLE, ARCHIBALD.

Went out as 2d Lieutenant; promoted 1st Lieutenant May 28, 1862; discharged May 20, 1863, to become Major in the Thirty-Fifth United States Colored Troops, in General Wild's Brigade.[6]

---

[1] Died Jan. 30, 1866, of consumption, contracted while in the service; for obituary sketch, see "Roll of Honor."

[2] Enlisted July 28, 1862; joined the regiment at New Berne, N. C.

[3] Afterward entered the navy; see chap. IX.

[4] Enlisted in the Seventeenth Regiment Aug. 11, 1862; joined it at New Berne, N. C.; served previously in the Twenty-Second Regiment; see page 28.

[5] For obituary sketch, see "Roll of Honor."

[6] Previous to entering the Seventeenth, served nearly two months in the Second Battalion of Infantry in the Forts of Boston Harbor. For further details concerning Major Bogle, see Chap. XIV.

PRIVATE.
McMAHAN, PHILIP.

Re-enlisted Jan. 5, 1864; transferred to new organization, July 16, 1864; mustered out July 11, 1865.

Co. K.

CAPTAIN.
SIMONDS, JOSEPH R.

Mustered out at expiration of service, Aug. 3, 1864.[1]

PRIVATES.
CROCKETT, ALBERT W.

Re-enlisted Jan. 5, 1864; taken prisoner at "Battle of

---

[1] We find the following complimentary notice of Captain Simonds in a little pamphlet which appeared in 1864, entitled "Soldiering in North Carolina; being the experiences of a 'Typo' in the Pines, Swamps, Fields, Sandy Roads, Towns, Cities, and among the Fleas, Wood-ticks, 'Gray-backs,' Musquitoes, Blue-tail Flies, Moccasin Snakes, Lizards, Scorpions, Rebels, and other Reptiles, Pests and Vermin of the 'Old North State.'" It was written by Thomas Kirwan, a member of his company. "The Captain Joseph R. Simonds, was a thoroughly patriotic and honest man, a good soldier, with many virtues, and a few faults and foibles, (and what man has not these to a greater or less extent?) He took great pride in the well-being and efficiency of his company; and its good name, and the praise of his superiors for cleanliness, superiority in drill, or having a small sick-list, were to him matters of just pride and gratulation, — and frequently after a creditable performance on drill or parade, he would snap his fingers with delight, and, after dismissal, invite them all to his quarters for a treat. He was careful about the quality of their food, and whenever he could (which was not often) would procure such articles of luxury and dietetic change as would be most likely to promote health. He was uniformly kind, obliging and considerate, and did not look upon his men as mere pieces of mechanism that moved when he pulled the wires. He considered them *men*, — socially his equals, though in reality under his command, and to a certain extent at his mercy. He rarely abused his authority — never maliciously; and though he occasionally did injustice to some deserving men — it was, I think, more from an error of judgment than through design."

Batchelder's Creek," Feb. 1, 1864; died at "Andersonville" Aug. 1, 1864.[1]

HAYNES, JOSEPH W.

Re-enlisted Jan. 5, 1864; transferred to new organization July 16, 1864; mustered out, close of war, July 11, 1865.

PEABODY, TORREY, JR.

Mustered out at expiration of service, Aug. 3, 1864.

GROVER, JOHN C.

Re-enlisted Dec. 28, 1863; transferred to new organization, July 16, 1864; mustered out, close of war, July 11, 1865.

EIGHTEENTH REGIMENT.[2]
Co. E.

PRIVATES.

CARLISLE, JOHN.

Non-resident.[3]

PRINCE, ALBERT G.

Wounded in neck at "Second Bull Run Battle," Aug. 30, 1862; taken prisoner, held five days and paroled; discharged Oct. 15, 1862.

---

[1] For biographical notice, see "Roll of Honor."
[2] The Eighteenth Massachusetts left the State August 28, 1861, and took part in the following engagements: Gaines' Farm, Second Bull Run, Sheppardstown, Fredericksburg, Chancellorsville, Gettysburg, Rappahannock Station, Wilderness, Spottsylvania, Cool Arbor, Petersburg and Weldon Railroad.
[3] Recruit enlisted Aug. 26, 1863.

Co. H.

PRIVATE.

ROWELL, STEPHEN P.

Discharged Jan. 11, 1862, for disability.[1]

TWENTIETH REGIMENT.[2]

Co. A.

PRIVATES.

McDONALD, ANGUS.

Discharged for disability.

HINCKLEY, GEORGE H.

Non-resident.[3]

TWENTY-SECOND REGIMENT.[4]

Co. G.

LIEUTENANT.

McKAY, GURDON.

Commissioned 2d Lieutenant Oct. 1, 1861; dismissed the service Aug. 3, 1863, for being absent without leave.

---

[1] Re-enlisted in Fiftieth Massachusetts, see chap. V.

[2] The Twentieth Massachusetts left the State Sept. 4, 1861, and was in the following engagements: Ball's Bluff, West Point, Fair Oaks, Peach Orchard, Savage's Station, Glendale, Malvern Hill, Chantilly, Antietam, Fredericksburg, Chancellorsville, Gettysburg, Bristoe's Station, Mine Run, Wilderness, Po River, Spottsylvania, Tolopotomy, Cool Arbor, Petersburg, Strawberry Plains, Deep Bottom, Ream's Station, Boydtown Road, Vaughn Road and Farmville.

[3] Enlisted Dec. 20, 1862; for form of certificate taken of non-residents at this time see appendix A.

[4] The Twenty-Second Massachusetts was recruited at Lynnfield, and left the State Oct. 8, 1861. Its first colonel was Hon. Henry Wilson. A flag was presented to this regiment, as it passed through Boston, by Hon. Robert C. Winthrop, in behalf of some citizens, and another in New York, by Hon. James T. Brady, in behalf of the "Sons of Massachusetts" resident in New

SERGEANT.
BATCHELDER, GEORGE W.

Promoted Sergeant Oct. 5, 1861; taken prisoner at "Battle of Gaines' Farm,"[1] June 27, 1862; first carried to "Libby Prison," where he was kept fourteen days, and thence to "Belle Isle," where he suffered the usual severe treatment at the hands of the rebels for sixty-four days; paroled Oct. 18, 1862; exchanged, date unknown; re-enlisted Feb. 1, 1864; transferred to Thirty-Second Massachusetts Regiment Oct. 17, 1864.[2]

WAGONER.
BARRON, HENRY.

Mustered out at expiration of service, Oct. 17, 1864.

CORPORAL.
DAVIS, EDMUND W.

Promoted Corporal June 17, 1862; taken prisoner at "Battle of Gaines' Farm," June 27, 1862; exchanged Aug. 5, 1862; discharged Oct. 20, 1862, at Philadelphia, Pa., for disability.[3]

---

[1] In Adjutant General Schouler's Reports this is called the "Battle of Gaines' Mills;" in Winch's "Chronicles of the Great Rebellion" it is called "Gaines' Mills" and "Gaines' Hill." Lossing calls it "Gaines' Farm." The Confederates called it, in their report, the "Battle of the Chickahominy." The national loss at this battle was about 8,000, 6,000 of which were killed and wounded. Rebels lost 5,000.

[2] See Thirty-Second Regiment, page 31.

[3] Died at Melrose, July 22, 1864.

York. This was a gallant regiment and experienced hard service. It was engaged in the following battles: Yorktown, Mechanicsville, Chickahominy, Malvern Hill, Gainesville, Antietam, Fredericksburg, Chancellorsville, Gettysburg, Rappahannock Station, Wilderness, Laurel Hill, Spottsylvania, Jericho Ford, Little River, Tolopotomy, Bethesda Church, Shady Grove Church and Siege of Petersburg.

PRIVATES.

BODWELL, HENRY A.

Left the regiment after "Second Bull Run Battle," Aug. 30, 1862, and enlisted in Co. K, Sixteenth Regiment Virginia Infantry, Sept. 22, 1862, and served until it was disbanded, June 3, 1863.[1]

GREEN, AUGUSTUS.

Killed at "Battle of Bethesda Church," June 3, 1864.[2]

GROVER, ANDREW J.

Discharged Sept. 18, 1862, for disability.[3]

MORRISON, CHARLES H.

Discharged Jan. 1, 1862, for disability.[4]

McALLISTER, DANIEL W.

Discharged Oct. 9, 1862, for disability.

PEABODY, TORREY.

Discharged Nov. 9, 1862, for disability.

PEABODY, FRANCIS.

Discharged April 21, 1862, for disability.[5]

---

[1] Afterwards served four years in the navy, see chap. IX.
[2] For obituary notice, see "Roll of Honor."
[3] Re-enlisted in Third Heavy Artillery, see chap. VI.
[4] Re-enlisted in Thirty-Eighth Regiment, see chap. IV.
[5] Re-enlisted in Seventeenth Regiment, see page 23.

TWENTY-THIRD REGIMENT.[1]

Co. K.

PRIVATES.

DONAGAN, MAURICE.

Deserted June 11, 1862; non-resident.

SHANNON, MARTIN.

Discharged Oct. 27, 1862, for disability.

TWENTY-FOURTH REGIMENT.[2]

Co. B.

CORPORAL.

BUFFUM, ADELBERT A.

Mustered out at expiration of service, Sept. 24, 1864.

Co. C.

PRIVATES.

LITTLEFIELD, CUSHING W.

Wounded in leg at Little Washington, N. C., Nov. 3, 1862 ; discharged June 28, 1863.

---

[1] The Twenty-Third Massachusetts left the State Nov. 11, 1861, and was in the following engagements : Roanoke, New Berne, Rawles' Mills, Kinston, Goldsboro', Wilcox Bridge, Winton, Smithfield, Heckman's Farm, Arrowfield Church, Drury's Bluff, Cool Arbor, and other engagements before Petersburg, and Kinston 2d.

[2] The Twenty-Fourth Massachusetts left the State Dec. 9, 1861, and took part in the following battles : Roanoke Island, Kinston, Whitehall, Goldsboro', Tranter's Creek, New Berne, James Island, Morris Island, Fort Wagner, Green Valley, Drury's Bluff, Richmond and Petersburg Railroad, Weir Bottom Church, Deep Bottom, Deep Run, Fussell's Mills, Siege of Petersburg, Four Mile Run Church and Darby Town Road.

WYMAN, WILLIAM.

Re-enlisted Jan. 4, 1864; wounded in hand — lost two fingers — in "Battle of Deep Bottom," Aug. 15, 1864 mustered out, at close of war, July 10, 1865.

TWENTY-SIXTH REGIMENT.[1]

Co. A.

PRIVATE.

STARBUCK, GEORGE M.

Non-resident.

THIRTIETH REGIMENT.[2]

Co. B.

PRIVATE.

LANE, FRANCIS W.

Non-resident.

Co. E.

PRIVATE.

SLOCOMB, HENRY W.

Re-enlisted Jan. 1, 1864; mustered out July 10, 1866.

---

[1] The Twenty-Sixth Massachusetts left the State Nov. 21, 1861. Its colonel was Edward F. Jones, of Baltimore fame. It had many of the men that belonged to the old Sixth Regiment, and that went through Baltimore, April 19, 1861. It was in the "Department of the Gulf" the greater part of its time of service. Was in battles of Winchester, Cedar Creek and Fisher's Hill, under General Sheridan.

[2] The Thirtieth Massachusetts was mustered in Jan. 4, 1862, and took part in the following engagements: Vicksburg, Baton Rouge, Plains Stores, Port Hudson, Cox's Plantation, Donaldsonville and Winchester, Cedar Creek and Fisher's Hill under Sheridan. It was the last Massachusetts Regiment in United States service, being mustered out July 10, 1866.

THIRTY-SECOND REGIMENT.[1]
Co. C.
LIEUTENANT.
BATCHELDER, GEORGE W.

Transferred as Sergeant from Twenty-Second Regiment, Oct. 17, 1864; promoted 2d Lieutenant Dec. 4, 1864; 1st Lieutenant, April 1, 1865; discharged, by reason of close of war, June 29, 1865.

PRIVATE.
HANIGAN, JOHN.

Mustered out Oct. 28, 1864; non-resident.

Co. A.
PRIVATE.
QUINN, JOHN F.

Discharged Dec. 4, 1862, for disability.

NINETY-NINTH NEW YORK REGIMENT.[2]
Co. B.
PRIVATE.
QUINN, JOHN H.

Transferred from Co. K; mustered out Feb. 30, 1865.

---

[1] The Thirty-Second Massachusetts was mustered into service Dec. 18, 1861. It was in the following battles: Malvern Hill, Gainesville, Second Bull Run, Chantilly, Antietam, Fredericksburg, Chancellorsville, Gettysburg, Rappahannock Station, Mine Run, Wilderness, Spottsylvania, North Anna River, Tolopotomy, Bethesda Church, Petersburg, Weldon Railroad, Vaughn Road, Dabney's Mills, Boydtown Road and White Oak Road.

[2] Known as the "Union Coast Guard." Massachusetts did not receive credit for the three hundred men she had in it. Melrose paid State aid to the families of Quinn and Gallagher.

Co. G.

PRIVATE.

GALLAGHER, RICHARD.
Mustered out Feb. 30, 1865.

SECOND BATTERY.[1]

LIEUTENANT.

ELLIS, JACOB M.[2]
Promoted Corporal Jan. 1, 1862; re-enlisted Feb. 15, 1864; promoted Sergeant Aug. 1, 1864; 2d Lieutenant, Jan. 8, 1865; discharged, close of war, Aug. 11, 1865.

SERGEANT.

HOWE, FRANCIS E.
Promoted Corporal Aug. 1, 1861; Sergeant, Jan. 1, 1862; discharged Jan. 8, 1863, for disability.

CORPORAL.

ANDREWS, EDWIN A.[2]
Mustered out at expiration of service, Aug. 16, 1864.

PRIVATES.

EASTMAN, WILLIAM H.
Taken prisoner at Bayou Bœuf, June 19, 1863; paroled

---

[1] The Second Massachusetts Battery—Nims'—left the State Aug. 8, 1861, and was in the following engagements: Vicksburg, Baton Rouge, Port Hudson, Sabine Cross Roads, Brashear City, Jackson, Claiborne, Ala., and Daniels' Plantation.

[2] Credited to Boston at Adjutant General's Office, but citizen of Melrose at time of enlistment and since the war. Melrose paid State aid.

July 3, 1863; exchanged Nov. 20, 1863; mustered out, Aug. 16, 1864.[1]

SEAVEY, LEONARD C.

Mustered out at expiration of service, Aug. 16, 1864.

STILPHEN, JOHN E.

Mustered out at expiration of service, Aug. 16, 1864.[2]

THIRD BATTERY.[3]

CORPORAL.

HOWARD, AVERY B.

Promoted Corporal May 14, 1862; mustered out, expiration of service, Sept. 16, 1864.

PRIVATE.

CROCKETT, GEORGE F.

Discharged Jan. 2, 1863, for disability.[4]

FOURTH BATTERY.[5]

PRIVATE.

SMITH, THOMAS.

Re-enlisted Jan. 2, 1864; mustered out, close of war, Oct. 14, 1865.

---

[1] For sketch of prison experience, see chap. XIV.

[2] Died June 25, 1865; for biographical notice, see "Roll of Honor."

[3] The Third Massachusetts Battery — Follett's, afterwards Martin's — left the State Oct. 7, 1861. It took part in the following engagements: Siege of Yorktown, Hanover Court House, Mechanicsville, Gaines' Farm, Malvern Hill, Antietam, Sheppardstown, Leestown, Fredericksburg, Chancellorsville, Middlebury, Gettysburg, Mine Run, Wilderness, Laurel Hill, Spottsylvania, North Anna River, Bethesda Church, Cool Arbor, Petersburg, Six Mile Station, and Petersburg and Weldon Railroad.

[4] Afterwards re-enlisted in same battery in the quota of Mansfield.

[5] The Fourth Massachusetts Battery — Manning's — left the State Nov. 20, 1861, and was in the following engagements: Pontichoula, Baton Rouge, Bonfouca, Bisland, Cotten, Port Hudson, Vermilion, and Siege of Mobile.

FIFTH BATTERY.[1]

ARTIFICER.

STANTIAL, THOMAS B.

Discharged July 25, 1862, by reason of the abolishment of the office.

PRIVATE.

SKINNER, CHARLES E.

Discharged Oct. 9, 1863, for disability.

FIRST CAVALRY.[2]

Co. G.

LIEUTENANT.

STEVENS, CHARLES H.

Entered the service as private in Co. B; promoted 1st Sergeant Co. G, March 8, 1863; 2d Lieutenant Jan. 2, 1864; acted as such during remainder of service, but not mustered in; wounded through left hand at Deep Bottom, Va., July 28, 1864; mustered out as Sergeant, Sept. 16, 1864.

---

[1] The Fifth Massachusetts Battery — Eppendort's, afterwards Phillips' — left the State Dec. 25, 1861. It took part in the following battles: Yorktown, Hanover Court House, Mechanicsville, Gaines' Farm, Malvern Hill, Second Bull Run, Fredericksburg, Chancellorsville, Gettysburg, Rappahannock Station, Mine Run, Wilderness, Spottsylvania, North Anna River, Bethesda Church, Petersburg, Weldon Railroad, and Hatcher's Run.

[2] The First Massachusetts Cavalry, — "the eyes of the army," — was mustered in Nov. 1, 1861, and was in the following engagements: Poolesville, South Mountain, Antietam, Fredericksburg, Chancellorsville, Brandy Station, Aldie, Upperville, Gettysburg, Williamsport, Culpepper, Auburn, Todd's Tavern, Fortifications of Richmond, Vaughn Road, St. Mary's Church, Cool Arbor, and Bellefield.

CORPORAL.

LYNDE, SHERMAN.

Promoted Corporal Feb. 1, 1864; mustered out, expiration of service, Oct. 31, 1864.

PRIVATES.

CHANDLER, ROSWELL W.

Discharged Oct. 31, 1862, for disability.

PRATT, DANIEL S.[1]

Mustered out Oct. 31, 1864.

At the end of the year 1861, Massachusetts had furnished for the war forty-one thousand two hundred and ninety-four (41,294) men ; of which number three thousand seven hundred and thirty-six (3,736) were for the three months' service, one hundred and forty-four (144) — one Battery — for six months' service, seven thousand six hundred and fifty-eight (7,658) in the navy, and the balance, twenty-nine thousand seven hundred and fifty-six (29,756) for the three years' service.

Melrose had furnished at this same time eighty-one (81) men; of which number five (5) were for the three months' service, three (3) were in the navy, and the balance, seventy-three (73), for the three years' service. Three of those in the three years' service were commissioned officers, viz: Second Lieutenant Archibald Bogle, of the Seventeenth Regiment; Second Lieutenant Gurdon McKay, of the Twenty-Second Regiment; and Captain Joseph R. Simonds, of the Seventeenth Regiment. Also, J. Wesley

---

[1] Served three months in 1861, in Co. F, Eighth Regiment, from Lynn.

Jones, First Lieutenant of the Twelfth U. S. Infantry, and Smith W. Nichols, Jr., Midshipman in U. S. Navy.

The position of Massachusetts at this time is well represented by the following extract:

Massachusetts regiments and batteries were in front of Washington and Fortress Monroe ; five regiments were at Annapolis, ready to embark in General Burnside's expedition against North Carolina. One regiment and a battery were at Ship Island in Mississippi, waiting orders from General Butler. Gunboats, officered and manned by Massachusetts men, kept watch and ward on the Southern coast, or carried the flag upon far off seas. Officers remained here on recruiting service ; and enlistments were made to complete new regiments, and to fill the depleted ranks of those at the seat of war. Wounded officers and soldiers were at home on furlough or discharged for disability. The "empty sleeve" was seen daily in our streets ; and maimed veterans hobbled up the steps of the State House to show their honorable discharge papers, and tell in modest words, of their toils and dangers.

IV.

1862.

Great God ! to whom our nation's woes,
Our dire distress, our angry foes,
In all their awful gloom are known,
We bow to Thee and Thee alone.

* * * * * *

We trust to Thy protecting power
In this, our country's saddest hour,
And pray that Thou wilt spread Thy shield
Above us in the camp and field.

* * * * * *

'Till, guided by Thy glorious hand,
Those armies reunite the land,
And North and South alike shall raise
To God their peaceful hymns of praise.

Park Benjamin.

On the first day of July, 1862, President Lincoln issued his third Proclamation, calling for troops, the Governors of eighteen loyal States having joined in an address to him, suggesting the necessity of so doing. This call was for three hundred thousand (300,000) volunteers, to serve for three years, or until the end of the war. These were to form new regiments and batteries, and fill up the depleted ranks of those then in the service.

The nation had passed through a year of successes and reverses, and this new call came just at the time of the disheartening result of the campaign before Richmond, when Gen. McClellan and his army were falling back to Harrison's Landing, on the James River.

The encouraging features at this juncture of affairs were that Gen. Banks and his army still held possession of the upper waters of the Potomac. Gen. Burnside had captured New Berne, and other places in North Carolina, which were strongly held. Admiral Farragut, with his "jolly tars," had passed and taken Forts Jackson and St. Philip, thus opening the Mississippi River, and Gen. Butler occupied New Orleans and other points in Louisiana ; and, notwithstanding the failure of this attempt to take the Confederate capital, long wished for and long expected, the loyal North

"bated no jot of heart or hope";

and never was the determination stronger than now to put down this nefarious Rebellion.

Brig.-Gen. William Schouler, — Adjutant-General of the State during the war, — in his "History of Massachusetts in the Civil War," speaks as follows of the situation at this time, and of the unremitted energy displayed by our great war Governor, John A. Andrew :

We well remember one night, when the news of McClellan's retreat reached Boston ; the papers were filled with accounts of the terrible disaster ; the names of the dead and wounded of Massachusetts' bravest and best were arrayed in the ghastly bulletins transmitted from the front.

That very night the Governor said : "We must issue a new order, call for more men, incite recruiting, inspire hope, dispel

THIRD CALL FOR TROOPS.

gloom; this is the time which requires boldness, firmness, and every personal sacrifice."

The order was issued; it aroused the latent energies of the people; young men, who had not before thought of volunteering, offered themselves as recruits, eager to press forward to fill the gaps which disaster and death had made in our ranks.

The proportion of the three hundred thousand (300,000) men assigned to Massachusetts was fifteen thousand (15,000). The annual returns of the assessors of the several towns and cities, of the men liable to perform military duty, were taken as a basis on which to arrange the different quotas; and as soon as the figures could be properly adjusted, an order was issued by Adjutant-General Schouler, giving the quota of each city and town in the State.

The quota of Melrose was found to be thirty-seven (37) men. On the evening of July 14th, immediately after the promulgation of this order, a war meeting was held at Lyceum Hall, at which Colonel John H. Clark was chosen Chairman, and Mr. Thomas Shelton, Secretary. A number of patriotic speeches were made by our citizens, and it was determined that the quota of Melrose should be speedily raised.

A proposition was submitted to the meeting by Mr. Rufus Smith, of the following tenor, viz:— That enough of the citizens of the town to fill the quota, then and there pledge themselves either to enlist, or furnish substitutes.

The following gentlemen gave their names, agreeing to abide by the proposition; four of them proposing to furnish two substitutes.

Rufus Smith, two men.
George W. Heath, "
David Fairbanks, "

Frank A. Messenger, two men.
N. B. Bryant, one man.
George A. Bacon, "
Charles H. Isburgh, "
John W. Fairbanks, "
Isaac Emerson, Jr., "
Theodore L. Knowles, "
George Emerson 2d, "
Moses Parker, M. D., "
R. Watson Emerson, "
Elbridge H. Goss, "
Thomas C. Evans, "
Anthony Crosby, "
Elisha W. Cobb, "
George W. Emerson, "
Daniel Russell, "

The names of the volunteers procured by the above gentlemen, as their substitutes, and the battery and regiments in which they served, are as follows. Sums ranging from twenty to fifty dollars each were paid for these substitutes, in addition to the bounty of one hundred dollars paid by the Town.

Nelson W. Bickford, Co. I, 38th Reg., Charles S. Jones, Co. G., 39th Reg., for Rufus Smith.

Francis Deshon, Co. K., 38th Reg., James R. Howard, Co. K., 38th Reg., for George W. Heath.

John P. Shelton, Co. A., 13th Reg., Ambrose Dawes, Co. A., 13th Reg., for Frank A. Messenger.

Charles L. White, Co. E., 1st H. Art., for George A. Bacon.

Nathan H. Brand, 9th Bat., for John W. Fairbanks.
Horace Prescott, 9th Bat., for Isaac Emerson, Jr.
Samuel Tobey, 9th Bat., for Thomas C. Evans.

William L. Tucker, 9th Bat., for George W. Emerson.
James A. Kennelly, Co. I, 38th Reg., for Elbridge H. Goss.
Benjamin Lynde, Co. K, 38th Reg., for Theodore L. Knowles.
George O. Noyes, Co. K, 38th Reg., for George Emerson, 2d.
William H. Martin, Co. K, 38th Reg., for R. Watson Emerson.
George E. Richardson, Co. K, 38th Reg., for Anthony Crosby.
Benjamin Tower, Co. K., 38th Reg., for Elisha W. Cobb.
James W. Emerson, Co. K, 38th Reg., for Daniel Russell.

The substitutes for those whose names do not appear in the latter list were non-residents; and they were obtained and put into the service by Captain James H. Wade, of the Thirty-Eighth Regiment.

The following article of agreement was drawn up and circulated, immediately after this meeting, and was very generally signed by our citizens. As will be seen hereafter, the vote to pay one hundred dollars ($100) bounty to each volunteer, and the appointment of the Committee referred to in this article, were duly authorized at a regularly called Town Meeting.

At a meeting of the citizens of Melrose, held this day, for the purpose of procuring the necessary quota of soldiers required from the Town, in accordance with the Governor's Order No. 26, a Committee was appointed consisting of the present Board of Selectmen, together with Messrs. Elbridge Gardner, Isaac Emerson, Jr., and John W. Fairbanks, who were empowered to draw upon the Town Treasurer moneys in the amount of one hundred dollars ($100) per man for every volunteer so required, recruited and accepted. And in order that the wishes of the citizens thus expressed should have the necessary legal and binding effect, and that the moneys thus raised should fall equally alike upon all in proportion to their substance, the Committee were directed to employ an officer to visit every tax-payer and request his or her assent and signature to this agreement; to wit:

Whereas it appears to us that it has become necessary to raise money for military purposes in an informal manner, and without any precedent in law,

We, the Tax-payers of Melrose, give our assent, and by our signatures do hereby bind ourselves to pay, without demurring, our property proportion of the aforesaid levy, waiving any informality in law; and do further agree that the same shall be considered as due from us as a portion of our Town Tax to be assessed, paid or collected in the customary and usual manner and form; and save the before-named Committee, as also all Town Officers engaged in raising and disbursing the same, harmless in their private capacity and estate.

MELROSE, July 14, 1862.

A Town meeting was called and held at Lyceum Hall, July 28th. Mr. William B. Burgess was chosen Moderator, and the proceedings of the citizens' meeting were read by the Secretary, and fully indorsed and accepted; and further measures were taken to induce and secure enlistments.

The following vote — offered by Mr. Henry A. Norris — was unanimously passed:

Voted, That the sum of thirty-seven hundred dollars ($3,700) be raised to pay thirty-seven (37) able-bodied men, who shall voluntarily enlist in the service of the United States under the recent call of the President of the United States for three hundred thousand (300,000) men; and that the Selectmen be authorized to disburse one hundred dollars ($100) to each man who shall enlist, as soon as he shall have been accepted by the military authorities of this State, and mustered into said service.[1]

It was also

Voted, That the sum of two hundred dollars ($200) be raised to aid the cause of enlistment, to be disbursed by a Committee chosen at this meeting, in such manner as said Committee deem best.

This Committee consisted of the Selectmen, — Colonel John H. Clark, and Messrs. William B. Burgess and George M. Fletcher, — and Messrs. Elbridge Gardner, Isaac Emerson, Jr., and John W. Fairbanks.

Encouraging and patriotic speeches were made by Hon. N. B. Bryant, Rev. George W. Quinby, Mr. Charles H. Isburgh, and others. A determination to bear our share of expense, and raise our proportion of men for the field, was manifested, and the best spirit prevailed during the entire meeting.

In order to encourage and obtain enlistments, Mr. Henry A. Norris offered to pay the sum of fifty dollars ($50) to the first five men who should enlist at this time.

Mr. Daniel W. Wilcox also offered to pay ten dollars ($10) each to the next ten men that should enlist from our town.

Hon. N. B. Bryant agreed to pay the sum of ten dollars ($10) each to all others who should sign the enlistment roll on that evening.

With these extra inducements a number of our young men enlisted at this time, the first one to sign his name to the roll being

William Francis Barry.

---

[1] For form in which this bounty was paid to those who enlisted at this time, see appendix B.

This meeting was adjourned until the evening of August 2d, when a very large and enthusiastic gathering was held, at which stirring and interesting addresses were made by Hon. Daniel W. Gooch, — then member of Congress from the Sixth District ;[1] Judge Cochran, of the Supreme Court of Maryland ; Sergeant E. G. Adams, of the Second New Hampshire Regiment ; Captain James H. Slade, of the Thirty-Eighth Massachusetts Regiment, and formerly of General Sigel's staff; Mr. Rufus Smith and Rev. George W. Quinby. The exertions and inducements put forth at these meetings were successful, and our quota was more than filled.

We now give the names of those who enlisted for three years, on the quota of Melrose, at this time, and during the rest of the year 1862, excepting those who went into the regiments organized the year before, and whose names have been already given on previous pages. No special effort has been made to gather items concerning non-residents.

---

[1] In January 1858, Mr. Gooch was elected Representative from the Seventh District for the remainder of the term commencing March 4, 1857. He was re-elected for the succeeding terms, commencing in 1859, 1861, 1863 — then by a new division of Representative Districts, called the Sixth instead of the Seventh District — and 1865. He was a member of the "Congressional Committee on the Conduct of the War" during its four years of investigations, and its Chairman on the part of the House. The following are among the speeches delivered at different times during his congressional service : "The Lecompton Constitution and the admission of Kansas into the Union," March 29, 1858; " Polygamy in Utah," April 4, 1860; " The Supreme Court and Dred Scott," May 3, 1860; "Organization of the Territories," May 11, 1860; "Any Compromise a Surrender," February 23, 1861 ; " Recognition of Hayti and Liberia," June 2, 1862 ; " Secession and Reconstruction," May 3, 1864. He resigned his seat in the House September 1, 1865, having been appointed Naval Officer for the Port of Boston by President Johnson, and was removed by him in less than a year from the time of his appointment.

ELEVENTH REGIMENT.[1]

Co. I.

PRIVATE.

WELLS, CHARLES A.

Wounded at "Battle of Gettysburg," July 2, 1863;[2] mustered out at expiration of service, June 24, 1864.

FIRST HEAVY ARTILLERY.[3]

Co. E.

PRIVATE.

WHITE, CHARLES L.

Wounded in hand — one finger shot off — at Warrenton Junction, Aug. 28, 1862, trying to save General Pope's supply train; transferred to Veteran Reserve Corps Oct. 23, 1863; mustered out Nov. 15, 1865.

---

[1] The Eleventh Massachusetts was recruited at Fort Warren, Boston Harbor, and mustered into the United States service June 13, 1861. It was in most of the principal battles participated in by the "Army of the Potomac" from the First Bull Run to the Siege of Petersburg and fall of Richmond.

[2] Federal loss in this battle, 23,186; 2,834 killed, 13,709 wounded, 6,643 missing. Rebel loss estimated at 26,500 in killed, wounded and prisoners.

[3] The First Massachusetts Heavy Artillery — changed from Fourteenth Regiment Infantry — left the State July 7, 1861, and was stationed in the Forts around Washington until the last campaign, when it took part in the following battles: Spottsylvania, North Anna River, Tolopotomy, Cool Arbor, Petersburg, Strawberry Plains, Deep Bottom, Poplar Spring Church, Boydtown Road, Hatcher's Run, Duncan's Run and Vaughn Road.

THIRTY-THIRD REGIMENT.[1]
Co. C.
PRIVATES.

DAVIS, LOAMI G.

Discharged March 15, 1863, for disability.[2]

KRANTZ, FREDERICK W.

Taken prisoner after "Battle of Gettysburg" by Stuart's cavalry while on a raid; held seven months, escaped, and joined his regiment at Lookout Valley; again taken prisoner while on the "march to the sea" and confined at "Salisbury Prison;" paroled April 3, 1865; discharged June 6, 1865.

THIRTY-EIGHTH REGIMENT.[3]
Co. I.
MUSICIAN.

KENNISTON, CHARLES.

Wounded at "Siege of Port Hudson," June 14, 1863; mustered out with regiment, June 30, 1865; non-resident.

---

[1] The Thirty-Third Massachusetts left the State Aug. 14, 1862, and was in the following battles: Fredericksburg, Chancellorsville, Beverly Ford, Gettysburg, Lookout Mountain, Missionary Ridge and the battles of General Sherman's Grand Army.

[2] Re-enlisted in Third Heavy Artillery, see chap. VI.

[3] The Thirty-Eighth Massachusetts left the State Aug. 26, 1862, and was in the following engagements: River, Mansura, Bisland, Port Hudson, Opequan, Fisher's Hill and Cedar Creek.

SERGEANT.

MORRISON, CHARLES H.

Deserted at "Camp Emory," Baltimore, Md., Nov. 7, 1862.[1]

CORPORAL.

KENNELLEY, JAMES A.

Discharged at Mower Hospital, Phila., Pa., May 3, 1865, for disability; non-resident.

PRIVATES.

BICKFORD, NELSON W.

Discharged Sept. 28, 1863, at Baton Rouge, La., for disability.

KELLEY, PATRICK.

Mustered out June 30, 1865; non-resident.

RICE, GEORGE.

Absent, sick, at muster-out of regiment; non-resident.

Co. K.

LIEUTENANT.

MARTIN, GEORGE T.

Went out 2d Lieutenant; promoted 1st Lieutenant April 14, 1863; resigned Aug. 12, 1863, on account of disability.[2]

---

[1] The whole number of deserters from the Union army during the war was 278,644; whole number of Massachusetts soldiers that deserted was 7,352; only two citizens of Melrose are here recorded as deserters.

[2] Re-entered the service in Fourth Heavy Artillery, see chap. VI.

SERGEANT.

MARTIN, WILLIAM H.

On detached service in Ordnance Department from April 11 till Aug. 1, 1863; mustered out June 30, 1865.

CORPORALS.

NOYES, GEORGE O.

Promoted Corporal March 10, 1863; wounded in hand at "Siege of Port Hudson," June 14, 1863; mustered out June 30, 1865.

TOWER, BENJAMIN.

Promoted Corporal Aug. 10, 1863; wounded at "Battle of Cedar Creek," Oct. 19, 1864; mustered out June 30, 1865.

PRIVATES.

DESHON, FRANCIS.

Mustered out June 30, 1865.

EMERSON, JAMES W.

Mustered out June 30, 1865.

HOWARD, JAMES R.

Discharged Dec. 5, 1863, for disability.[1]

LYNDE, BENJAMIN.

Died Aug. 18, 1863, at Baton Rouge, La., of chronic diarrhœa.[2]

---

[1] Died at Melrose Aug. 16, 1864; for obituary notice, see "Roll of Honor."
[2] For obituary notice, see "Roll of Honor."

RICHARDSON, GEORGE E.

Taken prisoner at "Battle of Cedar Creek," Oct. 19, 1864; died in prison at Salisbury, N. C., Nov. 3, 1864.[1]

THIRTY-NINTH REGIMENT.[2]

Co. G.

CORPORAL.

STONE, HENRY.

Discharged at Boston, Sept. 30, 1863, for disability.[3]

PRIVATES.

EARL, WILLIAM H.

Wounded in hand at Hagerstown, Md., July 15, 1863; transferred to navy,[4] April 21, 1864.[5]

JACKSON, WILLIAM H.

Discharged May 19, 1864, for disability.

JONES, CHARLES S.

Transferred to Veteran Reserve Corps, March 31, 1864; discharged June 24, 1865.

PIKE, JACOB F.

Mustered out June 13, 1865.

---

[1] For obituary notice, see "Roll of Honor."
[2] The Thirty-Ninth Massachusetts left the State Sept 6, 1862, and was in the following battles: — Mine Run, Wilderness, Spottsylvania, North Anna River, Tolopotomy, Bethesda Church, Petersburg, Weldon Railroad, Dabney's Mills, Gravelly Run and Five Forks.
[3] Re enlisted in Fifty-Ninth Regiment, see chap. VI.
[4] Authority for thus transferring given by Congress, Feb. 24, 1864.
[5] For navy items, see chap. IX.

STEBBENS, THADDEUS S.

Discharged Dec. 25, 1863, at Finley Hospital, Washington, D. C., for disability.

Co. I.

PRIVATES.

BURNS, FRANCIS.
Non-resident.

FERGUSON, JOHN.
Non-resident.

SAWYER, OBADIAH.
Non-resident.

WILSON, JOHN.
Non-resident.

NINTH BATTERY.[1]

CORPORAL.

TUCKER, WILLIAM L.

Promoted Corporal Oct. 23, 1864; mustered out with battery, June 6, 1865.

PRIVATES.

BRAND, NATHAN H.

Died March 6, 1864, at Emory Hospital, Washington, D. C., of cholera morbus.

---

[1] The Ninth Massachusetts Battery left the State Sept. 3, 1862, and was in the following engagements: Gettysburg, Mine Run, Spottsylvania, North Anna River, Tolopotomy, Bethesda Church, Petersburg, Weldon Railroad and Hatcher's Run.

CHAPIN, JOSEPH A.

Discharged Aug. 29, 1864, to receive promotion as Hospital Steward in United States Army, by General Order No. 284, Adjutant General's Office, Washington, D. C.[1]

PRESCOTT, HORACE.

Mustered out June 6, 1865.

TOBEY, SAMUEL.

Wounded at "Battle of Gettysburg," July 2, 1863 ; mustered out June 6, 1865 ; non-resident.

THIRTEENTH BATTERY.[2]

CORPORAL.

ELLIS, ALVAN T.

Promoted Corporal Dec. 30, 1862 ; deserted Dec. 11, 1863, at Hampton, Va.; non-resident.[3]

SECOND CAVALRY.[4]

Co. B.

PRIVATES.

HARRIS, WILLIAM.

Non-resident.

---

[1] Served fifteen months at Fort Independence, Boston Harbor.

[2] The Thirteenth Massachusetts Battery left the State Jan. 20, 1863. It was in the "Department of the Gulf," and took part in the following engagements: Port Hudson, Carrion Crow Bayou and Pleasant Hill.

[3] In the Adjutant General's Office at the State House, he is credited to Boston ; but Melrose put him into the service, and paid his bounty.

[4] The Second Massachusetts Cavalry was mustered in the early part of 1863, and was in the following engagements: South Anna Bridge, Ashley's Gap, Drainesville, Aldie, Fort Stevens, Fort Reno, Rockville, Poolesville, Summit Point, Halltown, Opequan, Winchester, Luray, Waynesboro, Tom's Brook, Cedar Creek, South Anna, White Oak Road, Berryville Pike, Charlestown, Dinwiddie's Court House, Five Forks, Saylor's Creek, Appomattox Court House.

Co. C.

CLARK, JAMES.[1]

Non-resident; mustered out June 6, 1865.

Co. D.

BURKE, PATRICK.

Non-resident.

GILLISPIE, JOHN.

Non-resident; died from wounds at Washington, D. C., July 20, 1864.

ROBERTSON, WILLIAM.

Non-resident.

Co. H.

HOLLIS, HENRY P.[2]

Mustered out June 6, 1865.

Co. I.

BRANDON, EDWARD A.[1]

Non-resident; mustered out June 6, 1865.

Co. K.

KING, DAVID H.[1]

Non-resident; mustered out June 6, 1865.

---

[1] Enlisted May 25, 1864.
[2] Enlisted Nov. 30, 1863.

THIRD CAVALRY.[1]

Co. D.

CAPTAIN.

SIMONDS, JOSEPH F.

Mustered in as Sergeant of Co. E; wounded severely in the shoulder during a cavalry charge in the "Red River Expedition," May 18, 1864; promoted 1st Sergeant, July 8, 1864; 2d Lieutenant, Sept. 20, 1864; wounded in hand at "Battle of Opequan," Sept. 19, 1864; promoted 1st Lieutenant May 28, 1865; at the close of the war the regiment was ordered to the West, to quell Indian disturbances; wounded — shot through both thighs — at Fort Kearney, Aug. 25, 1865; promoted Captain Oct. 5, 1865; discharged Oct. 8, 1865.

Co. G.

PRIVATE.

HUGHES, JAMES.[2]

Non-resident.

---

[1] The Third Massachusetts Cavalry was originally the Forty-First Regiment of Infantry. It left the State Nov. 15, 1862, and took part in the following engagements: Irish Bend, Henderson's Hill, Cane River, Georgia Landing, Port Hudson, Sabine Cross Roads, Muddy Bayou, Piney Woods, Red River Campaign, Opequan, Fisher's Hill, Snag Point, Winchester, Cedar Creek, and others.

[2] Enlisted April 14, 1864.

V.

1862.

NINE MONTHS' MEN.

In Freedom's name our blades we draw,
   She arms us for the fight!
For country, government, and law,
   For Liberty and Right.
The Union must — shall be preserved,
   Our flag still o'er us fly!
That cause our hearts and hands has nerved
   And we will do or die.
                      George P. Morris.

"We are coming, Father Abra'am,
   Three hundred thousand more,
From Mississippi's winding stream
   And from New England's shore."

On the 4th of August, 1862, President Lincoln issued his proclamation calling for three hundred thousand (300,000) more troops, to serve for nine months; a draft to be made if the quotas were not filled by volunteers by the 15th of August.

The proportion assigned by the War Department to Massachusetts was nineteen thousand and eighty (19,080) men. The quota of Melrose was seventy-nine (79) men.

To this call, as heretofore, Melrose responded promptly, sending its full quota of seventy-nine (79) men into the field in eight different regiments.

OUR NINE MONTHS' MEN.   55

A war meeting was called and held at the vestry of the Orthodox Church on the evening of August 11th, to consult in relation to supplying these additional troops. Colonel John H. Clark was chosen Chairman, and Mr. Charles H. Isburgh, Secretary. Speeches were made by Colonel Clark, Mr. George F. Stone, and several other citizens; and a vote was passed recommending that the Town pay a bounty of one hundred and fifty dollars ($150) to each and every person that should enlist and enter the service for nine months.

A warrant for a Town Meeting was immediately issued, to be held August 21st, to take the matter into consideration. Colonel John H. Clark was chosen Moderator. As will be seen by the following vote, offered by Mr. Stephen W. Shelton, the recommendation of the citizens' meeting was fully indorsed and adopted:

Voted, That the Town raise an amount of money equal or equivalent to the sum of one hundred and fifty dollars ($150) per man, for every man who is, or who may be required from this Town to answer to the recent call of the President of the United States for additional troops for nine months' service, to serve in the army of the United States; and that the Treasurer is authorized and required, under the direction of the Selectmen, to borrow that amount of money and pay the same to such parties who may volunteer, and are properly and legally accepted by the proper and legal authorities for such service.

It was also voted, on motion of Mr. Rufus Smith,

That a Rallying Committee of twenty-five men be appointed by the Chairman of this meeting, with full powers to call meetings and perform such other duties as they may deem necessary; and that an appropriation of three hundred dollars ($300) for incidental expenses be made by the Town, to be expended under the direction of said Committee.

The following citizens were appointed to serve on that Committee:

Rufus Smith,
Michael A. McCafferty,
Nelson Cochran,
Moses Parker, M. D.,
Samuel O. Dearborn,
Henry A. Norris,
Henry B. Newhall,
Fernando C. Taylor,
John S. Sewall,
Daniel Norton, Jr.,
Josiah P. Mendum,
George A. Bacon,
R. Watson Emerson,
Frank A. Messenger,
Napoleon B. Bryant,
Isaac Emerson, Jr.,
Joel Snow,
George W. Emerson,
Philip B. Holmes,
Levi S. Gould,
Walter Babb,
Allen C. Goss,
Addison W. Banfield,
Isaiah A. Young,
Stephen W. Shelton.

The Selectmen were afterwards joined to this Committee.

Several large and spirited war meetings were held at various places in the town, under the auspices of this Rallying Committee. The first one took place on Monday evening, August 25th, at Lyceum Hall. Good music was furnished by the Malden Band, and some fine singing by a quartette. Addresses were made by Lieutenant-Colonel Wardwell, of the Thirty-Eighth Massachusetts Regiment, Hon. Daniel W. Gooch, Hon. Elihu C. Baker, Messrs. George W. Copeland, Guppy, and others.

Meetings were also held on Wednesday, Thursday and Saturday evenings of this week, at which addresses were made by our citizens, and by speakers from abroad; and volunteers came rapidly forward, and this quota of seventy-nine (79) was filled.

The last week of August was almost wholly given up

to recruiting purposes. The Governor recommended a suspension of business during the afternoons, and the recommendation was very generally complied with.

Owing to the measures taken at these various meetings, the following paper — whereby the signers agreed to pay their just proportion of all taxes, and to indemnify all town officers for any action taken in carrying out the wishes of the town — was circulated among the citizens for signatures :

AGREEMENT.

Be it remembered, that whereas the Town of Melrose, at several meetings called for that purpose, have, with great unanimity, passed sundry votes providing for the payment of bounty to our volunteers, and for the support of their families, and other incidental war purposes, which votes may, upon nice and technical grounds, be regarded as invalid in law, — Now, therefore, we the undersigned, Tax-payers in the Town of Melrose, hereby waive all objection to the form, substance, or validity of said proceedings ; and agree to pay all taxes assessed against us respectively arising from said votes.

And we severally hereby release any present or future officer of said Town from all actions, or causes of action, on account of the assessment or collection of the aforesaid tax ; all of which we feel in duty bound to do, as true and loyal citizens, resolved to make any sacrifice necessary for the most vigorous prosecution of the war, and for the honor and dignity of our glorious flag.

Of our nine months' volunteers, twenty-nine enlisted in the Forty-Second Massachusetts Regiment, all but one of them being in Co. G ; and they experienced the sad fate of falling into the hands of the rebels, at the "Battle of Galveston," January 1st, 1863. But they were not, thank God! destined to undergo the horrors of an "Andersonville," "Salisbury," or "Belle Isle," as they were soon afterward paroled.

The following are the names of our nine months' men, with their regiment and company :

FIFTH REGIMENT.[1]
Co. A.
PRIVATE.

CHASE, EDE K.
Mustered out with the regiment, July 2, 1863.

Co. H.
PRIVATE.

SUMNER, STEPHEN.
Mustered out with the regiment, July 2, 1863.

FORTY-SECOND REGIMENT.[2]
Co. G.
CORPORAL.

BUTTRICK, JOHN W.
Taken prisoner at " Battle of Galveston," Jan. 1, 1863 ; in

---

[1] The Fifth Massachusetts, — which served in the three months' campaign at the beginning of the Rebellion, — now volunteering for nine months, left Boston Oct. 22, 1862, for New Berne, N. C. Its period of service was passed in the " Department of North Carolina," and it was in the following engagements : Whitehall, Kinston, Goldsboro', New Berne, Blount's Creek, and Moseley Creek, besides numerous expeditions and reconnoissances, marching six hundred miles over the poor roads of North Carolina, during its term of service.

[2] The Forty-Second Massachusetts left the State Nov. 21, 1862, for the "Department of the Gulf." Three companies — D, G and I — were in the "Battle of Galveston," Jan. 1, 1863, and taken prisoners ;* afterwards paroled, but not exchanged ; therefore did not perform any more active service. The balance of the regiment served in the Louisiana campaigns.

---

* "When Colonel Burrill offered his sword to the officer designated by General Magruder to receive the surrender, he was desired to keep it, in respect to his brave and able defence of his position against such an overwhelming force ; and, on being informed that the little band that stood before them were *all* the troops there, the rebels could scarcely believe it, and were surprised they had held their position so well and so long."

FORTY-SECOND REGIMENT.

prison at Houston, Texas ; paroled while on steamer "General Quitman," near Alexandria, La., Feb. 18, 1863 ; mustered out with the regiment, Aug. 20, 1863.

MUSICIAN.

IRESON, DAVID A.[1]

WAGONER.

JUDKINS, ROLAND C.[1]

PRIVATES.

BARRETT, CHARLES.[1]
BARRETT, CHARLES L.[1]
BARNARD, JOHN M., JR.[1]
BOARDMAN, CHARLES.[1]
BRIDGES, HENRY.

Deserted at New York City, Dec. 6, 1862 ; non-resident.

BRYANT, THOMAS O.[1]
BURNHAM, PASCHAL E.

Discharged March 27, 1863, for disability.

CLARK, FREDERICK F.[1]
CORSON, FREDERICK U.[1]
DAVIS, JOHN E.[1]
DAVIS, JAMES L.[1][2]

---

[1] Same military history as that of Corporal Buttrick.
[2] Also served ninety days in Seventh Un. Co. Infantry, in 1864 ; see chap. VIII.

DOUBLE, EDMUND B.[1]
Wounded in hand at "Battle of Galveston," Jan. 1, 1863.

EMERSON, JAMES G.[1,2]

HETON, JOHN.[1]

HYDE, GEORGE S.[1]

IRESON, ALONZO D.[1]

LYNDE, AMOS W.[1,2]

LYNDE, CHARLES B.[1]

MARSTON, JAMES M.
Deserted Dec. 6, 1862, at New York City; non-resident.

SWEETSER, THOMAS T.[1]
Wounded in the mouth at "Battle of Galveston."

MARSHALL, SAMUEL.[1]

UPHAM, CHARLES H.[1]

VINTON, EDWIN A.[1,3]

YORK, JOSIAH R.[1,2]

YORK, WILLIAM B.[1,2]

Co. H.

PRIVATE.

WILDE, BENJAMIN F.
Deserted Nov. 25, 1862, at New York City.

---

[1] Same military history as that of Corporal Buttrick.
[2] Also served ninety days in Seventh Un. Co. of Infantry in 1864; see chap. VIII.
[3] Also served one hundred days in Eighth Regiment in 1864; see chap. VIII.

FORTY-THIRD REGIMENT.[1]
Co. A.
PRIVATE.

SMITH, WAYLAND R.
Mustered out with the regiment, July 30, 1863.

FORTY-FOURTH REGIMENT.[2]
Co. D.
PRIVATE.

SIMONDS, JOSEPH W.
Mustered out with the regiment, June 18, 1863.[3]

---

[1] The Forty-Third Massachusetts was in the "Department of North Carolina," and was in the battles of Kinston, Whitehall, and several marches and skirmishes.

[2] This regiment was also in the "Department of North Carolina," and was in the Tarboro' expedition, the battles of Kinston, Whitchall, Goldsboro' and Siege of Washington, N. C. It had in its ranks the astronomer Tuttle, of Cambridge, the two brothers Cobb, artists, and Rev. Mr. Gibbs, who relinquished the pastorate of the Universalist Church in West Cambridge. The following "army song" was written by "Selim," and dedicated to the Forty-Fourth :

TUNE — "Scots wha hae wi' Wallace bled."

From Katahdin's snowy crest,
To Mount Vernon's sacred rest,
Through imperial valleys West,
   Shout the battle-cry.

Hark ! it is your country's call !
Lo ! she bids her brave sons all
Make the band of traitors fall,
   In recreant graves to lie.

Would you see our broad domain
By giant treason rent in twain,
In border-strifes your children slain?
   Back as cowards fall.

Would you see our banner bright
Wave untorn in Freedom's light,
Brave the world's united might?
   Strike, then, once for all.

Come from homes you love so dear,
Come with hearts that know no fear,
Come with might in bow and spear.
   Down bid slavery go.

By the prayers our fathers breathed,
By the trusts to us bequeathed,
By the hopes our hearts which heaved,
   Smile oppression low.

Hail our *Union's* new birthnight !
See it girt with grander might,
Ray out now a purer light
   To the nations round.

When our last victory is won,
When the work of blood is done,
And to our loved homes we come,
   To God shall praises sound.

[3] Also served one hundred days in the Eighth Regiment, in 1864 ; see chap. VIII.

Co. E.

PRIVATE.

ROBERTS, CHARLES H.
Discharged Jan. 14, 1863, for disability.

Co. G.

PRIVATE.

HART, ABNER B.
Mustered out June 18, 1863.

Co. H.

PRIVATE.

DAWES, RICHARD C.
Mustered out June 18, 1863.[1]

Co. I.

PRIVATES.

ANDERSON, LEONARD B.
Mustered out June 18, 1863.

CROCKER, JOSEPH C.
Mustered out June 18, 1863.[2]

---

[1] Appointed Acting Ensign in the navy Dec. 16, 1863, but he was then living in Brookline. He served until Jan. 11, 1867, when he was honorably discharged.

[2] Also served nine months as clerk in the Quartermaster's Department, Headquarters 18th Army Corps, Army of the James.

FORTY-FIFTH REGIMENT.[1]

Co. A.

MUSICIAN.

FREELAND, JOSEPH V.

Mustered out with the regiment, July 7, 1863; non-resident.

Co. D.

SERGEANT.

BARRY, ROYAL P.

Promoted Corporal Sept. 27, 1862; Sergeant, June 19, 1863; mustered out July 7, 1863.

PRIVATES.

CUTTING, WILLIAM H., JR.

Mustered out July 7, 1863.

EVANS, THOMAS C.

Wounded in both hands and leg at "Battle of Kinston," Dec. 14, 1862; discharged Feb. 27, 1863.

FOSS, JAMES T.

Wounded at "Battle of Kinston," Dec. 14, 1862; mustered out July 7, 1863.

LEIGHTON, WILLIAM F.

Mustered out July 7, 1863.

CHIPMAN, GEORGE A.

Mustered out July 7, 1863.[2]

---

[1] The Forty-Fifth Massachusetts was in the "Department of North Carolina," and in the battles of Kinston, Whitehall, and several skirmishes and reconnoissances.

[2] Also served one hundred days as Lieutenant, Co. A, Sixth Regiment, in 1864; see chap. VIII.

MARSHALL, JAMES.
Mustered out July 7, 1863.

McLAUGHLIN, GEORGE W.
Mustered out July 7, 1863.[1]

PERKINS, JOHN, JR.
Wounded in thigh at "Battle of Kinston," Dec. 14, 1862; discharged May 21, 1863.

JUNKINS, EDWIN W.
Mustered out July 7, 1863.

Co. I.

PRIVATES.

DORRING, JOHN.
Mustered out July 7, 1863; non-resident.

FOSS, GEORGE A.
Mustered out July 7, 1863; non-resident.

FERGUSON, JOHN.
Mustered out July 7, 1863; non-resident.

HARRIS, JOHN.
Mustered out July 7, 1863; non-resident.

MYARS, JOHN.
Mustered out July 7, 1863; non-resident.

---

[1] Was a minor at time of enlistment. For form of parent's consent in such cases see Appendix C.

FORTY-EIGHTH REGIMENT.[1]

Co. D.

SERGEANT.

TODD, THOMAS.
Mustered out Sept. 3, 1863 ; non-resident.

MUSICIAN.

RICHARDSON, ALFRED C.
Died Aug. 8, 1863, at Baton Rouge, La. ; non-resident.

PRIVATE.

CRANE, WILLIAM P., JR.
Mustered out Sept. 3, 1863 ; non-resident.

Co. G.

SERGEANT.

HARE, ANDREW.
Mustered out Sept. 3, 1863.

FIFTIETH REGIMENT.[2]

Co. D.

SERGEANT.

ROWELL, STEPHEN P.
Mustered out with the regiment, Aug. 24, 1863.

---

[1] The Forty-Eighth Massachusetts left New York for the " Department of the Gulf," Jan. 4, 1863, and was engaged in the "Siege of Port Hudson," and marches and skirmishes in that Department.

[2] The Fiftieth Massachusetts was in the " Department of the Gulf," and left the State Nov. 19, 1862. Took part in Siege of Port Hudson, and marches and expeditions in that Department.

MUSICIAN.

NICHOLS, WILLIAM R.
Mustered out Aug. 24, 1863; non-resident.

Co. E.

PRIVATES.

BARRON, ELLIOT F.
Mustered out Aug. 24, 1863.

BROWN, JONAS G.
Died June 18, 1863, in Regimental Hospital at Baton Rouge, La., of malarial fever.[1]

COX, JAMES P.
Mustered out Aug. 24, 1863.

DIX, JOSEPH O.[2]
Mustered out Aug. 24, 1863.

FARRELL, MICHAEL.
Mustered out Aug. 24, 1863.

FULLER, GEORGE P.
Mustered out Aug. 24, 1863.

LYMAN, HENRY H.
Mustered out Aug. 24, 1863.

McALLISTER, GEORGE H.
Mustered out Aug. 24, 1863.

---

[1] For obituary sketch, see "Roll of Honor."
[2] Also served three months in 1861, in Co. B, Fifth Regiment, from South Reading.

THE FIFTIETH REGIMENT.

O'DONAGHUE, JOHN.
Deserted Nov. 22, 1862, at New York City; non-resident.

PRENTICE, CHARLES.
Mustered out Aug. 24, 1863.

SHELTON, THOMAS.[1]
Mustered out Aug. 24, 1863.

SIMONDS, CHARLES H.
Mustered out Aug. 24, 1863; non-resident.[2]

HAMILTON, ROBERT.
Mustered out Aug. 24, 1863; non-resident.

HARRINGTON, CHARLES T.
Mustered out Aug. 24, 1863; non-resident.

HAWKES, JOHN.
Mustered out Aug. 24, 1863; non-resident.

KINGMAN, WILLIAM W.
Mustered out Aug. 24, 1863; non-resident.

KNIGHTS, HENRY C.
Mustered out Aug. 24, 1863; non-resident.

Co. F.

PRIVATES.

GALLAGHER, JOHN.
Deserted Oct. 20, 1862, at Boxford, Mass.; non-resident.

---

[1] Also served one hundred days in the Eighth Regiment in 1864; see chap. VIII.

[2] Resident of Malden; re-enlisted in Co. K, Fifty-Ninth Regiment; lost a leg before Petersburg, June 17, 1864.

WILSON, JOHN.
Deserted Oct. 20, 1862, at Boxford, Mass.; non-resident.

At the commencement of the year 1863, Massachusetts had sent into the field forty-six thousand nine hundred and twenty (46,920) three years' men, sixteen thousand eight hundred and thirty-seven (16,837) nine months' men, and three thousand seven hundred and thirty-six (3,736) three months' men; making a total of sixty-seven thousand four hundred and ninety-three (67,493) men; thirteen thousand six hundred and eighteen (13,618) men had also entered into the naval service of the United States, for which Massachusetts had received no credit, making a total number of men furnished by Massachusetts of eighty-one thousand one hundred and eleven (81,111).

General Schouler says of Massachusetts at this time:

She had given martyrs to the great cause on nearly every battlefield; many had their limbs severed from their bodies; many households had been made desolate; many stood by the butts of their muskets, keeping watch and ward, facing the enemy from the falls of the Potomac to the delta of the Mississippi. Some were in prison, some were in hospitals, some were in tents, some swinging in their hammocks at the mouths of rivers, to prevent blockade runners from supplying the enemy.

And Governor Andrew, in his address to the Legislature at the beginning of 1863, eloquently refers to the part taken by Massachusetts men: after recapitulating the many battlefields from "Big Bethel" and "Cedar Mountain" to "Baton Rouge" and "Antietam," he continues:

Through all the capricious fortunes of the war the regiments of Massachusetts have borne her flag by the side of the banner of the Union. And, beyond the Atlantic slope, every battle-field has drunk the blood of her sons, nurtured among her hills and sands, from which in adventurous manhood they turned their footsteps to the West. Officers and enlisted men have vied with each other in deeds of valor. The flag, whose standard-bearer, shot down in battle, tossed it from his dying hand, nerved by undying patriotism, has been caught by the comrade, who in his turn has closed his eyes for the last time upon its starry folds as another hero-martyr clasped the splintered staff and rescued the symbol at once of country and of blood-bought fame.

How can fleeting words of human praise gild the record of their glory? Our eyes suffused with tears, and blood retreating to the heart, stirred with unwonted thrill, speak with the eloquence of nature, uttered but unexpressed. From the din of the battle they have passed to the peace of eternity. Farewell! warrior, citizen, patriot, lover, friend, — whether in the humbler ranks or bearing the sword of official power, whether private, captain, surgeon or chaplain, for all these in the heady fight have passed away, — hail! and farewell! Each hero must sleep serenely on the field where he fell in a cause "sacred to liberty and the rights of mankind."

Melrose had sent into the service up to this time, — January 1, 1863, — one hundred and twenty-six (126) three years' men, five (5) of whom were commissioned officers; seventy-nine (79) nine months' men, and five (5) three months' men; and had also furnished seven (7) men for the navy; one of whom had been transferred from the army; one discharged and enlisted in the army, and four of whom were commissioned officers; making a total number furnished of two hundred and sixteen (216) men.

The officers in the army were: Second Lieutenant Gurdon McKay, of the Twenty-Second Regiment; Second

Lieutenant George T. Martin, of the Thirty-Eighth Regiment; First Lieutenant Archibald Bogle, of the Seventeenth Regiment; Captain Joseph R. Simonds, of the Seventeenth Regiment, and First Lieutenant J. Wesley Jones, of the Twelfth U. S. Infantry. In the navy, Acting Master's Mate N. Mayo Dyer, Acting Ensign James F. Perkins, Acting Ensign Edward A. Small, and Lieutenant Smith W. Nichols, Jr.

The total quota of Melrose to this date, of three years' and nine months' men, was one hundred and eighty-four (184), and we had furnished two hundred and ten (210) men for those periods of service.

On the 22d of September of this year, — 1862, — was issued the great Proclamation by President Lincoln, declaring that the slaves of all persons in States which, on the 1st day of January, 1863, should be in rebellion, " shall be thenceforth and forever free." Concerning this act it has been eloquently said :

" As yet the policy of the Nation was undefined. Nor did it reach the dignity of positive justice, clearly pronounced, until, by the great Proclamation of Liberty, the Government became anchored to an immortal thought, and decreed Emancipation. By that act the President ascended a height more lofty than Federal Hill. He rose to the serene heights of Zion, received light and knowledge and power from an Eternal Source, fixed by a word the moral judgment of mankind in sympathy with our national cause, secured the verdict of history and the prayers of the good in every land, and humbly awaited ' the gracious favor of Almighty God.' "

VI.

1863.

THREE YEARS' MEN.

"The Sun of Liberty shall ne'er
In clouds and darkness set;
Her sons are brave, — they know no fear, —
And God is with us yet."

An Enrollment or Conscription Act having been passed by Congress, for the purpose of recruiting the forces in the field, and making up deficiencies on the calls previously made, a new enrollment of the men liable to do military duty was ordered, and a draft of such enrolled men to be made in July, 1863.

These enrolled men were divided into two classes. The first class comprised all persons subject to do military duty between the ages of twenty and thirty-five years, and all unmarried persons subject to do military duty between thirty-five and forty-five. The second class comprised the married men who were subject to do military duty and were more than thirty-five, but under forty-five years of age.

On the 25th of May, Provost-Marshal Herrick appointed Mr. Stephen Shelton "Enrolling Officer for Sub-District No. 9, Town of Melrose," who immediately entered upon the duties of his office;[1] and by this enrollment it was ascertained that there were in our town, at this time, exclusive of those then in the service, one hundred and sixty-two (162) persons of the first class, and one hundred and twenty-one (121) of the second class.[2] In the whole State it was ascertained that there were one hundred and seven thousand, three hundred and eighty-six (107,386) persons of the first class, and fifty-six thousand, seven hundred ninety-two (56,792) of the second class; a total of one hundred and sixty-four thousand, one hundred and seventy-eight (164,178).

This draft was to be made from the enrolled of the first class.

The result of this first draft of the Melrose men is given on another page. Owing to the great number of exemptions that were made, the additions to the men in the service, by means of the draft, were small; consequently, to carry on this gigantic struggle with treason, it was found necessary to issue another call, which was made by the President, October 17, 1863, for three hundred thousand (300,000) more troops, to serve for three years, or during the war.

The quota of Massachusetts, on this last call, was found to be fifteen thousand, one hundred and twenty-six (15,-126) men; and that of Melrose to be twenty-four (24) men.

It was determined that another draft in Melrose should be avoided if possible. A Town meeting was held Novem-

---

[1] Mr. Shelton was re-appointed to the same position May 6, 1864, and he made the necessary returns of the additions and changes in the enrollment for that year. For letter of instructions, see appendix H.

[2] For the names of the enrolled, see appendix D.

ber 14th, at which Hon. N. B. Bryant was chosen Moderator. It was voted that a Committee of four be appointed by the Chair, which, in conjunction with the Selectmen, — John H. Clark, William B. Burgess and George M. Fletcher, — should constitute a Recruiting Committee, with full powers to act in such manner as would best enable the Town to fill its quota under the recent call of the President. Stephen W. Shelton, Isaac Emerson, Jr., Rufus Smith and Charles H. Isburgh were appointed to act on this Committee, and three thousand dollars ($3,000) were appropriated to defray its expenses.

During the latter part of the year 1863, and the beginning of 1864, re-enlistments of the men already in service commenced, and the Recruiting Committee secured quite a number of such re-enlistments,[1] thus reducing the quota.

The Fifty-Ninth Veteran Regiment was also forming at this time, and a number of the men that enlisted in this regiment were obtained; also a number, — some of them our own citizens, — that entered the Third Heavy Artillery.

We now give the rest of the names of those who entered, or re-entered, the service, in the Massachusetts regiments, at or soon after this time, counting on our quota. Wherever re-enlistments of our men took place in regiments already mentioned on previous pages, such re-enlistments are there stated, and do not appear here. As heretofore, no special effort has been made to obtain items concerning non-residents.

---

[1] All who thus re-enlisted were called "Veteran Volunteers," received a thirty-days' furlough, a United States bounty of four hundred dollars, and, as an honorable distinction, "service chevrons" were authorized by the War Department. Over 136,000 tried soldiers were thus secured to the service. 10,000 re-enlisted in Massachusetts.

FIFTEENTH REGIMENT.[1]

Co. A.

PRIVATE.

ARNOLD, CHARLES H.
Non-resident.

Co. B.

PRIVATE.

WALSH, THOMAS.
Transferred to Fifteenth Battalion, July 12, 1864; non-resident.

FIFTY-NINTH REGIMENT.[2]

PRIVATES.

BARRY, JOHN.
Non-resident.

FRISBY, JOHN.
Non-resident.

HAGGERTY, DANIEL.
Non-resident; discharged for disability, Dec. 15, 1863.

LEVER, RICHARD.
Killed at "Battle of Spottsylvania," May 12, 1864.

JENKINS, GEORGE.
Non-resident.

---

[1] The Fifteenth Massachusetts left the State Aug. 8, 1861. Was in battles of Ball's Bluff, of the Peninsula, and most of the other battles participated in by the "Army of the Potomac."

[2] The Fifty-Ninth Veteran Massachusetts left the State April 26, 1864. It took part in the following engagements: Wilderness, Spottsylvania, North Anna River, Cool Arbor, Petersburg, Weldon Railroad, Poplar Spring Church, Hatcher's Run and Fort Stedman.

MULCOTT, ADOLPHUS.
Non-resident
O'REGAN, MICHAEL.
Non-resident.

Co. B.

PRIVATES.

HALPINE, BARTHOLOMEW.
Non-resident.
LEWIS, WALTER H.
Non-resident.
JACKSON, HENRY M.
Non-resident.
JOHNSON, WILLIAM A.
Non-resident.
PERKINS, BENJAMIN W.
Non-resident; discharged April 18, 1865.

Co. D.

PRIVATES.

MARRA, JAMES.
Non-resident.
PEASLEY, CHARLES D.
Non-resident.

Co. F.

PRIVATES.

ALDRIDGE, WILLIAM H.
Non-resident.
RYAN, MICHAEL.
Non-resident.
YOUNG, JOHN W.
Non-resident.

76   THE MELROSE MEMORIAL.

Co. G.

LIEUTENANT.

MORSE, GEORGE J.

Commissioned 2d Lieutenant Oct. 22, 1863; promoted 1st Lieutenant March 4, 1864; killed at the "Battle of Spottsylvania," May 12, 1864.[1]

Co. H.

SERGEANT.

STONE, HENRY.

Wounded through the hand at the "Battle of the Wilderness," May 6, 1864; taken prisoner at Weldon Railroad, Aug. 20, 1864; held in "Libby Prison" a month and then exchanged; mustered out with the regiment, July 30, 1865.

THIRD HEAVY ARTILLERY.[2]

Co. C.

PRIVATES.

CHEEVER, AUGUSTUS L.

Discharged March 9, 1865, for disability.

GROVER, ANDREW J.

Mustered out with the regiment, Sept. 18, 1865.

---

[1] For biographical sketch see "Roll of Honor."
[2] The Third Massachusetts Regiment of Heavy Artillery was composed of unattached companies, part of which were on duty in the coast defences of this State; in the fall of 1864 the regiment was sent to Washington, and served in its Forts until mustered out, Sept. 18, 1865.

GROVER, GEORGE W., JR.
Mustered out Sept. 18, 1865.

HAMMOND, GEORGE.
Transferred to navy, July 28, 1864.[1]

RICHARDSON, WILLIAM H.
Mustered out Sept. 18, 1865.

Co. F.

PRIVATES.

DAVIS, JOHN W.
Deserted at Fort Stephens, D. C., June 23, 1865; non-resident.

DAVIS, LOAMI G.
Left the regiment, June 18, 1865, by permission.

FARGO, CHARLES O.
Discharged March 10, 1865, for disability.[2]

Co. K.

PRIVATES.

REARDON, LAWRENCE.
Mustered out Sept. 18, 1865; non-resident.

TURCK, JOHN.
Discharged July 29, 1864, for disability; non-resident.

---

[1] See chap. IX.
[2] Served previously in the Tenth Maine Regiment; severely wounded in the hip at "Battle of Cedar Mountain," Aug. 9, 1862; discharged Feb. 10, 1863.

FOURTH HEAVY ARTILLERY.[1]

Co. C.

LIEUTENANT.

MARTIN, GEORGE T.

Commissioned Senior 1st Lieutenant Aug. 16, 1864; died at Massachusetts General Hospital, March 13, 1865, of pyæmia.[2]

Co. K.

LIEUTENANT.

NICHOLS, GEORGE G.[3]

Commissioned 1st Lieutenant Twenty-Fifth Un. Co. Heavy Artillery,—afterwards Co. K, Fourth Regiment,—Aug. 18, 1864; appointed Regimental Quartermaster Dec. 17, 1864; appointed Acting Assistant Quartermaster, Third Brigade, DeRussey's Division, on Staff Colonel William S. King, Commanding Brigade, Dec. 20, 1864; mustered out, June 17, 1865.

FIFTY-FOURTH REGIMENT.[4]

Co. A.

PRIVATES.

BUSH, HENRY.

Died from burns, Feb. 23, 1863; non-resident.

---

[1] The Fourth Massachusetts Heavy Artillery, like the Third, was composed of unattached companies and sent to Washington, and served in its defences until its muster-out, June 17, 1865. It was raised for one year's service.

[2] For biographical sketch see "Roll of Honor."

[3] Served nine months in 1862-3, in Forty-Second Regiment, but on Boston's quota.

[4] The Fifty-Fourth Massachusetts was the first colored regiment raised in Massachusetts, and left the State May 28, 1863, and took part in the following engagements: Fort Wagner and the several engagements before Charleston, Olustee, James Island, Honey Hill and Boykin's Mills.

THE FIFTY-SIXTH REGIMENT. 79

JOHNSON, WILLIAM H.
Non-resident.[1]

FIFTY-SIXTH REGIMENT.[2]
Co. B.

PRIVATE.

YORK, BENJAMIN F.

Taken prisoner at "Mine Explosion," July 30, 1864; at Danville, Va., eight months; exchanged April 1, 1865; mustered out June 16, 1865.

At the end of the year 1863, Massachusetts had furnished for the army in the field a total of eighty-three thousand, nine hundred and thirty-two (83,932) men; sixty-three thousand, three hundred and fifty-nine (63,359) of which were for the three years' service, sixteen thousand, eight hundred and thirty-seven (16,837) for the nine months' service, and three thousand seven hundred and thirty-six (3,736) for the three months' service; and from the commencement of the Rebellion to the end of this year, seventeen thousand, three hundred and four (17,304) men had entered the navy, for which Massachusetts had, as yet, received no credit on its quotas; this made a grand

---

[1] The whole number of negro troops commissioned and enlisted during the war was 186,017; the largest number in the service at any one time was 123,156. The State in which the largest number of colored soldiers was recruited or drafted was Louisiana, viz: 24,052; the smallest number, Texas, viz: 45. Massachusetts furnished 4,987; Melrose, 2.

[2] The Fifty-Sixth Massachusetts Veteran Regiment left the State March 21, 1864, and took part in the Wilderness, Spottsylvania, North Anna River, Cool Arbor, Petersburg, Weldon Railroad, Poplar Spring Church, Hatcher's Run and Siege of Petersburg.

total of one hundred and one thousand, two hundred and thirty-six (101,236) men furnished by the State, up to the end of the year 1863, for the United States service.

The following commissioned officers from Melrose were in the service at this time: In the army, Second Lieutenant George J. Morse, of the Fifty-Ninth Regiment; First Lieutenant J. Wesley Jones, of the Twelfth U. S. Infantry; Captain Joseph R. Simonds, of the Seventeenth Regiment; Captain J. Spencer Drayton, and Major Archibald Bogle, of the Thirty-Fifth U. S. Colored Troops. In the navy, Acting Ensigns N. Mayo Dyer, James F. Perkins and Edward A. Small, and Lieutenant Smith W. Nichols, Jr.

Of the position held by Massachusetts in this great struggle at this time, Governor Andrew thus eloquently speaks in his address to the Legislature on the 8th of January, 1864:

But the heart swells with unwonted emotion when we remember our sons and brothers, whose constant valor has sustained on the field, during nearly three years of war, the cause of our country, of civilization, and liberty. Our volunteers have represented Massachusetts, during the year just ended, on almost every field and in every department of the army where our flag has been unfurled. At Chancellorsville, Gettysburg, Vicksburg, Port Hudson and Fort Wagner, at Chickamauga, Knoxville and Chattanooga, — under Hooker, and Meade, and Banks, and Gilmore, and Rosecrans, Burnside and Grant, — in every scene of danger and of duty, along the Atlantic and the Gulf, on the Tennessee, the Cumberland, the Mississippi and the Rio Grande, — under Dupont, and Dahlgren, and Foote, and Farragut, and Porter, — the sons of Massachusetts have borne their part, and paid the debt of patriotism and valor. Ubiquitous as the stock they descend from, national in their opinions and universal in their sympathies, they have fought shoulder to shoulder with men of all sections and of every extraction. On the ocean, on the rivers, on the land, on the heights where they thundered down from the clouds of Lookout Mountain the defiance of the skies, they have graven with their swords a record imperishable.

The muse herself demands the lapse of silent years to soften, by the influences of time, her too keen and poignant realization of the scenes of war — the pathos, the heroism, the fierce joy, the grief, of battle. But, during the ages to come, she will brood over their memory. Into the hearts of her consecrated priests will breathe the inspirations of lofty and undying beauty, sublimity and truth, in all the glowing forms of speech, of literature and plastic art. By the homely traditions of the fireside, — by the head stones in the churchyard, consecrated to those whose forms repose far off in rude graves by the Rappahannock, or sleep beneath the sea, — embalmed in the memories of succeeding generations of parents and children, the heroic dead will live on in immortal youth. By their names, their character, th service, their fate, their glory, they cannot fail ;

> "They never fail who die
> In a great cause ; the block may soak their gore ;
> Their heads may sodden in the sun, their limbs
> Be strung to city gates and castle walls ;
> But still their spirit walks abroad. Though years
> Elapse, and others share as dark a doom,
> They but augment the deep and sweeping thoughts
> Which overpower all others, and conduct
> The world at last to Freedom."

VII.

1864-5.

Our glorious banner no traitor shall mar,
By effacing a stripe, or destroying a star!
Francis De Haes Janvier.

At the annual Town Meeting in March, 1864, Mr. Isaac Emerson, Jr., was excused, at his own request, from serving longer on the Recruiting Committee, and Mr. William E. Fuller was elected Selectman in place of Mr. George M. Fletcher; and the Recruiting Committee now consisted of the following gentlemen: — Colonel John H. Clark, Chairman and Recruiting Agent,[1] William B. Bur-

---

[1] PROVOST-MARSHAL'S OFFICE,
6TH DISTRICT, MASS.,
LAWRENCE, November 6, 1863.

To the Chairman of the Board of Selectmen of Melrose: —

Sir, — You are hereby informed that, under the authority of the Provost-Marshal General U. S., and by direction of Major F. N. Clarke, A. A., Provost-Marshal General of this State, I have appointed you a Recruiting Agent for your town, in accordance with the Regulations for the Bureau of the Provost-Marshal General of Oct. 28, 1863.

Please report to me personally, if you accept the appointment. If you do not accept, so inform me by mail immediately.

Very respectfully,
Your ob't servant,
H. G. HERRICK,
Captain and Provost-Marshal, 6th Dist. Mass.

gess, William E. Fuller, Stephen W. Shelton, Rufus Smith and Charles H. Isburgh. At a subsequent Town Meeting, held April 11th, it was voted that this same Recruiting Committee continue its labors, and four thousand dollars ($4,000) were appropriated for its use. This Committee acted throughout the continuance of the war; and by its spirited and strenuous exertions, — and also of the Committee as previously constituted, — no other draft[1] was ever needed in order to fill our several quotas under the calls of the President, issued in October, 1863, and February, March, July and December, 1864, in which calls a million and a half of men were asked for. A second draft was made, of the enrolled men, in April, 1864, but none of the drafted were required to report, as the quotas were then filled.[2]

Various measures were taken to aid this Committee in its efforts to procure men, with which to fill our different quotas. On the 6th of June, 1864, a Town Meeting was held, at which Colonel John H. Clark was chosen Moderator; and, on motion of Mr. Walter Babb, it was voted:

That the Town of Melrose appropriate the sum of ten thousand dollars ($10,000) for the purpose of procuring recruits for any future calls there may be made by the President of the United States for soldiers, and to make up any deficiencies that there is, or has occurred, in the last call for volunteers; and that the present Recruiting Committee of the Town of Melrose proceed immediately to recruit or procure men in anticipation of the next call, or calls, that may be made by the President of the United States. And that the Selectmen be instructed to

---

[1] One draft took place in July, 1863; for names of the citizens drawn, and the disposition of the same, see chap. X.

[2] For names of the citizens drawn at this time, see chap. X.

procure the bodies of all those of our citizen soldiers who have or may lose their lives in this war, and have them transported to their relatives or friends.

And it was also voted :

That the Town Treasurer be instructed to borrow, from time to time, such sums of money as might be required of the amount appropriated.

The raising of money for this purpose, in this manner, was illegal, as the Legislature of Massachusetts had provided, by the act of March 16, 1864, that cities and towns might raise money by taxation, or otherwise, for the purpose of procuring volunteers, and pay to each one enlisted into the service as a part of the quota of said cities and towns, a sum not exceeding one hundred and twenty-five dollars ($125).

A petition was drawn up, signed by thirty-four citizens, and presented to the Supreme Judicial Court, asking for an injunction on the proceedings at the above Town Meeting. Such an injunction was issued by Chief Justice George T. Bigelow, on the 11th of June, 1864. This was afterwards so far modified as to permit the paying of one hundred and twenty-five dollars ($125), by the Recruiting Committee, to each recruit enlisted and accepted by the United States authorities under any call of the President made between the first day of March, 1864, and the first day of March, 1865, as a part of the quota of the town of Melrose under said calls.

At this time recruits for the army cost a larger sum than one hundred and twenty-five dollars ($125); therefore a citizens' meeting was called, to take into consideration the best manner of raising a sum of money, as a recruiting fund, to aid the Committee in the furnishing of men for our quotas. There was a very large attendance at this meeting, and it was decided to raise the money needed by subscription. A paper was drawn up, which was headed by Mr. Wingate P. Sargent; and at this and subsequent times, a sum of nearly six thousand dollars ($6,000) was raised for recruiting purposes, to be expended under the auspices of the Recruiting Committee.

At the second meeting, held for the purpose of raising this fund, the following gentlemen were chosen a Committee to collect the amounts already subscribed, and to solicit additional subscriptions from the citizens. Messrs. Wingate P. Sargent, Daniel Norton, Jr., Levi S. Gould, Isaac Emerson, Jr., Thomas A. Long and Joseph D. Wilde. Mr. Sargent was appointed Treasurer, and, after the collections were made, the money was paid over by him to Colonel Clark, as Chairman of the Recruiting Committee.

The names of the subscribers to this fund, and the amounts paid, are as follows :

Wingate P. Sargent	$250 00
Daniel Norton, Jr. .	130 00
Rufus Smith . .	100 00
Alverse L. White .	100 00
Isaac Emerson, Jr. .	100 00
Wickham C. McNish	100 00
Samuel E. Sewall .	100 00
Daniel W. Gooch .	100 00
Daniel W. Foster .	100 00
Samuel S. Houghton	80 00
Joseph D. Wilde .	75 00
Elisha F. Sears .	75 00

Ralph Warren	75 00
Charles H. Isburgh	75 00
George A. Mansfield	75 00
Nathaniel J. Bartlett	75 00
George G. Wheeler	60 00
Jeremiah Crowley	50 00
William H. Allen	50 00
Edgar M. Stevens	50 00
Levi S. Gould	50 00
Ira H. Bickford	50 00
Frank O. Dame	50 00
George Hart	50 00
William F. Morse	50 00
Oliver Whyte	50 00
Gardner Wheeler	50 00
Walter Littlefield, Jr.	50 00
Henry A. Norris	50 00
Napoleon B. Bryant	50 00
Andrew P. Trott	50 00
R. Watson Emerson	50 00
Augustus Barrett	50 00
John Baldwin	50 00
Joseph H. Greene	50 00
William H. Stone	50 00
Simeon Locke	50 00
Alonzo V. Lynde	50 00
George Emerson	50 00
George F. Stone	50 00
Frank A. Messenger	50 00
Oren H. Peck	45 00
Joseph A. Fairbanks	40 00
George M. Fletcher	30 00
S. W. Heald	30 00

CITIZENS' RECRUITING FUND.

James M. Beckett	30 00
Edward R. Knights	30 00
John L. Allen	30 00
Jarvis P. Hudson	25 00
Albert P. Perkins	25 00
Thomas A. Long	25 00
Erastus F. Bradford	25 00
Benjamin F. Greene	25 00
George N. Noyes	25 00
Dr. George Macomber	25 00
Joel Bowker	25 00
Charles H. Blaisdell	25 00
Daniel Jefferson	25 00
Dr. Moses Parker	25 00
Allen C. Goss	25 00
Fernando C. Taylor	25 00
Joseph E. Westgate	25 00
James A. Barrett	25 00
George C. Sargent	25 00
Samuel S. Bugbee	25 00
Anthony Crosby	25 00
John H. Clark	25 00
George Newhall	25 00
William O. Lynde	25 00
Charles Larrabee	25 00
John S. Higgins	25 00
John Shelton	25 00
C. Edgar Buffum	25 00
Henry A. Leonard	25 00
Rufus Leavitt	25 00
Robert J. Chute	25 00
Obadiah S. Edgerly	25 00
Sargent F. Severence	25 00

Liberty Bigelow	25 00
John Conway, Jr.	25 00
Jonathan Barrett	25 00
Charles Boardman	25 00
John W. Cobb	25 00
Elbridge Gardner	25 00
Peter Edgerly	25 00
Jeremiah Martin	25 00
Horatio N. Perkins	25 00
George F. Boardman	25 00
Josiah P. Mendum	25 00
Stephen Shelton	25 00
Lewis G. Coburn	25 00
Frederick W. A. Rankin, Jr.	25 00
Thomas J. Kimball	25 00
John S. Sewall	20 00
Elbridge H. Goss	20 00
John W. Tower	20 00
George R. Forsythe	20 00
P. Russell Ellis	20 00
Sylvanus Upham	20 00
Charles Furneaux	20 00
Edward B. Newhall	20 00
John Smith	20 00
Nelson Cochran	20 00
John W. Buttrick	20 00
Daniel O. Morton	20 00
Leonard Lynde	20 00
Henry B. Newhall	20 00
Artemas Barrett	20 00
George W. Bartlett	20 00
Robert W. Pierce	20 00
George W. Pollock	20 00

CITIZENS' RECRUITING FUND.

George B. Sargent	20 00
Caleb Howard	20 00
Christopher Kirmes	20 00
Joseph McIntire	20 00
James Astle	20 00
John L. Andrews	20 00
William F. Poole	20 00
Lyell T. Terwillager	20 00
Alfred W. Sprague	20 00
William H. Wells	20 00
George A. Chipman	20 00
Isaiah A. Young	20 00
Benjamin Underwood	20 00
Charles A. Messenger	20 00
Walter Babb	20 00
Solomon Severy	15 00
John Q. Adams	15 00
Alonzo Patterson	15 00
Samuel O. Dearborn	15 00
Peter Batchelder	15 00
Joel Atwood	15 00
George C. Stantial	15 00
Thomas W. Chadbourne	15 00
Asa H. Jones	15 00
Samuel M. Tourtellot	15 00
George Hemminway	14 00
Samuel Barker	10 00
Martin Ellis	10 00
Walter R. Collins	10 00
William B. Burgess	10 00
Charles E. Keith	10 00
Samuel F. Summers	10 00
John Robson	10 00

Dr. Benjamin F. Abbott	10 00
William W. Vaughn	10 00
G. W. Gilman	10 00
Calvin Stone	10 00
William D. Stratton	10 00
Sullivan C. Atwood	10 00
Calvin N. Chapin	10 00
Hiram D. Richardson	10 00
Azel E. Steele	10 00
Elbridge Green	10 00
Benjamin Roach	10 00
Charles P. Lynde	10 00
Rev. Nathan P. Selee	10 00
James S. Sturtevant	10 00
William M. Gilmore	10 00
James Small	10 00
Alvin Lynde	10 00
William Clark	10 00
J. B. Daniels	10 00
Lawrence K. Munn	10 00
Charles F. Bowker	10 00
Moses A. Noyes	10 00
Addison Lane	10 00
Edmund B. Little	10 00
William L. Pierce	10 00
Royal P. Barry	10 00
Lewis H. Richardson	10 00
Jabez G. Hayward	10 00
Francis Fountain	10 00
George Sargent	10 00
Dexter Pratt	10 00
George C. Brown	10 00
Dr. Abel Astle	10 00

CITIZENS' RECRUITING FUND.

George Lynde	10 00
Josiah H. Barker	5 00
Martin B. Loring	5 00
J. T. Marcy	5 00
George W. Fisher	5 00
Albert A. Gould	5 00
Benjamin R. Walker	5 00
Augustus Brooks	5 00
William Finnegan	5 00
Dennis Finnegan	5 00
Joseph C. Bowker	5 00
Emery Close	5 00
Ansel B. Pierce	5 00
George Woodward	5 00
John Hurley	5 00
Edward Moore	5 00
Thomas Cowhey	5 00
Thomas Freeman	5 00
Solomon L. Howes	5 00
Paschal E. Burnham	5 00
John P. Buttrick	5 00
E. B. Southwick	5 00
Henry Robinson	5 00
Charles F. Upham	5 00
Jasper F. Ferdinand	5 00
John Gateley	5 00
Ai Rowe	5 00
Walter Murphy	5 00
Henry J. Robinson	5 00
Daniel Conway	5 00
Joel Snow	5 00
Carlon Buffum	5 00
Osmore Jenkins	5 00

Robert Wheeler	5 00
William A. Lamson	5 00
Aaron Green	5 00
Oliver T. Wentworth	3 00
Reuben T. Haley	3 00
Nathaniel Howard	3 00
Samuel D. Blanchard	2 00
Total	$5,650 00

With the above amount, so liberally contributed by our citizens, the Recruiting Committee were enabled to obtain all the men required to fill our several quotas, by adding to the amount paid to each recruit by the Town, — one hundred and twenty-five dollars ($125), — whatever sum was necessary; the average cost of a recruit at this time, in addition to the State and United States bounty,[1] being about two hundred and fifty dollars ($250).

Very few of our own citizens enlisted during the last year of the war, although quite a number that were already in the service re-enlisted; such re-enlistments counting on our quotas the same as new enlistments.

The names of most of the recruits obtained by the Committee, at various times and at various places, during the last year of the rebellion, may be found in the alphabetical list at the end of the volume.

---

[1] Massachusetts paid no bounty until 1863; then $50; Oct. 17, 1863, it was increased to $325. The United States paid $100 bounty until Oct. 17, 1863; then $300 to new recruits, and $400 to veterans until July 18, 1864; afterwards $100, $200 and $300 to one, two and three years' volunteers.

VIII.

1864.

ONE HUNDRED DAYS' MEN.

"All hail the Stars and Stripes!"[1] the cry
From forest home to ocean shore,
Ten thousand times ten thousand hands
Are raised to free that flag once more.
To each proud heart new hope is sent,
To each strong arm new strength is given;
And, raised aloft from every home,
The Stars and Stripes float nearer heaven.

George T. Brown.

In July, 1864, the Secretary of War made a requisition upon Massachusetts for five militia regiments, to serve for the period of one hundred days, during the time the re-enlisting troops were having their furloughs; and, as usual, the Old Bay State responded with alacrity, and the regiments were recruited and equipped with all possible despatch.

These one hundred days' men were not to be credited to the quota of Massachusetts, but it was conceded that whoever should serve for this length of time should not be liable to the draft then pending. Five thousand four hun-

---

[1] The last words of Luther C. Ladd, of the Sixth Regiment, who was killed while marching through Baltimore, April 19, 1861.

dred and sixty-one (5,461) men went forth from the State under this call.

As heretofore, under the various demands made, Melrose responded with its proportion of men, and sent a few into four of the five regiments then raised, viz: The Fifth, Sixth, Eighth and Sixtieth; and their names are as follows:

FIFTH REGIMENT.[1]

Co. K.

PRIVATE.

GROVER, W. W.

Mustered out with the regiment, Nov. 16, 1864.

SIXTH REGIMENT.[2]

Co. A.

LIEUTENANT.

CHIPMAN, GEORGE A.[3]

Mustered out with the regiment, Oct. 27, 1864

PRIVATES.

BURNHAM, OLIVER R.

Mustered out Oct. 27, 1864.

---

[1] The Fifth Regiment was mustered into the service July 28, 1864, and was stationed at Fort Marshall, near Baltimore, Md.

[2] The Sixth Regiment was mustered into the service July 20, 1864, and was stationed at Arlington Heights, Va., and at Fort Delaware, Md., a depot for Confederate prisoners.

[3] Also served nine months in Forty-Fifth Regiment in 1862-3; see chap. V.

McLAUGHLIN, HIRAM.
Mustered out Oct. 27, 1864.
WAITT, JOHN R.
Mustered out Oct. 27, 1864.
WYMAN, GEORGE W.
Mustered out Oct. 27, 1864.
WYMAN, WESTON.
Mustered out Oct. 27, 1864.

Co. E.

PRIVATES.

PAGE, MOSES S.[1]
Mustered out Oct. 27, 1864.
SPAULDING, HENRY H.
Mustered out Oct. 27, 1864.

EIGHTH REGIMENT.[2]

SERGEANT-MAJOR.

TYLER, WILLIAM N.[3]

Sergeant of Co. E at first; promoted Sergeant-Major July

---

[1] Acted as Postmaster of the regiment while at Arlington Heights, and Assistant Postmaster and Inspector of Rebel correspondence at Fort Delaware.

[2] The Eighth Regiment, — like the Fifth and Sixth, as stated on previous pages, — was one of the three months' regiments that responded so quickly when the first call for troops was made in April, 1861, and marched to Washington by the way of Annapolis, Md., overcoming many obstacles.* The Eighth was now mustered into service July 26, 1864, and was stationed at Baltimore and Cockeysville, Md.

[3] Also served three months in the Fifth Regiment in 1861, and nine months in the Fiftieth Regiment, in 1862-3, but on the South Reading quota.

---

* The National Intelligencer said of it, the day after its arrival in Washington, "We doubt whether any other single regiment in the country could furnish such a ready contingent to reconstruct a steam engine, lay a rail-track, and bend the sails of a man-of-war."

19, 1864; mustered out with the regiment, Nov. 10, 1864.

Co. E.

CORPORAL.

SHELTON, THOMAS.[1]
Mustered out Nov. 10, 1864.

PRIVATES.

ANDERSON, JOHN H. L.
Mustered out Nov. 10, 1864.

LYALL, DAVID S.
Mustered out Nov. 10, 1864.

QUINN, PATRICK.
Mustered out Nov. 10, 1864.

PRATT, HENRY W.
Mustered out Nov. 10, 1864.

SIMONDS, JOSEPH W.[2]
Mustered out Nov. 10, 1864.

VINTON, EDWIN A.[3]
Mustered out Nov. 10, 1864.

VINTON, GRAY.
Mustered out Nov. 10, 1864.

---

[1] Also served nine months in Fiftieth Regiment, in 1862-3, see chap. V.

[2] Also served nine months in Forty-Fourth Regiment, in 1862-3, see chap. V.

[3] Also served nine months in Forty-Second Regiment, in 1862-3, see chap. V.

NINETY DAYS' MEN. 97

SIXTIETH REGIMENT.[1]
Co. G.

PRIVATES.

PILLING, JAMES L.
Mustered out Nov. 30, 1864.

UPHAM, HENRY W.
Mustered out Nov. 30, 1864.

NINETY DAYS' MEN.

Massachusetts also sent into the field this same year, — 1864, — thirteen unattached companies of infantry, comprising twelve hundred and forty-seven (1,247) men, to serve for a period of ninety days; and in the Seventh Unattached Company,[2] Captain Albert E. Proctor, Melrose had seven (7) men, as follows:

LIEUTENANT.

NICHOLS, GEORGE G.
Commissioned 1st Lieutenant May 6, 1864; mustered out with the regiment, Aug. 4, 1864.[3]

CORPORAL.

LYNDE, AMOS W.[4]
Mustered out Aug. 4, 1864.

---

[1] The Sixtieth Massachusetts Regiment was mustered in Aug. 1, 1864, and was stationed at Indianapolis, Ind.

[2] The Seventh Unattached Company was mustered into service May 4, 1864, and was stationed at Gallop's Island, Boston Harbor.

[3] Also served nine months in Forty-Second Regiment, but on Boston's quota. Re-commissioned in Fourth Heavy Artillery, see chap. VI.

[4] Also served nine months in the Forty-Second Regiment, in 1862-3, see chap. V.

THE MELROSE MEMORIAL.

WAGONER.

YORK, JOSIAH R.[1]

Mustered out Aug. 4, 1864.

PRIVATES.

DAVIS, JAMES L.[1]

Mustered out Aug. 4, 1864.

EMERSON, JAMES G.[1]

Mustered out Aug. 4, 1864.

EMERSON, JOSEPH S.

Mustered out Aug. 4, 1864.

YORK, WILLIAM B.[1]

Mustered out Aug. 4, 1864.

ONE YEAR'S MEN.

Melrose had one man in the regiment,— the Sixty-First, — which was also organized during this same year, — 1864, — to serve for a period of one year. It was mustered into the service in October, and took part in the various engagements before Petersburg.

Co. F.

PRIVATE.

PEMBERTON, LEWIS E.

Mustered out Aug. 3, 1865.

---

[1] Also served nine months in the Forty-Second Regiment, in 1862-3, see chap. V.

IX.

1861-5.

NAVY.

And is the old flag flying still,
That o'er your fathers flew,
With bands of white and rosy light,
And field of starry blue?
Ay! look aloft! its folds full oft
Have braved the roaring blast,
And still shall fly when from the sky
This black typhoon has past!

Oliver Wendell Holmes.

Melrose was well represented in the naval service during the great Rebellion. From the breaking out of the war until April 13, 1865, Massachusetts furnished for the naval and marine service twenty-six thousand three hundred and ten (26,310) men. July 4, 1864, Congress passed an act allowing all men in the naval service to be credited on their proper quotas. Those whose place of residence could be ascertained were assigned to their several cities and towns. It was found that there were seven thousand six hundred and five (7,605) men whose places of residence could not be ascertained; and these, in September, 1864, were credited *pro rata* to the different towns and cities of the Commonwealth. The number apportioned to Melrose was twenty-eight (28), and their names are as follows. The name of the vessels on which a portion of them served, or their location, is given in the alphabetical list at the end of the volume.

Bosson, Samuel,
Kingdom, John,
Kohler, Charles,
Ludirzen, George S.,
Lombard, Charles E.,
Lee, George E.,
Lamb, John R.,
Lange, Andrew,
Lafferty, James,
Launzen, Christian,
Lane, John,
Lalley, Thomas J.,
Lewis, Thomas,
Lemont, Henry,

Ward, Reuben D.,
Waters, Henry,
Watts, Simon C.,
Weeks, Seymour,
Weldon, George E.,
Wharton, Joseph,
Wilbur, William H.,
Wilkins, Charles B.,
Wilkinson, Robert,
Williams, Charles J.,
Williams, George,
Williams, Walter,
Wilson, Thomas E.,
Woodman, Robert.

Those of our own citizens that served in the navy, at different times and for different periods, are as follows:

BODWELL, DANIEL A.[1]

Enlisted in Marine Corps, U. S. Navy, Aug. 24, 1863; served on gunboats "Augusta" and "Chicopee"; was in Farragut's victory in Mobile Bay, Aug. 5, 1864; discharged Aug. 24, 1867.

DYER, N. MAYO.[2]

Appointed Acting Master's Mate, May 2, 1862, and ordered to the Charlestown Navy Yard for instruction in

---

[1] Served a year in the Twenty-Second Massachusetts Regiment, see chap. III.

[2] Served a year in the Thirteenth Massachusetts Regiment, see chap. II.

gunnery, etc. July 7, ordered to the U. S. S. "R. R. Cuyler," Lieutenant Commanding Francis Winslow, and on the 29th July sailed for the East Gulf Squadron, touching at Nassau, where the Confederate steamer "Florida" — then called the "Oreto" — was lying, and under English colors. Cruised off that port for several days, until compelled to visit Key West for coal, and repairs to machinery. Sailed from Key West Aug. 21, for Nassau. "Oreto" had left that port, and on the 4th of September she entered Mobile Bay. Yellow fever broke out on board, and the surgeon, executive and commanding officers being sick, Aug. 26th the "Cuyler" started for New York. Aug. 27th, Dyer was placed in charge of the prize schooner "Anna Sophia," captured that day, and ordered to New York, where he arrived Sept. 1st. Rejoined the "R. R. Cuyler" at Portsmouth, N. H., Sept. 10, Captain Winslow and Lieutenant Phillips having died during his absence.

Oct. 7, the "Cuyler" sailed from Portsmouth, — Lieutenant Commander Homer C. Blake in command, — for the West Gulf Squadron, via Key West, arriving at Pensacola, Fla., Oct. 20, joining the blockading fleet off Mobile the 27th. On the escape of the "Oreto" from Mobile in January, 1863, the "Cuyler" started in chase, and cruised about the West Indies for two months in search of her, returning off Mobile the middle of March.

On the night of May 17, in charge of a boat's crew, Dyer boarded and captured the rebel schooner "Isabel" ashore under Fort Morgan, setting fire to her and bringing off her crew and papers.[1] May 20, 1863, he was promoted, by Admiral Farragut, to Acting Ensign, subject

---

[1] For Lieutenant Dyer's own account of this daring exploit, see chap. XVI.

to the approval of the Navy Department. May 30, ordered to the command of the steamer "Eugenie," and remained on blockade duty, with occasional trips to New Orleans, until the latter part of November; Sept. 12, capturing the blockade runner "Alabama," and being under fire of Forts Morgan and Gaines several times, — receiving a shell from Fort Morgan through the pilot house on one occasion, slightly wounding him in the hand.

During the winter of 1863-4 he was on duty in the Mississippi River, excepting one expedition to the Mermantau River, — coast of Louisiana, — resulting in the capture of a schooner and sloop, and their destruction, bringing off nine prisoners and valuable papers; for which he was promoted, in July, to Acting Master by the Navy Department, to date from Jan. 12, 1864. His health being poor at this time, he obtained permission to return North for two months; but on arriving at New Orleans, and learning that the attack on the defences of Mobile Bay would probably take place before the expiration of his furlough, he returned off Mobile and applied for orders to some vessel assigned for the attack.

July 19, he was ordered to the steamer "Metacomet," Lieutenant Commander James E. Jouett, which vessel on the 5th of August was the consort of the flag-ship "Hartford," — Rear Admiral Farragut, — leading the line past the rebel works into Mobile Bay, and to the attack of the rebel fleet inside. The rebel steamer "Selma" struck to the "Metacomet," and Dyer was placed in charge *pro tempore*.[1] August 26, the rebel defences of the bay having all surrendered, he accepted leave and returned North. Rejoined the squadron Oct. 29, when he was ordered to

---

[1] For Lieutenant Dyer's account of this fight, see chap. XVI.

the flag-ship "Hartford." Nov. 30, he was ordered to the command of U. S. S. "Rodolph," and to duty in Mississippi Sound, co-operating with the land forces under General Granger. The "Rodolph" was destroyed by a torpedo in Blakely River, in the approach upon Mobile, April 1, 1865,[1] from which time until May 10 he was engaged upon special duty connected with the clearing of torpedoes from Mobile Bay and Channel.

April 22, 1865, he was promoted Acting Volunteer Lieutenant. May 10, upon the surrender of the rebel fleet to the forces under Rear Admiral Thacher, he was given command of the late rebel steamer "Morgan." In June, detached and placed in command of the "Elk," and July 12, placed in command of the U. S. S. "Stockdale," and ordered to Mississippi Sound. The "Stockdale" being sold, Sept. 4, he was ordered to the U. S. S. "Moharka" as Executive Officer. Oct. 8, detached and placed in command of the U. S. S. "Glasgow," temporary flag-ship of Rear Admiral Thacher.

In April, 1866, received permission to return North, and May 19, was ordered to special duty in the Bureau of Navigation, Navy Department, Washington, D. C.

---

[1] "On this day, April 1, 1865, another vessel was sunk by a torpedo. At 1, P. M., the tin-clad steamer 'Rodolph,' Acting Master N. M. Dyer, in obedience to signal from flagship, weighed anchor, passed within hail, and, receiving orders to take a barge alongside containing apparatus for raising the 'Milwaukie,' proceeded with it inside the Blakely bar. The 'Rodolph' crossed the bar, and was standing up toward the wreck of the 'Milwaukie,' when, at 2.40, P. M., being directly between the 'Chickasaw' and 'Winnebago,' she exploded a torpedo under her starboard bow, and rapidly sank in twelve feet of water. It appeared that a hole had been made in her ten feet in diameter. By this casualty four of her crew were killed and seven wounded, of whom five were colored men " — *History of the Campaign of Mobile, by Brevet Major-General C. C. Andrews.*

March 12, 1868, he was commissioned a Lieutenant in the regular service, and is now on duty in the Pacific Squadron.

EARL, WILLIAM H.[1]

Transferred from the Thirty-Ninth Massachusetts Regiment, April 21, 1864; served on gunboat "Mendota"; discharged June 12, 1865.

FULLER, WILLIAM A.

Appointed Acting Third Assistant Engineer, March 23, 1864; assigned to gunboat "Fort Donelson"; discharged Dec. 18, 1865.

HAMMOND, GEORGE.

Transferred from the Third Heavy Artillery, June 29, 1864; served on gunboat "Juniata"; was in the attacks on "Fort Fisher," Dec. 24–25, 1864, and Jan. 13, 14, 15, 1865; afterwards in North and South Atlantic Blockading Squadrons; discharged 1865.

HARVEY, FRANKLIN.

Enlisted Dec. 19, 1861; served two years on gunboat "Miami"; was in the attack on Forts "St. Philip" and "Jackson," April 15–23, 1862, under Admiral Farragut; discharged Dec. 21, 1863.

MACEY, JOHN S.[2]

Enlisted Nov. 15, 1863; served one year on gunboat "Phillippi"; discharged Dec. 1, 1864.

---

[1] Served on U. S. frigate "Sabine" six months, in 1861-2.
[2] Served previously in the Seventeenth Regiment Massachusetts Volunteers, see chap. III.

MARTIN, JEREMIAH, JR.

Appointed Paymaster's Clerk, on U. S. S. "Tritonia," Dec. 19, 1864; transferred to U. S. ship "J. C. Kuhn," July 3, 1865; discharged Sept. 14, 1865.

McLAUGHLIN, FRANK M.

Enlisted March 27, 1865; served three years and a half on gunboats "Kearsarge," "Mohican," and "Mohongo," as Ship's Yeoman; discharged Aug. 29, 1868.

MITCHELL, GEORGE.

Enlisted Feb. 15, 1862; served three years on gunboats "Tioga," "Sonoma," and "Britannia"; was in attack on "Fort Fisher," Dec. 24-25, 1864; discharged Feb. 15, 1865.

NICHOLS, SMITH W., JR.[1]

At the opening of the Rebellion, assigned as Midshipman to the U. S. frigate "Wabash"; at home on leave of absence, on account of sickness, two or three months during the summer of 1861; after which appointed Assistant Instructor on the U. S. Receiving Ship "Ohio"; Aug. 1, 1862, appointed Lieutenant by President Lincoln; commissioned Feb. 21, 1863; appointed Executive Officer of U. S. Sloop "Macedonian" in latter part of 1862; transferred to Schoolship "Savannah," at New York, in spring of 1863, where he remained until ordered to the U. S. Steam-sloop "Shen-

---

[1] Appointed Acting Midshipman in the United States navy, Sept. 27, 1858, on the recommendation of Hon. D. W. Gooch. Entered the Naval Academy at Annapolis, Md. In the monthly report for December, 1860, he is spoken of by the Superintendent, G. S. Blake, as a "correct and promising young gentleman."

andoah "; was Executive Officer of the "Shenandoah" during the attacks on "Fort Fisher," Dec. 24-25, 1864, and Jan. 13, 14, 15, 1865.[1] After the fall of "Fort

---

[1] Captain Daniel B. Ridgely, commanding the "Shenandoah" during these attacks on "Fort Fisher," thus mentions Lieutenant Nichols in his reports. Under date "Off Beaufort, N. C., December 31, 1864," referring to the first attack, he says :

" It affords me much gratification to speak of the cool bearing of Lieutenant S. W. Nichols, the Executive Officer, and other officers, and the crew of this ship, during the two days' bombardment."

After the second attack, under date "Off Fort Fisher, January 17, 1865," in his detailed report he says :

* * * " At 9.48, A. M., sent the first and second launches and first cutter with the storming party, consisting of fifty-four men and fourteen marines, under command of Lieutenant S. W. Nichols, the Executive Officer, Ensign. Sands, and Boatswain J. H. Polley. * * * I enclose Lieutenant Nichols' report of the storming party from this ship, which will speak for itself. I take great pleasure in bearing testimony to the cool bearing of Lieutenant Nichols, the Executive Officer, and the other officers and crew of this ship during the bombardment.
I am, very respectfully,
Your obedient servant,
DANIEL B. RIDGELY, *Captain*."
REAR-ADMIRAL DAVID D. PORTER,
Commanding North Atlantic Squadron.

The following is the report of Lieutenant Nichols referred to by Captain Ridgely :
UNITED STATES STEAMER SHENANDOAH,
OFF NEW INLET, N. C., Jan. 17, 1865.

SIR :— I have the honor to report, that on leaving this ship on the morning of the 15th instant, in charge of assaulting party of this ship, consisting of fifty-four men and a sergeant's guard of marines, with Ensign J. H. Sands and Boatswain J. H. Polley, I passed within hail of the "Malvern," and was there ordered to Lieutenant Commander Breese, on shore. Arrived on shore, leaving two men as boat-keepers in each of the three boats, reported to Lieutenant Commander Breese, and was by him placed in the third division, under command of Lieutenant Commander Selfridge. The marines were ordered elsewhere. On the charge our men were orderly; kept together; did not drop, except when ordered to do so, and when the stockade in front of the fort was reached, were among the foremost, and were among the last to fall back. Robert Esler, second-class fireman, remained with me and other officers and men behind the stockade until dark, when we all succeeded in getting away.

I found that marines, Charles Smith, Adolph Burton, Wilmer D. Lyne, James Whyte, Thomas S. Brown, all of this ship, had remained near Fort Fisher until dark, not having fallen back with their own line. On arriving down the beach, I found that Ensign Sands and Boatswain Polley had rallied all the men of this ship during the retreat, had found all

Fisher," ordered in the iron-clad "Passaic" to Philadelphia; at close of war ordered home, waiting orders. The latter part of 1865, again ordered to the U. S. Steamer "Shenandoah," one of the fleet belonging to the Asiatic Squadron, commanded by Rear Admiral H. H. Bell, where he now is. Promoted Lieutenant Commander, July 25, 1866.

PERKINS, JAMES F.

Appointed Acting Ensign Nov. 14, 1862 ; assigned to U. S. S. "Tritonia," "Barrataria," "Horace Beals," and "Portsmouth"; was in Farragut's victory at Forts "St. Philip" and "Jackson," and "Siege of Vicksburg"; discharged Sept. 20, 1865.[1]

---

[1] For form of discharge papers, see Appendix I.

---

the wounded of our own men, seven in number, and had sent them on board and rendered good service to other wounded men of the assaulting party. Our men here maintained the sailor discipline, obeying their officers cheerfully, ready and willing to do whatever was required of them. None left the shore except those ordered to take off the wounded. Ensign Sands and Boatswain Polley deserve the highest praise for the zeal and energy shown throughout. At night the sailors and marines relieved the garrison at army headquarters. On being relieved in the morning, was ordered up the beach to bury the dead. Arriving there and finding the burial party of sufficient force, returned to the boats, thence to the ship. I am happy to state that none of our men were killed, and that the color-bearers, two in number, returned each with his flag.

In conclusion, sir, I would beg leave to state that all of our men behaved in such a gallant manner that I would consider it invidious to make any distinction. Each and all deserve the highest commendation for their coolness and courage under the most trying circumstances, and fully sustained the hard-earned reputation of the American sailor.

I am, sir, very respectfully,
Your obedient servant,
SMITH W. NICHOLS, JR.
Lieutenant U. S. Navy.

CAPTAIN D. B. RIDGELY,
Commanding "Shenandoah."
Forwarded.

DANIEL B. RIDGELY,
Captain U. S. N.

SMALL, EDWARD A.

Appointed Acting Ensign June 16, 1862; ordered to U. S. S. "Cambridge" in North Atlantic Squadron; detached Oct. 17, 1864, and ordered to Frigate "Wabash"; was in the attacks on "Fort Fisher," Dec. 24, 25, 1864, and Jan. 13–15, 1865; promoted Acting Master Feb. 22, 1865; ordered on special duty until May 15, 1865, and then to the ship "New Hampshire," in the South Atlantic Squadron; discharged Oct. 14, 1865.

"The good ship Union's voyage is o'er,
    At anchor safe she swings,
And loud and clear, with cheer on cheer
    Her joyous welcome rings:
Hurrah! Hurrah! it shakes the wave,
    It thunders on the shore, —
One flag, one land, one heart, one hand,
    One Nation, evermore!"

X.

1863.

THE DRAFT.

Strike for that broad and goodly land,
Blow after blow, till men shall see
That Might and Right move hand in hand,
And glorious must their triumph be.
William Cullen Bryant.

The Act of Congress for "enrolling and calling out the national forces, and for other purposes," was approved March 3, 1863. The main objects of this law were to enroll and hold liable to military duty all citizens capable of bearing arms not exempted therefrom by its provisions, to call forth the national forces when required, and to arrest deserters and return them to their proper commands.

The original act required the enrollment to be composed of two classes: the first comprising all persons subject to do military duty between the ages of twenty and thirty-five years, and all unmarried persons subject to military duty above the age of thirty-five and under the age of forty-five; the second, comprising all other persons subject to military duty, that is, all married persons between thirty-five and forty-five years of age, who fulfilled the required conditions. The law provided that the second class should not be called out in any district until the first class was exhausted. This distinction of classes was abolished Feb. 24, 1864, and all persons liable to military duty consolidated into one and the same class.

Under this law, and by direction of Provost-Marshal General James B. Fry, four drafts were made throughout the loyal States during the Rebellion. The first commenced about the 1st of July, 1863, and was for one-fifth of the persons enrolled in the first class. The second commenced about the 15th of April, 1864, and was for deficiencies under calls for seven hundred thousand (700,000) volunteers. The third commenced about the 19th of September, 1864, for deficiencies under call of July 18, 1864, for five hundred thousand (500,000) volunteers. The fourth commenced about the 20th of February, 1865, for deficiencies under call of Dec. 19, 1864, for three hundred thousand (300,000) volunteers.

The whole number of persons drawn, in the United States, during the first draft, was		292,441
Failed to report	39,415	
Discharged for various causes	460	
		39,875
		252,566
Whole number exempted		164,395
		88,171
Held to personal service	9,881	
Furnished substitutes	26,002	
Paid commutation	52,288	
		88,171

THE FIRST DRAFT.

The whole number of persons drawn in Massachusetts during this draft was ... 32,077
Failed to report 2,880
Discharged for various causes . 6
             2,886
             29,191
Whole number exempted   22,359
             '6,832
Held to personal service . 807
Furnished substitutes . . 2,322
Paid commutation . . . 3,703
             6,832

The whole number of persons drawn in this District, — the Sixth, — during this draft was . . . 2,712
Failed to report 167
             2,545
Total number exempted .   2,148
             397
Held to personal service   52
Furnished substitutes .   102
Paid commutation . .   243
             397

Captain H. G. Herrick, of Saugus, was appointed Provost-Marshal for this District, and his headquarters were at Lawrence; and on the days of drafting, busy and interesting scenes were presented at his office, there being a great desire manifested during the progress of the draft, to witness the operation, and to ascertain who were the unlucky ones whose names should be taken from the wheel of,— *not* fortune, but, to them, of *mis*fortune. The drafting in this District commenced July 9th, and Melrose,

— Sub-District No. 9, — was reached July 13th. Forty-nine (49) names were drawn from the wheel [1] The provisions of the act were such that any person drafted, if found acceptable, could be exempted from service by furnishing a substitute, or paying three hundred dollars ($300) commutation.

The following is a list of the drafted persons, giving those who furnished substitutes, those who paid commutation, those who failed to report, and those who were exempted for various causes. No one was drafted and accepted from our town who served in person.

Furnished substitutes:
Jonathan C. Howes,
Henry W. Barrett,
George W. Emerson.

Paid commutation: [2]
William F. Gordon,
Joseph A. Fairbanks,
Osgood W. Upham,[3]
Charles Robbins.

Exempted because only son of a widow, liable to military duty:
Nathaniel J. Bartlett,
William Donalavy.[4]

---

[1] The whole number in enrolled men of Melrose liable to do military duty, as returned by the assessors in May of each year of the war, was as follows: In 1861, 366; 1862, 440; 1863, 368; 1864, 359; 1865, 365.

[2] The amount of commutation money paid at this time, in Massachusetts, was $1,110,900 by 3,703 men; and during the war, $1,610,400 by 5,318 men. The amount paid during the war, throughout the loyal States, was $26,366,316.78, paid by 87,874 men.

[3] For form of certificate of exemption, see Appendix E.

[4] Afterwards entered the marine service for five years, but not on the quota of Melrose.

Exempted because had two brothers then in United States' service :
Richard H. Shelton,
Stephen W. Shelton.

Exempted because over thirty-five, and married :
William H. Stone.

Exempted because not naturalized :
James Astle.

Exempted for disability :
Charles E. Keith,
Joseph Goodwin,
Curtis S. Gordon,
Daniel L. Chase,
Frederick W. A. Rankin, Jr.,
William Cook,
Jonathan Barrett,
James W. Dodge,
Elbridge H. Goss,
Lucius L. D. Porter,
William F. Morse,
Charles A. Waite,
Moses S. Page,
Lewis H. Richardson,
Albert F. Shelton,[1]
Andrew P. Trott,
Oren Brown,
Leander T. Freeman,
Theodore L. Knowles,
Walter Babb,

---

[1] Was discharged Dec. 23, 1862, from the Thirteenth Regiment on account of wound received at "Battle of Antietam," Sept. 17, 1862.

Charles H. Blaisdell,
Edmund W. Davis,[1]
John H. B. Henderson,
William A. Fuller,
Oren H. Peck,
William Morse,
Joseph S. Emerson,
John L. Allen,
John Thompson,[2]
Joshua Emery, Jr.,
John H. Crocker,[3]
Bradford Edmands.

Failed to report:

Augustus L. Cheever,[4]
George W. Grover, Jr.,
Edward Finnegan,
George Hammond.[5]

Whole number drawn   49
Furnished substitutes .   3
Paid commutation   4
Failed to report . . .   4
Exempted for disability .   32
Exempted for other causes .   6
    — 49

---

[1] Was discharged Oct. 20, 1862, from the Twenty-Second Regiment on account of disability.

[2] Afterwards entered the navy, but not on quota of Melrose.

[3] Was discharged Dec. 30, 1862, from the Thirteenth Regiment on account of disability.

[4] Enlisted in Third Heavy Artillery, July 15, 1863, two days after the draft.

[5] Enlisted in Third Heavy Artillery, July 25, 1863, twelve days after the draft.

There were three Shelton families in our town at the time of the draft, in one of which were five brothers; three of these brothers were drafted, one of whom had been in the service. The other two brothers were then in the service.

The Boston Journal of July 14th, — the next day after the draft, — contained the following item:

MELROSE.
CELEBRATING THE DRAFT.

The drafted men of this quiet village had a jolly time of it last evening. A party of them arrayed in fantastic uniforms, and with strange weapons, with an American flag, a drum, horns, tin pans, and other musical instruments, made a tour of the town, calling on all their fortunate compatriots, and somewhat in this way: The procession halts in front of a residence where the lights are low, and a passer-by would know that somebody there had been drafted. The commander shouts in a stentorian voice, "Conscript So-and-so, you're wanted! Ten days is played out; five minutes is the word. Conscript, come forth!"

A provost guard forthwith wait upon the honored personage, and he is placed, with cheers and congratulations, in the procession, which, amid the clamor of unheard of music, moves on to the residence of the next fortunate man. There was no escaping this conscription. Every man had to take his place, and everybody seemed to enjoy the fun. At a late hour the melancholy horns were moaning in the suburbs; and there was a general impression with the citizens, as they retired to rest, that it was rather a jolly thing, than otherwise, to be drafted.

1864.

Calls for five hundred thousand (500,000) men were

116   THE MELROSE MEMORIAL.

made Oct. 17, 1863, and Feb. 1, 1864, and our quota assigned by Provost-Marshal Herrick.[1]

The second draft was made, under the call of March 14th, 1864, and resulted as follows:

The whole number of persons drawn throughout the United States, during this draft, was		113,446
Failed to report . . .	27,193	
Discharged for various causes	1,296	
		28,489
		84,957
Whole number exempted		39,952
		45,005
Held to personal service	3,416	
Furnished substitutes	8,911	
Paid commutation .	32,678	
		45,005

---

[1] PROVOST-MARSHAL'S OFFICE,
6TH DISTRICT, MASS.,
LAWRENCE, Feb. 16, 1864.

Col. J. H. Clark, Melrose, Mass.:

Dear Sir: — The quota of Melrose, exclusive of any deductions, under the "call for 500,000 men, and to make up deficiencies," is 50.

From this is to be deducted the number of men enlisted and mustered, not heretofore credited, and also 4 men drafted and commuted for, and 3 furnished substitutes.

You will be credited for all men who shall have enlisted from your town, and who shall have been duly mustered, up to and including Feb. 29.

Very respectfully,
Your obedient servant,
H. G. HERRICK,
Capt. and Pro.-Mar. 6th Dist. Mass.

The whole number of persons drawn in Massachusetts
during this draft was 9,505
Failed to report 2,287
Discharged for various causes . . 44
                                    ─────
                                    2,331
                                    ─────
                                    7,174
       Whole number exempted   4,711
                                    ─────
                                    2,463
Held to personal service   105
Furnished substitutes   743
Paid commutation   1,615
                             ─────
                                    2,463

The whole number of persons drawn in this District,[1]
during this draft, was   .   350
       Whole number exempted   273
                                   ───
                                    77
Held to personal service   . 2
Furnished substitutes   . 19
Paid commutation .   . 56
                                  ───
                                   77

The draft in this District commenced on the 14th of May, and, on the 17th, the following names were drawn

---

[1] Our quota was as follows:

PROVOST-MARSHAL'S OFFICE, }
6TH DIST. MASS.,
LAWRENCE, March 25, 1864. }

Sir: — The *Quota* of your Town, under the President's call of March 14, 1864, for 200,000 men, will be as follows: Sub-Dist. No. 9, . . 19 men.
By order of Board of Enrollment, 6th Dist. Mass.,
S. W. HOPKINSON,
Commissioner.

CHAIRMAN SELECTMEN OF MELROSE.

for Melrose; but as there was no deficiency at this time, all the quotas of our town having been filled, the drafted persons were not required to appear for examination.[1]

Four of the citizens that were drafted in 1863 were also drafted at this time.

John Thompson,
William Donalavy,
Samuel A. Robinson,
Joseph Goodwin,
Alonzo Patterson,
William F. Paul,
William A. Fuller,[2]
George W. Farnsworth,
William Clark,
Augustus Ripley,
Lyell T. Terwillager,
Jarvis P. Hudson,
James Biffin,
John Perkins, Jr.,
Fernando C. Taylor,
Timothy Upham,
David A. Alden,
John H. L. Anderson,
Gardner Wheeler,

---

[1] PROVOST-MARSHAL'S OFFICE,
6TH DISTRICT, MASS.,
LAWRENCE, May 31, 1864.

Col. J. H. Clark, Melrose, Mass.:

The deficiency of Melrose is full, as appears from a list of Supplementary Credits furnished this morning by Major Clarke. The drafted men need not appear. You are authorized to so notify them.

Very respectfully,
H. G. HERRICK.
Capt. and Pro.-Mar., 6th Dist. Mass.

[2] Was then in the navy, Acting Third Assistant Engineer.

THIRD AND FOURTH DRAFTS.

Sylvanus Magoon,
Joseph Holbrook,
Edward B. Newhall,
Thomas Hawkins,
Daniel R. Woodward

On the third and fourth drafts, there were no names drawn in Massachusetts, her quotas being more than full. The following is the general result of those drafts:

Whole number of persons drawn under the call of July 18, 1864, was . . . 231,918
Failed to report 66,159
Discharged for various causes   27,223
                                ——— 93,382
                                     138,536
Whole number of exemptions .   82,531
                                     ———
                                     56,005
Held to personal service   26,205
Furnished substitutes .   28,502
Paid commutation . .   . 1,298
                                ——— 56,005

Whole number of persons drawn under the call of Dec. 19, 1864, was . . .   139,024
Failed to report 28,477
Discharged for various causes . 64,419
                                ——— 92,896
                                     46,128
Whole number exempted   28,631
                                     ———
                                     17,497
Held to personal service   6,845
Furnished substitutes .   10,192
Paid commutation   460
                                ——— 17,497

SUBSTITUTES

FOR

ENROLLED MEN.

During the year 1864, an arrangement was made, by which any person liable to do military duty could, in anticipation of the draft then pending, furnish a substitute. Four of our citizens availed themselves of this privilege, paying for their substitutes sums ranging from five hundred and seventy-five to seven hundred dollars.[1] In this manner men were added to our forces in the field, and our quota was reduced to an equal extent.

The following are the names of those who thus furnished substitutes, and also the names and reputed residence of their respective substitutes:

Enrolled Men.	Substitutes.	Residence.
George Emerson, 2d,	Samuel Wilson,	Nova Scotia.[2]
George W. Heath,	William Beamen,	" "
James O. Lynde,	John H. Reynard,	Canada.
Daniel W. Wilcox,	Andrew Tyrill,	Nova Scotia.

---

[1] The prices demanded for substitutes during the rebellion differed somewhat from those paid in former wars, as will be seen by the following receipts, — the original of which are now in possession of our townsman, Mr. Artemas Barrett. The substitutes in each case were for citizens of North Malden, — now Melrose, — and one of these citizens was the grandfather of Mr. Barrett.

January 13, 1761.

Received of Phinehas Sprague june'r. eight Pounds lawful money it being for my going a Solger to forte cumberland and 1 had a promes not of Six Pounds be fore.

Pr, me   JOHN BATTS.

CAMBRIDGE, August 17, 1781.

Rec'd of Mr. Joseph Barrett the sum of Twelve Pounds Solid Coine in full of all accounts Debts Dues and Demands against Mr. Joseph Lyonde (Lynde) or Mr. Joseph Barretts. Class for Procuring a man for three years service in the Army. Recd by me   BENJ PERKINS.

[2] For form of certificates given in such cases, see appendix F.

Representative Recruits.

During the latter part of the year 1864, Massachusetts and some of the other loyal States sent recruiting agents into the rebellious States, at points occupied by our forces, for the purpose of enlisting colored volunteers, under the Act of Congress approved July 4th, 1864.

An arrangement was also made by which any person not liable to be drafted into the military service of the United States, by reason of age or disability, could deposit with the Treasurer of the State in which such person resided, the sum of one hundred and twenty-five dollars ($125), and be assigned one of the volunteers thus enlisted, such volunteer to be called a "Representative Recruit." The recruits thus obtained, and not assigned as "Representative Recruits," were apportioned among the various towns and cities of the Commonwealth for which the enlistments were made.

The whole number of volunteers secured by these agents was two thousand four hundred and eighteen (2,418); of which number Massachusetts enlisted twelve hundred and fifty-seven (1,257).

The whole number of "Representative Recruits" assigned to different individuals in all the States was twelve hundred ninety-two (1,292), of which number Massachusetts furnished five hundred and fifty-three (553).

Three citizens of our town availed themselves of this privilege of putting into the service a "Representative Recruit," receiving from the State a certificate signed by the Governor, John A. Andrew, and the Provost-Marshal of the State, Joseph M. Day, giving the names of the "sable volunteers" thus assigned them.[1]

---

[1] For form of receipt and certificate given, see appendix G.

The names of these three gentlemen were:
David Fairbanks,
Daniel Russell,
Dexter Bryant.

The names of their representatives were, respectively: Samuel Harris, enlisted at Natchez, Mississippi, in the Seventy-First United States Colored Infantry; Davis Jones, enlisted at Washington, Louisiana, in the Fifty-Eighth United States Colored Infantry; William Parsons enlisted in Tennessee, in the Fiftieth United States Colored Infantry.

It was afterwards ascertained that the cost of these "Representative Recruits" was only about one hundred dollars ($100); and by permission of the depositors, the balance of the sum deposited, twenty-five dollars ($25), was transferred to the hands of Surgeon-General Dale, to be appropriated for the benefit of discharged disabled Massachusetts soldiers, or their families. An acknowledgment of the receipt of this sum was given by the Surgeon-General to each depositor. In this manner the sum of ten thousand six hundred and ninety dollars ($10,690) was added to the fund for the relief of sick and disabled soldiers.

XI.

1861-5.

Our native land ! to thee,
  In one united vow,
To keep thee strong and free,
  And glorious as now —
We pledge each heart and hand ;
By the blood our fathers shed,
By the ashes of our dead,
By the sacred soil we tread !
  God for our native land !

George W. Bethune.

The whole number of men furnished by the State of Massachusetts during the war, for the service of the United States, for the several terms of service, of all arms, and including both army and navy, was one hundred and fifty-nine thousand, one hundred and sixty-five (159,165). The following table, from the Report of the Adjutant-General for the year 1865, gives the number of men thus furnished more in detail :

Organizations, Terms, etc.	Number.	Aggregate.
THREE MONTHS' SERVICE, 1861.		
Four (4) Regiments, Infantry,		
One (1) Battalion, Riflemen,		
One (1) Battery, Light Artillery,		3,736
THREE YEARS' MEN IN THE ARMY.		
Forty (40) Regiments, Infantry,		
Five (5) Regiments, Cavalry,		

Three (3) Regiments, Heavy Artillery,
One (1) Battalion, Heavy Artillery,
Two (2) Companies, Sharpshooters,
Sixteen (16) Batteries, Light Artillery, 54,187
Recruits, including drafted men, for above
   organizations, 26,091
Men for Regular Army, Veteran Reserve
   Corps, and other organizations, 9,790
Re-enlistments in the State organizations, 6,202
                                                      96,270

ONE YEAR'S MEN IN THE ARMY.

Two (2) Regiments, Infantry,
Two (2) Unattached Companies, Infantry,
One (1) Regiment, Heavy Artillery,
Eight (8) Un. Companies, Heavy Artillery,
Seven (7) Companies, Cavalry, 4,728

NINE MONTHS' MEN.

Seventeen (17) Regiments, Infantry, 16,685

ONE HUNDRED DAYS' MEN.

Five (5) Regiments, Infantry,
Nine (9) Un. Companies, Infantry, 5,461

NINETY DAYS' MEN.

Thirteen (13) Un. Companies, Infantry, 1,209

MEN IN THE NAVY.

Number for One Year, 8,074
Number for Two Years, 3,204
Number for Three Years, 13,929
Number, term not given, 956
                                                    26,163

Number enlisted from Dec. 1, 1864, up to
and including August, 1865, viz:
White Volunteers, 2,741
Colored Volunteers, 1,308
Regulars, 432
Seamen, 154
Marines, 12
Veteran Reserve Corps, 266
                                                    4,913

            Total, 159,165

Of the enlisted men, of whom muster-out rolls have been received at the Adjutant-General's office, twelve thousand, eight hundred and twenty-six (12,826) were killed, or died in service. Three thousand two hundred and seventy-eight (3,278) were killed on the battlefield, eighteen hundred and twenty-two (1,822) died of wounds, fifty-five hundred and ninety-four (5,594) died of disease, and twenty-one hundred and thirty-two (2,132) died in rebel prisons.

The whole number of commissioned officers furnished by Massachusetts during the war was fifty-eight hundred and sixty-nine (5,869), four hundred and thirty-two (432) of whom laid down their lives for their country, most of them on the field of battle. Two hundred and sixty (260) were killed, one hundred and four (104) died of wounds, seventy-five (75) died of disease, and three (3) died in rebel prisons. The above figures show that two thousand three hundred and forty (2,340) more men died of disease and in rebel prisons than were killed or died of wounds.

Of the thirty-five (35) general officers furnished by Massachusetts, nine (9) have been killed or fatally wounded in action, and sixteen (16) who have fallen in battle survive their wounds. Only ten (10) have escaped injury.

The whole number of men furnished by Melrose for the war, for the several terms of service, of all arms, including both army and navy, and including the eight (8) citizens that enlisted on other quotas, was four hundred and fifty-four (454). Of these, twenty-one (21) enlisted men lost their lives; five (5) were killed on the battle-field, one (1) was accidentally shot, thirteen (13) died of disease contracted in the service, and two (2) died in rebel prisons.

The number of commissioned officers furnished by Melrose was eighteen (18); two (2) of whom lost their lives, one (1) on the field of battle, and one (1) died of disease contracted in the service.

The whole number of men apportioned to Massachusetts, under the several calls for troops during the war, was one hundred and seventeen thousand, six hundred and twenty-four (117,624). The number furnished, reducing all the different times of service to the standard of three years, was one hundred thirty-one thousand, one hundred and sixteen (131,116) men, which shows a surplus of thirteen thousand, four hundred ninety-two (13,492.)

All of the three hundred and thirty-five cities and towns in the Commonwealth, with the exception of twelve small towns, furnished a surplus of men; and it is a source of great satisfaction to be able to say, that when the rebellion closed, Melrose, one of the youngest towns in the State,[1] had a surplus, according to a communication from

---

[1] Melrose was incorporated May 3d, 1850. It was formerly the northern part of Malden, one of the oldest towns in the State, having been set off as a town in 1649. Captain Edward Johnson, of Woburn, in his "Wonder-Working Providence of Sions Saviour in New England," published in London in 1654, — and recently re-printed in very fine style, with a learned historical Introduction and an Index by our townsman, Mr. William F. Poole, — says that Malden was settled " by certain persons, who issued out of Charles Town, and indeed had her whole structure within the bounds of this more elder Town, being severed by the broad spreading river of Mistick the one from the other, whose troublesome passage caused the people on the North side of the river to plead for Town-priviledges within themselves, which accordingly was granted them; the soyl is very fertile, but they are much straitened in their bounds, yet their neerness to the chief Market Towns, makes it the more comfortable for habitation; the people gathered into a Church some distance of time before they could attain to any Church-Officer to administer the Seals unto them, yet in the mean time at their Sabbath assemblies they had a godly Christian named M. Sarjant, who did preach the Word unto them, and afterwards they were supplied at times with

the District Provost-Marshal, H. G. Herrick, of seventy-
four (74) men [1] over and above all the different quotas

> [1] PROVOST-MARSHAL'S OFFICE,
> 6TH DISTRICT, MASS.,
> LAWRENCE, December 31, 1864.
> This is to certify that, as appears by the records of this office, the surplus
> of the Town of Melrose, over all calls, is seventy-four (74) men.
> H. G. HERRICK,
> *Captain and Provost-Marshal, 6th Dist. Mass.*

some young Students from the Colledg,* till the year 1650, one Mr. Marma-
duke Mathews, coming out of Plimouth Patten,† was for some space of time
with a people at the Town of Hull, which is a small Port-town peopled by
fishermen, and lies at the entrance of the Bays mouth, where this Mr.
Mathews continued preaching, till he lost the approbation of some able
understanding men, among both Magistrates and Ministers, by weak and
unsafe expressions in his teaching, yet notwithstanding he was called to the
office of a Pastor by the brethren of this Church of Christ at Malden,
although some neighbor-churches were unsatisfied therewith, for it is the
manner of all the Churches of Christ here hitherto, to have the approbation
of their Sister-Churches, and the civil Government also in the proceedings
of this nature, by the which means Communion of Churches is continued,
peace preserved ; and the truths of Christ sincerely acknowledged." The
brief record of what may be regarded as the act of incorporation by the
General Court is as follows : " In answer to the petition of several inhabi-
tants of Mistick side, their request is granted, viz. to be a distinct town of
themselves, and the name thereof to be Maulden." The two-hundredth
anniversary of the settlement of Malden was celebrated May 23, 1849. An
oration was delivered by Hon. James D. Green, and a poem by Rev. Gilbert
Haven, Jr. A year afterward these were published, together with other historical matter relating to the town, and the Committee of Publication thus
refer to Melrose, which was set off from Malden the same year : " The new
town of 'fair Melrose,' the only daughter of Malden, goes forth to set up a
separate municipal existence, with the parental consent and blessing ; and
will doubtless reflect lasting credit on her parentage." Its population at
this time was 1,260 ; and in 1860 it had increased to 2,527. In 1865, the
year the war closed, our population was 2,865.

*Harvard College.
†Plymouth Colony.

from the many calls for troops, by the President of the United States.

And, notwithstanding the necessary outlay of money on account of this gigantic rebellion, there was no reduction in the amounts of money voted for the School, Poor, Highway, and other appropriations; but, on the contrary, a steady increase throughout the continuance of the war.

As has been stated, Melrose furnished during the war four hundred and fifty-four (454) men for the different periods of service. Three hundred and seventy-seven (377) different names appear on the alphabetical list; of these, five (5) were in the three months' service in 1861, all but one of whom re-enlisted. Eleven (11) of those that entered the service in 1861 and 1862 for three years re-enlisted, and counted twice in filling our quotas. Eight (8) re-entered the service after recovering from the wounds or sickness, on account of which they had been discharged; and in this list is included also the names of the twenty-eight (28) men in the navy, credited to us from the State at large; also the names of the substitutes put into the service by enrolled citizens, and the "Representative Recruits" furnished by our citizens not liable to draft.

Quotas.

The following is a statement of the number of men called for at different times during the rebellion by the President of the United States, the total quotas assigned, and the number obtained from all the States. Also the quotas of Massachusetts, with the number of men furnished on each, compiled from the Report of the Provost-Marshal General, James B. Fry. Also the quotas of Melrose and the number of men furnished, as correctly as it is possible to state them.

QUOTAS.

Date of Proclamation.	Number called for.	Period of service.	Total quotas assigned.	Number obtained.	Quota of Massachusetts.	Men furnished.	Quota of Mel-rose.	Men furnished.
April 15, 1861	75,000	3 months.	73,391	93,326	1,560	3,736	. .	5
May & July, 1861*	582,748	3 years.	611,827	714,231	34,868	32,177	76	76
May & June, 1862	. . .	3 months.	. . .	15,007	. . .	. . .	. .	. .
July 2, 1862	300,000	3 years.	334,835	431,958	19,080	1,510	37	56
August 4, 1862	300,000	9 months.	334,835	87,588	19,080	16,685	79	79
June 15, 1863	100,000	6 months.	militia.	16,361	. . .	103	. .	. .
July, 1863, Draft	. . .	}	. . .	. . .	. . .	. . .	. .	7
October 17, 1863	300,000	} 3 years.	467,434	374,807	26,597	21,413	50	
February 1, 1864	200,000							
March 14, 1864	200,000	3 years.	186,981	284,021	10,619	18,876	19	166
April 23, 1864	85,000	100 days.	113,000	83,652	4,000	6,809	.	28
July 18, 1864	500,000	1, 2, 3 years.	346,745	384,882	21,965	31,739	58	
December 19, 1864	300,000	1, 2, 3 years.	290,000	204,568	1,306	3,728		
	2,942,748		2,759,049	2,690,401	139,095	151,785		

Citizen in the Navy (not included in above count) 1
Allotted by Navy Commissioners 28

319 : 446

*Congress passed acts on the 22d, 25th and 31st July, 1861, authorizing the President to accept the services of volunteers, either as cavalry, infantry or artillery, in such numbers not exceeding 1,000,000, as he might deem necessary for the purpose of repelling invasion and suppressing insurrection.

† "Of the number of troops mustered into the United States' service for a less period than six months (including all three months' men), not heretofore credited on any quota since the commencement of the Rebellion, but which would have been proper credit upon any subsequent call, in accordance with provisions of section 15th of acts of March 3d, 1865, Massachusetts furnished 4,983 men for three months, 6,809 for one hundred days, and 121 for four months. Total, 11,913; equal to 3,157 years of service, or 1,052 men for three years."

XII.

1861–5.

Relief of Soldiers and their Families.

In all of the cities and towns of the Commonwealth, large contributions of money, clothing, and other articles, were being made during the entire period of the war. In many, in most of these cities and towns, there was one or more organized societies for the disbursement of these contributions. Melrose had no such regularly organized association, although much was done for the benefit of the soldier and his family by the Town and by individuals. Of the unnumbered private donations of money, of boxes and packages of soldiers' necessities and luxuries, sent by patriotic mothers and sisters, who can fully estimate their value, or the benefit derived therefrom?

The generous sympathy and munificent gifts, not only of our own citizens, but of the entire people, for the soldiers and their cause, were wonderful. These gifts were "from every department of social, business and religious life; from every age, sex and condition of our community; by gifts, by toil, by skill and handiwork; out of the basket and the store, and out of the full hearts of the community, — they have poured through countless channels of benevolence." [1]

---

[1] As an instance of this hearty generosity, only one of many; nine car-loads of hospital stores left Boston after battles of "Groveton," "Second Bull Run," and "Chantilly," which ended the campaign under Major-General John Pope.

CITIZENS' SUBSCRIPTION. 131

At the first regularly called Town Meeting that was held after the breaking out of the Rebellion, — May 6, 1861, — three thousand dollars ($3,000) were appropriated for the relief of volunteers and their families, according to the vote already given on a previous page, the Selectmen being appointed a Committee of disbursement.

At the annual Town Meeting in March, 1862, twenty-five hundred dollars ($2,500) were appropriated for the same purpose, to aid the families of volunteers, as provided by Chap. 222, Statutes of 1861, wherein it was enacted that the State should reimburse the cities and towns, to a certain amount per family, the sums thus paid ; and regularly, at each annual Town Meeting, during the continuance of the war, a vote of similar import was unanimously passed.

In July, 1862, at the solicitation of Mr. William F. Poole, a subscription of three hundred and forty dollars ($340) was made by the following gentlemen, for the "purpose of promoting recruiting in Melrose ; for equalizing the bounties of those patriotic citizens who have already enlisted ; and for the benefit of the families which the quota from Melrose shall leave behind them."

Hon. Samuel E. Sewall	$75 00
Hon. Daniel W. Gooch	50 00
Andrew J. Morse	50 00
George W. Heath	50 00
John S. Higgins	30 00
Philip B. Holmes	25 00
William F. Poole	25 00
Lewis G. Coburn	25 00
Charles Kastner	10 00
	$340 00

This amount was disbursed, mostly in aid of the families of volunteers, by the Treasurer of the fund, Mr. Andrew J. Morse.

Guiding Star Lodge, No. 28, Independent Order of Good Templars, sent to the seat of war, on two different occasions during the years 1861 and 1862, a box and barrel of general hospital stores, blankets, drawers, reading matter, etc. The first lot was sent to the encampment of the Thirteenth Massachusetts Regiment, to the care of John H. Crocker, of Co. A, and the latter to the hospitals in Washington.

At the annual Town Meeting in March, 1863, it was voted that the poll-tax of all the soldiers in the field, belonging to Melrose, and all who should go during the year ensuing, should be abated; and also that the poll-tax of all who from wounds or disability had been discharged from the service of the United States, should be abated.

At the Town Meeting held June 8, 1863, it was voted to set off and appropriate a portion of "Wyoming Cemetery" as a free burial-place for all soldiers engaged in the war, and for the families of such soldiers as might choose to use the same.

For the two or three days immediately following the "Battle of Gettysburg," July 1-3, 1863, — and very great was the excitement in our town and throughout the North at this time, as we all remember, — the studies in our schools were suspended, and teachers and scholars spent the school hours in preparing lint for hospital use. In this manner a large quantity was gathered and sent to the hospitals on and around the battle-field.

At a meeting held Nov. 14, 1863, it was voted that the Recruiting Committee, — which consisted of the Selectmen, Colonel John H. Clark, William B. Burgess and

CONTRIBUTIONS OF THE CHURCHES. 133

George M. Fletcher, and Messrs. Stephen W. Shelton, Isaac Emerson, Jr., Rufus Smith and Charles H. Isburgh, — should "look after the interests of the families of volunteers who are now, or may be hereafter, in the service of the United States, and see that they are properly provided for." A subscription fund was also raised at this time to "give all the families of volunteers belonging to Melrose, then in service, means to provide for them such a Thanksgiving dinner as they are most deservedly entitled to."

At the fall election of this year, — 1863, — Mr. Isaac Emerson, Jr., was chosen, for the second time, Representative to the Massachusetts Legislature. Instead of giving a reception to his constituents and friends at his residence, as he did the previous year, he donated the sum of one hundred dollars ($100) to the "Christian Commission." Consequently the "guard at the front" received the benefit, rather than the members of the "home guard."

At different times during the war, a number of contributions were taken up in our various churches in aid of those wonderful monuments of the free-will offerings of the loyal North, the "Christian" and "Sanitary Commissions."[1]

The contributions of the "Orthodox Congregational Church" for the "Christian Commission," during the years 1863, 4, 5, amounted to three hundred and thirty dollars and six cents ($330.06), besides eighty-five dollars

---

[1] The total value of cash, stores and publications distributed by the "Christian Commission" during the war, was $5,478,280.31 ; $2,524,512.56 of which was donated in cash. Total amount received and distributed by the "Sanitary Commission" was $4,924,048.09.

and twenty cents ($85.20) contributed for the benefit of sick and wounded soldiers in the hospitals at Washington, which amount was sent to and distributed by Mrs. Gooch, — wife of Hon. Daniel W. Gooch, then our Representative in Congress from this District, — whose visits and kindnesses will long be remembered by many a soldier.

The "Universalist Church" contributed fifty dollars ($50) to the "Sanitary Commission," besides sending several boxes of articles suitable for the sick and disabled soldiers in Washington. These were sent to and distributed by Mrs. Emma Nichols Marden.

The "Methodist Episcopal Church" and the "Baptist Church" also contributed to the same object, but no record was made of the amount, therefore the sums cannot be given here.

A vocal and instrumental concert was given May 30, 1864, at Lyceum Hall, under the auspices of Mr. John H. B. Henderson, the proceeds of which were for the benefit of our sick and wounded soldiers. The sum of eighty-seven dollars ($87) was paid into the treasury of the "Christian Commission."

During the first year of the war, many of our ladies met in Lyceum Hall, a number of days in succession, for the purpose of making and collecting garments and articles of all kinds suitable for the sick and wounded soldiers in our hospitals. A large collection of comforts and luxuries was thus made and collected.

Barrels, boxes and bundles of such necessary articles, including garments, hospital stores, reading matter, etc., were also collected at later times in the war by some of our public-spirited and patriotic ladies, and forwarded to either the "Christian" or "Sanitary Commissions." That these various collections were ever welcomed by, and were

A SOLDIER'S GRATITUDE. 135

the source of great comfort to our brave boys, suffering from wounds received on the battle-field, or from diseases contracted in the service, is made evident by the following letter from Lieutenant O. D. Robinson, of the Ninth New Hampshire Regiment, written to a lady in our town, soon after the reception of one of these boxes :

MT. PLEASANT HOSPITAL,
WASHINGTON, D. C., June 24, 1864.

Mrs * * *

Dear Madam :— Last week a large box arrived at this Hospital filled with minor boxes and bags, each of which contained numerous comforts and luxuries for "sick and wounded soldiers," and I can assure you that the valuable gifts found plenty of eager recipients. To me was given a bag containing a nice pair of woollen socks, a linen handkerchief, pocket Testament, etc., etc. In the Testament was a brief note bearing the signature to which I am addressing this humble missive.

I trust, Dear Madam, the gifts you have so freely donated have not been given in vain, and I *hope* not unworthily bestowed. Many who that day received presents from friends unknown before, will soon return to their native homes to rest from the toils and hardships of war, having been disabled by wounds received in the recent battles. Others from the same cause may live but a few days to enjoy their gifts ; while others still, like myself, will soon return to engage anew in the bloody contest. I have not been wounded, but having participated in the bloody fights of Wilderness, Spottsylvania, North Anna River and Cool Arbor, having endured in common with others the hardships and exposures attendant upon such a campaign, and then suffering from a fresh attack of intermittent fever, contracted last summer in the swamps of Louisiana and Mississippi, I was compelled to leave the field for a few days to obtain rest and medical treatment. I arrived in Washington on the 10th inst., and shall return in the course of three or four days. Of socks I was nearly destitute, and had lost my pocket Testament, which is always my constant companion. Accept my thanks for these same articles received through your benevolence. I prize them the more, because, receiving them as I do from those I have never seen or known even by reputation, I feel that thousands of hearts are in sympathy with us in this unprecedented struggle, and that the Matrons and Daughters throughout New England are the *Mothers* and *Sisters* of those who are fighting for our Nation's honor and institutions.

But I am intruding too largely upon your time and more upon your patience. It was my intention to write but a note. I shall go back to my comrades refreshed after my short respite, and encouraged to faithfully perform my duty, by the kindness I have received from friends present and absent.

I am, Dear Madam, a *true friend* to all lovers of our Country and our Country's Flag.

LIEUTENANT O. D. ROBINSON,
Co. E, 9th N. H. V.[1]

Our fellow-citizen, Rev. John C. Ingalls, spent the winters of 1861, 2, 3 in Washington, D. C.; and on one occasion, during this time, he raised the sum of twelve hundred dollars ($1,200) in the cities of Philadelphia, New York, Boston and Portland, for the benefit of the sick and wounded soldiers at the Emory Hospital in Washington. He also acted as Chaplain of this hospital for a number of weeks, without pay, during the sickness of its regular Chaplain. Besides which, he raised the money for building a chapel for the use of this same hospital.

---

[1] Lieutenant Robinson was afterwards promoted Captain of his company, and remained in the service until the close of the war.

XIII.

Our "Roll of Honor.'

" High on the world's heroic list,
    Shall every name be seen, —
And time among the cherished dead
    Shall keep their memories green.

" The patriot's heart shall warmer glow,
    When standing by their grave;
And dearer still shall be the flag
    They welcomed death to save."

"How bright are the honors which await those who, with sacred fortitude and patriotic patience have endured all things that they might save their native land from division and from the power of corruption. The honored dead! They that die for a good cause are redeemed from death. Their names are gathered and garnered. Their memory is precious."

All generations shall commemorate their valor and their patriotism. No ties of kindred can impose limitations upon the grief and gratitude in which they shall be held and treasured. The country shall be their monument.[1]

Of the two hundred and three (203) Melrose citizens that served in the ranks of our armies during the Rebellion, "who helped open the Mississippi, who were present

---

[1] Governor Alexander H. Bullock, at the funeral of Lieutenant-Colonel George E. Marshall, of the Fortieth Massachusetts Regiment, at Fitchburg April 19, 1866.

at Vicksburg, Port Hudson, New Orleans and Mobile, who saw the starry flag as it ascended Missionary Ridge, and witnessed the flight of Bragg and his host; who marched from Atlanta to the sea, and who were among those who so long struggled between Washington and Richmond, and who at last saw the rebel flag go down upon the Appomattox," twenty-three (23) of them, or about one in nine, were either killed on the battle-field or died in consequence of services rendered in the great contest. Six (6) were killed by the bullet on the field, and the rest died in camp, in hospital, or after returning to their homes.

Two (2) commissioned officers and twenty-one (21) enlisted men constitute the oblation made by Melrose to Treason.

Our "Roll of Honor" — containing the names of all of our citizens that we have been able to learn, whether they served on our quotas or not, but who gave their lives for their country — is as follows ; name, regiment, company, cause and date of death :

THE "UNRETURNING BRAVE."

OFFICERS.

LIEUT. GEORGE J. MORSE.

Private Co. A, Thirteenth Regiment; 2d Lieutenant in 2d U. S. Col. Troops; 1st Lieutenant Co. G, Fifty-Ninth Regiment; killed at the " Battle of Spottsylvania," May 12, 1864.

LIEUT. GEORGE T. MARTIN,

1st Lieutenant Co. K, Thirty-Eighth Regiment; Senior 1st Lieutenant Co. G, Fourth Heavy Artillery; died at Massachusetts General Hospital, March 13, 1865, of pyœmia.

PRIVATES.

HENRY F. FULLER.

Co. A, Seventeenth Regiment; died at Baltimore, Md., Oct. 6, 1861, of typhoid fever.

MARTIN GREENE.

Co. G, Second Regiment; died of wounds received at "Battle of Cedar Mountain," Aug. 9, 1862.

WILLIAM H. MACEY.

Co. F, Third Maine Regiment; died at Alexandria, Va., Aug. 30, 1862, of typhoid fever.

SIDNEY B. MORSE, 2D.

Co. D, Thirteenth Regiment; died at Finley Hospital, Washington, D. C., Sept. 16, 1862, of typhoid fever.

WILLIAM F. BARRY.

Co. A, Thirteenth Regiment; killed at "Battle of Antietam," Sept. 17, 1862.

JOHN P. SHELTON.

Co. A, Thirteenth Regiment; killed at "Battle of Antietam," Sept. 17, 1862.

THOMAS H. STEVENS.

Co. A, Sixteenth Regiment; died at Boston, March 26, 1863, of chronic diarrhœa.

JONAS G. BROWN.

Co. E, Fiftieth Regiment; died at Baton Rouge, La., June 18, 1863, of malarial fever.

BENJAMIN LYNDE.

Co. K, Thirty-Eighth Regiment; died at Baton Rouge, La., Aug. 18, 1863, of chronic diarrhœa.

NATHAN H. BRAND.

Ninth Battery; died at Emory Hospital, Washington, D. C., March 6, 1864, of cholera morbus.

RICHARD LEVER.

Co. A, Fifty-Ninth Regiment; killed at "Battle of Spottsylvania," May 12, 1864.

AUGUSTUS GREEN.

Co. G, Twenty-Second Regiment; killed at "Battle of Bethesda Church," June 3, 1864.

EDMUND W. DAVIS.

Co. G, Twenty-Second Regiment; died at Melrose, July 22, 1864, of consumption and heart disease.

ALBERT W. CROCKETT.

Co. K, Seventeenth Regiment; died in "Andersonville Prison," Aug. 1, 1864.

JAMES R. HOWARD.

Co. K, Thirty-Eighth Regiment; died at Melrose, Aug. 16, 1864, of chronic diarrhœa.

FRANCIS PEABODY.

Co. K, Seventeenth Regiment; died at New Berne, N. C., Oct. 3, 1864, of yellow fever.

GEORGE E. RICHARDSON.

Co. K, Thirty-Eighth Regiment; died in "Salisbury Prison," Nov. 3, 1864.

THE "UNRETURNING BRAVE." 141

BENJAMIN F. WILDE.

Co. H, Forty-Second Regiment; re-enlisted in Regular Infantry; afterward in Eleventh New York Cavalry; accidentally shot in fall of 1864.

JOHN E. STILPHEN.

Second Battery; died at Melrose, June 25, 1865, of hemorrhoids.

GEORGE W. LYNDE.

Co. A, Seventeenth Regiment; died at Melrose, Jan. 30, 1866, of consumption.

WILLIAM F. KRANTZ.

Co. C, Thirty-Third Regiment; Veteran Reserve Corps; died at Melrose, June 13, 1866, of dropsy and heart disease.

We cannot speak individually of all the "fallen brave" whose names are here given, although all deserve equal mention. They have rendered up their lives in behalf of what to us was a mighty and vital question, and we would hold their memory in veneration, remembering that

"They never fail
Who die in a great cause."

And with the scholarly and lamented Everett, standing on the blood-stained field of Gettysburg, at the consecration of its National Cemetery, we would feel as never before how justly "from the dawn of history to the present time, men have paid the homage of their gratitude and admiration to the memory of those who nobly sacrifice their lives, that their fellow-men may live in safety and in honor."

"The muffled drum's sad roll has beat
    The soldier's last tattoo ;
No more on life's parade shall meet
    That brave and fallen few.
On Fame's eternal camping-ground
    Their silent tents are spread,
And glory guards with solemn round
    The bivouac of the dead."

HENRY FRANKLIN FULLER.

Private in Co. A, Seventeenth Regiment Massachusetts Volunteers; died at Baltimore, Md., Oct. 6, 1861, of disease contracted in the service.

Henry Franklin Fuller, the youngest son of William E. and Mary (Boardman) Fuller, was born in Melrose, March 5, 1844.

The old family names of Melrose, or what was the northern part of Malden, were well represented in the great struggle between Right and Wrong; and in the list of dead we find the names of Brown, Fuller, Howard and Lynde.

Fuller was one of our youngest soldiers, and was the first one, belonging to Melrose, that laid down his life in the service of his country.

The disaster of the first "Bull Run Battle" had been realized, when young Fuller, like so many more of our noble and brave, felt called upon to offer himself to go forth to battle; and on the 6th of August, he went to "Camp Schouler," at Lynnfield, and enlisted in Co. A, Seventeenth Massachusetts Regiment. For some two months previous to this time, the duty of thus offering himself to the cause of liberty had been revolving itself in his mind, but he did not enlist until the above date.

The Seventeenth Regiment left the State on the 23d of August, and proceeded to "Camp Andrew," at Baltimore, Md., where Fuller underwent the hardships incident to the uncomfortable state of the camping-ground, which, according to the following extract from a letter, written by Captain Joseph R. Simonds to the Selectmen of Malden,[1] was anything but agreeable or conducive to good health.

How would the soldier at home like lying upon the bare earth every night for six weeks, with nothing but a thin rubber blanket under him, and a thinner woollen one over him, and a knapsack for a pillow?

Up to the time of Fuller's death, the regiment had been engaged in no battle or expeditions; but whatever duties were incumbent upon him, he performed faithfully and well, until the 1st of October, when he was taken sick with the typhoid fever, which terminated his life October 6, 1861.

His body was brought home and buried in the Melrose Cemetery.

> "He, the young and strong, who cherished
> Noble longings for the strife,
> By the roadside fell and perished,
> Weary, with the march of life."

---

[1] Captain Simonds, of our town, was in command of Co. K, Seventeenth Regiment, known as the Malden company, and in which Melrose had several men.

SIDNEY BRADFORD MORSE, 2D.

Private in Co. D, Thirteenth Massachusetts Regiment; Color Corporal, July 5, 1862; died at the Finley Hospital, Washington, D. C., Sept. 16, 1862, of disease contracted in the service.

"There is a history in almost every home of Massachusetts, which will never be written; but the memory of kindred has it embalmed forever. The representatives of the pride and hope of uncounted households, departing, will return no more."

Sidney Bradford Morse, 2d, was the second son of George H. and Sarah (Bird) Morse, and was born Dec. 28, 1844, in Charlestown, Mass. He was one of the youngest of our soldier boys; but he was old enough to fully comprehend the danger which threatened our country, and was at once aroused at the dark clouds gathering over it. At the time of the breaking out of the Rebellion he was employed in his father's agricultural warehouse, in Boston; and upon the day our Massachusetts men were shot down in the streets of Baltimore, — the 19th of April, 1861, — young Sidney hurried home, saying to his mother that he had a request to make of her, which was that he, — together with his older brother George, — might be permitted to enlist, in response to the President's call, and help uphold our dear old flag, and put down their country's enemies. Of course the mother hesitated, — what *mother* would not? — before she could yield to his importunities, and say:

> Go, save our country! she is first —
> Stand guard until you fall;
> Or till the danger overcome
> Shall respite the alarum-drum —
> I will delay recall.

> Go, where along the lurid front
> The Union vanguards tramp!
> Do your whole duty, danger spurn,
> When Freedom's laurelled, then return —
> These arms shall be your camp!

Upon receiving an affirmative reply, Sidney embraced his mother, and ardently thanked her, saying that however much he may have deemed it his duty to go, he never should have gone with the sin of disobedience to her resting upon him; saying also: "I have neither houses nor land to give, but I am willing to give my life for my country!" And truly did his actions verify the assertion.

He enlisted at once, — as did also his brother George, — in the Fourth Battalion of Rifles, which was soon afterwards sent to Fort Independence, Boston Harbor, where it was recruited to a full regiment, — the Thirteenth, — under the command of Colonel Samuel H. Leonard.

He left Boston with his regiment, July 30, 1861, and performed a soldier's duties with earnestness and devotion through the various hard marches, severe skirmishes and daily fatigues of the fall and winter campaign under General Banks, on the Upper Potomac, and thence down through Virginia to the still severer marchings and fightings of General Pope's campaign, ending with "Groveton," "Second Bull Run," and "Chantilly," in August, 1862; being constantly exposed to hardship, day and night; yet passing through all thus far uninjured, but very much worn and fatigued; so much so, that he was repeatedly urged to go into the camp hospital and recruit; but he would not leave his post, and on the night before the "Second Bull Run Battle," he was found on the picket line, entirely exhausted, and taken to the rear. He was placed on an open car, with other sick and wounded soldiers, and started for Washington; but, owing to the great confusion of those days of battle, he was two nights and one day on the way, entirely uncared for; no food, not even a drink of water; and when he arrived at the "Finley Hospital," a typhoid fever was raging fearfully. From that time, the fever had taken so firm a hold of him, he grew worse and worse until the day of his death, — Sept. 16, — about a fortnight after reaching Washington.

The Hospital Chaplain, Rev. W. W. Winchester, for several days previous to Sidney's death, repeated passages of Scripture to him, and talked with him concerning that other and "better land"; and during his last moments, — his father having arrived and being present, — he read the beautiful Twenty-Third Psalm; Sidney, then, as always before, greatly enjoying the consolations of Holy Writ; after which his spirit took its flight to the soldier's home with perfect calmness and serenity.[1]

Although but a lad of seventeen and a half years of age, young Morse was a brave and a thorough soldier. It is the universal testimony of officers and comrades, that, young though he was, he made one of the best and truest; never shrinking from any post, however dangerous; and he bore the hardships incident to camp life, and the fatigues of the long and wearisome marches of the Regiment through various parts of Virginia, with perfect cheerfulness and heroic fortitude. He was sick long before he was found exhausted, and should have left the

---

[1] Mr. Winchester says, in a letter of condolence to Sidney's parents:
"May God bless and comfort the mothers who give their sons! I stand amazed at the fortitude which they sometimes exhibit, when they speak of the sacrifices which they make. God sees how they give those dearer to them than their heart's blood, and God will reward with blessings richer and purer than any this earth can afford."

field; but he was too earnest and ardent in his work to allow himself to do so, and would not leave, so long as he had strength. At the time he left his regiment he held the position of Right General Guide, with rank of Corporal.

The letters of young Morse were full of love and confidence, fearlessness of death, and words of kindness and sympathy for his parents in case he should fall in battle, or die in the hospital; often saying, that if he should lay down his life it would be in a just and holy cause. His remains were embalmed and brought to Melrose, and buried in Mount Auburn Cemetery; the funeral ceremonies being held September 27, at the Universalist Church, a large and sympathizing congregation being present.

Patriotism! bravery! duty! all are embraced in the action and career of the young and noble soldier, Sidney Bradford Morse.

"With us his name shall live,
Through long succeeding years,
Embalmed with all our hearts can give —
Our praises and our tears."

WILLIAM FRANCIS BARRY.

Private in Co. A, Thirteenth Massachusetts Regiment; killed at the "Battle of Antietam," Sept. 17, 1862.

> *Who* dies in vain
> Upon his country's war-fields, and within
> The shadow of her altars?

William Francis Barry, another of our youngest soldiers, was the second son of Royal P. and Elizabeth (Serrat) Barry, and was born in Boston on the 13th of December, 1843. At the breaking out of the Rebellion he was a clerk in the house of E. W. Wheelock & Co., Boston, dealers in tailors' trimmings. One year later, after the reverses to the Union army under General McClellan, before the gates of Richmond, and at the time when the President was calling for still further re-enforcements, young Barry felt it his duty to go forth and battle for his country. In conversation upon the subject at this time, he said:

"I don't wish to leave home, but rather stay, — but just such young men as I am are called for; I am well and strong; and it is my duty to go."

When reminded that by so doing he might lose his life, his noble answer was:

"What is life without a country?"

It was not an easy task for the widowed mother to part with her beloved boy; but, with thousands of other mothers, she realized the country's necessities, and, listening to the spirit of the following lines, finally acceded to his request:

> "Can you selfishly cling to your household joys,
>   Refusing this smallest tithe to yield,
> While thousands of mothers are sending boys
>   Beloved as yours to the battle-field?
> Can you see my country call in vain,
>   And restrain my arm from the needful blow?
> Not so; though your heart should break with pain,
>   You will kiss me, mother, and let me go."

And, with others, — among whom was his bosom friend and companion, Charles W. Shelton, — he enlisted at the war meeting held Monday evening, July 28th, 1862, was sworn into the United States' service, Aug. 4th, at Boston, and sent to " Camp Cameron," at Cambridge, a rendezvous for recruits for the regiments then in the field.

Previous to this time, when the Fourth Battalion of Infantry offered its services to the Government for a short term of enlistment, young Barry entered its ranks; but as it was not deemed best to accept any troops for so short a time, its services were rejected.

On the 13th of August, he was ordered, with other recruits, to the seat of war, passing through and spending a day in Washington; and joined his regiment, then on the Rapid Ann River, Va., on the 18th, a short time previous to the battles of "Groveton," "Second Bull Run," and "Chantilly," which ended the campaign under General Pope. The exigencies of the service were such at this time that recruits were at once sent to the front, and into active service, many of them young and without previous drill or military experience of any kind whatever; this was the case with young Barry and his companions from Melrose that enlisted in this emergency.

The day after he joined the ranks, according to his letters home,

> "Those fallen leaves that keep their green,
> The noble letters of the dead,"

his regiment marched twenty-three miles, during which many of the most experienced gave out; but the raw recruits bore up manfully under the severe trial.

The Thirteenth participated in the engagements on the Rappahannock River, from Aug. 20th to the 24th; Thoroughfare Gap, on the 28th, when he says, "Three men were shot down near me"; and in the disastrous battle of "Second Bull Run," on the 30th, when, according to his pocket diary, "The bullets whistled like hail, and a round shot struck within three feet of me and threw dirt all over me; but I came off without a scratch"; and in a letter written while in camp at Hall's Hill, Va., four miles from the capital, he says:

> We went on to the field on the double quick and with hurrah. I never was so excited in my life as then. On the Battle-field I felt just as cool as a man could be. I was n't frightened at all until we got some ways back on the retreat. I was helping to carry off a wounded man. The bullets, shell and shot struck all round. A person feels much more frightened at thinking of the danger after he has been through it than when he is in the midst of it.

Of the day after this battle, he says in his diary:

> Centreville was the most mixed up place that ever I saw. Artillery, cavalry, ammunition, ambulances, hacks, and everything under the sun. Every house, barn and place of shelter crowded with wounded. Men of every regiment in the field, hunting and inquiring for it, — nobody knew anything.

Then came the Maryland campaign, with its hard marches, the "Battle of South Mountain," and ending with the "Battle of Antietam." The last entry in his diary is dated September 8; but a letter to his brother Royal, found on his body after he was killed, was dated Ridgeville, Md., Sept. 12, five days previous to the battle; and the following extract from this, his last letter, gives a slight idea of the hardships incident to this campaign:

The recruits joined us three days ago; they stand it very well so far. Yesterday we marched about eight miles; day before, seventeen; the first was a pretty hard one; the day was sultry, and the sweat poured off in streams. Near the end of the march we got pretty well used up. My shoulders got so sore that it was hard work to tell which to put the gun on. When we went into camp for the night it was raining, and it rained all night. I woke up in the night several times, and found my feet in a pool of water; I would draw them up and go to sleep again.

On the fatal day, the 17th of September, the Thirteenth Massachusetts was in the thickest of the fight, during the early part of the day, and suffered severe losses in killed and wounded. Young Barry fought as well and as bravely as the oldest veteran, until he was shot directly through the heart. His friend, Charles W. Shelton, writing from Keedysville, Md., on the 19th, two days after the battle, after very touchingly alluding to their intimacy, his sorrow at his death, and his deep sympathy for his afflicted mother, says:

He was Willie Barry on the battle-field. The coolest, bravest, noblest of the many patriots who that day gave themselves a sacrifice to Liberty and Country!

His body was buried on the battle-field. Through the

kind exertions of Mr. Stephen W. Shelton it was exhumed and brought to Melrose; and on the 29th of September, very interesting and appropriate funeral ceremonies were held in the Baptist Church, the Rev. Mr. Edmands delivering the commemorative discourse; after which all that was mortal of brave young Willie Barry was laid at rest in Wyoming Cemetery.

> " So prompt at duty's call,
>   So dauntless and so brave ; —
> To shield his bleeding Country's life.
>   His blood, his life he gave.
>
> " Rest, Soldier, Patriot, Friend !
>   In your young manhood rest ; —
> Your Country's blessing o'er your bier,
>   Her flag above your breast.
> * * * * * *
> " A grateful land uprears
>   Her tribute to your praise :
> Yours are the holiest of her tears,
>   The greenest of her bays."

JOHN PARKER SHELTON.

Private in Co. A, Thirteenth Regiment Massachusetts Volunteers ; killed at the "Battle of Antietam," Sept. 17, 1862.

" How sweetly they sleep, who have died for their country,
And never will wake for the combat again,
But mantled with glory, they peacefully slumber,
And rest from their toil in the graves of the slain."

John Parker Shelton was the only son of John and Ann (Kendall) Shelton, and was born in Boston, June 8th, 1844.

He graduated as a medal scholar from the Chauncy School, in Boston, about the time of the breaking out of the Rebellion ; after which he entered as clerk in a wholesale clothing house in that city, where he was at the time of his enlistment, Aug. 7th, 1862. Most of our young men who went to the war during its first years were of our best families, of good education and of high character ; enlisting from a true sense of duty and pure love of country ; not from the novelty of the occupation or mere love of excitement, or for pecuniary gain, but only and solely to save our land from Treason's grasp. Thus was it with young Shelton. He enlisted at a time when our regiments and batteries had been depleted by many battles, skirmishes and marches, just after the terrible blow and disheartening result of the Peninsular campaign, while General McClellan and his army were at Harrison's Landing on the James River.

" He gave the tribute of a tear
To those fond hearts who held him dear,
And southward turned — a volunteer —
The oft-told story.

JOHN PARKER SHELTON.

To right the wrong, wipe off the shame,
He cared not that the trump of Fame
Should sound aloud his humble name.
  In tropes of glory.

For Union, and for equal laws,
For Liberty — the grand old cause ;
How could he speak these names and pause,
  Faltering, uncertain ?
He knew not what Fate had in store,
Nor cared her purpose to explore,
But calmly waited on, before
  Her awful curtain."

With others who had enlisted in the Thirteenth at this time he was forwarded to his regiment, and joined it at Mechanicsville, near Washington, after the defeat of our army under General Pope; when the "Second Bull Run Battle" had been fought, and Lee's invasion of Maryland had begun. Ten days afterward the great "Battle of Antietam" took place. Young Shelton's action in this, his first and only battle, is so well told by his friend and companion, — Ambrose Dawes, — that his letter concerning him is here introduced :

NEW YORK, July 4, 1867.
Mr. E. H. Goss:

Dear Sir: — It is with great pleasure, not, indeed, unmixed with sadness, that I comply with your request to give you some account of the last hours of our mutual friend and neighbor, John P. Shelton. The noble courage, heroic devotion and pure patriotism of that young life, nipped as it was in the bud, cannot be too highly appreciated. During the few short days he was with the regiment he endeared himself to many, and his vivacious temperament did much towards keeping up the spirits of his companions during that dark hour when " Bull Run " was lost, and before " Antietam " was gained.

Enlisting with no other thought but love of country, he went forth to fight the good fight, leaving behind him everything which makes it "life to live," and carrying nothing with him but the prayers of dear ones to shield him from the bullets of the enemy. I remember his coming to me just upon the eve of the battle, — perhaps ten minutes before it opened, — looking very pale, — as we probably all did, — and saying that he felt very strangely, and as if he should never return from that field alive. I clasped his hand in mine, and encouraged him as well as I could, for I felt no fears of that kind myself, and we marched together into the fight. Some little time after the battle commenced, he turned to me, his face flushed with excitement, and said : " I am hit in the foot, but shall stick to it and have another pop at them." We advised him to quit the field in vain. This was the last time I saw him. Soon after I saw young Barry fall with a bullet through the forehead. I went up to him, but he was dead, and drawing him behind a tree out of reach of bullets, we left him. Then I received a slight wound, and from loss of blood, being too weak to fight any more, left the field. Shelton remained till the regiment was ordered to the rear, to make room for re-enforcements, after fighting nearly three hours, and then, instead of selfishly looking out for himself, he volunteered to help a dying comrade off the field, although he himself could use but one foot. Thus slowly helping this poor fellow out of danger, a bullet hit him in the spine, which caused paralysis in the lower limbs.

He was taken up, in a dying condition, in a blanket, by four men, one a member of our regiment, and sent, by mistake or from necessity, to one of Sedgewick's Hospitals instead of Hooker's, and thus was lost track of. Being informed that he had repeatedly asked to see me, I hastened to where he had been left ; but unfortunately he had been removed to some other place ; and although I travelled from hospital to hospital I could not find him. We know that he lived but about forty-eight hours, and expired with no friends around him, in one of the most uncomfortable places on earth, — a field hospital. You know the rest; how his body was found and brought home to his bereaved and heart-broken parents, and buried in the beautiful cemetery at Wyoming. No better man, no more generous spirit fell in the war. He gave his life freely in the cause of duty. Why regret that he died such a glorious death? Rather envy him that he died for his country in the cause for which Reno, and Mansfield, and Wadsworth, and Reynolds, and last, but not least, the Martyred Lincoln, laid down their lives. Let us hope that they did not die in vain; that their blood may be sanctified to our country, and from their ashes rise the Phœnix, Liberty and Union, forever and ever. And now, my dear sir, I thank you for allowing me the privilege of testifying to the noble life and glorious death of my truest friend and companion.

I have the honor of being,
Very Respectfully,
Your Obedient Servant,
AMBROSE DAWES.

As is intimated in the above letter, no definite information concerning young Shelton was obtained by his sorrow-stricken family for nearly three weeks after the battle. As soon as the sad tidings were telegraphed, Mr. Simon G. Cheever, — an intimate friend of the family, — started immediately for the battle-field, using every exertion to find him, or learn aught of his situation; issuing descriptive posters and scattering them throughout the region, and making all possible inquiries; but to no purpose; no trace of him was learned. Nothing was ascertained until a letter was received from Surgeon S. G. Palmer, of General Howard's Division, who wrote from head-quarters, in camp near Harper's Ferry, Oct. 2, — the battle was Sept. 17th, — stating that young Shelton died of his wounds at the hospital on Hoffman's Farm; — in the rear of that portion of the battle-field where Sumner's corps, — to which the Thirteenth Regiment belonged,—was engaged, and where about a thousand of the wounded had been brought;—and that he had been buried in a pleasant spot beneath a walnut tree, by the side of many others, about an eighth of a mile from the farm house; at the same time sending home what few effects were found upon his body. When these facts were learned, his cousin, Mr. Stephen W. Shelton, and his brother-in-law, Mr. George W. Copeland, at once proceeded to the battle-field and brought his body home. He was buried in Wyoming Cemetery on the 16th of October, the funeral services being held in the Baptist Church. An appropriate sermon was preached by the pastor, Rev. Mr. Colby, and he was assisted in the solemn ceremonies by the Rev. William H. Munroe, rector of the Episcopal Church.

As has been said, "Antietam" was young Shelton's first and only battle; he had not been in even a skirmish before; and it is the testimony of all,—officers and privates,—that he fought well and manfully,—the bravest of the brave,—on that bloody field. Would that he had not been called to render up his young life so early in the great conflict!

"There is a tear for all that die,
  A mourner o'er the humblest grave;
 But nations lift the funeral cry
  And freedom weeps above the brave.

"For them is sorrow's purest sigh
  O'er ocean's heaving bosom sent;
 For them are tears in every eye;
  All earth becomes their monument.

"A theme to crowds that knew them not,
  Lamented by admiring foes,
 Who would not choose their glorious lot,
  Who would not die the death they chose?"

JONAS GREEN BROWN.

Private in Co. E, Fiftieth Massachusetts Regiment ; died at Baton Rouge, La., June 18, 1863, of disease contracted in the service.

Jonas Green Brown, son of Joseph and Keziah (Gerry) Brown, was born in Melrose, June 20, 1824.

In August, 1862, when the President called for three hundred thousand more troops, to serve for nine months, Brown enlisted in Captain Littlefield's South Reading Company, Fiftieth Regiment, of which Carlos P. Messer, of Haverhill, was Colonel. The nucleus of the Fiftieth was the Seventh Massachusetts Militia Regiment, and it was composed of companies from Essex and Middlesex Counties. The Colonel and Lieutenant-Colonel, — John W. Locke, of South Reading, — were Captains in the three months' service when the Rebellion broke out. The Fiftieth was sent into the "Department of the Gulf," and assigned to the command of Acting Brigadier-General N. A. M. Dudley, First Division, Third Brigade, Nineteenth Army Corps, and was encamped at Baton Rouge. On the 14th of March it accompanied Major-General Banks' expedition to the rear of Port Hudson, which was undertaken for the purpose of allowing Admiral Farragut, with his two war steamers, "Hartford" and "Albatross," to pass the batteries. This object was successfully accomplished, and the Fiftieth returned to Baton Rouge. It was afterwards actively engaged in the "Siege of Port Hudson," and, after the surrender of that stronghold, was encamped within its fortifications ; but previous to the siege, and while at Baton Rouge, Brown was attacked with diarrhœa, — May 17th, — and died June 18th, 1863.

An extract from Captain Littlefield's letter to the widow, — indorsed by Lieutenants Warren and Draper, — testifies to the regard in which Brown was held by his officers and fellow-soldiers :

We feel that an all-wise Providence has in His, to us sometimes mysterious dispensations, seen fit to take from our number a brother soldier, whom we esteemed for his virtues and respected for his personal worth ; while from you He has taken a loved partner and support, and from your children a kind father and protector. No words can express to you what we feel in our hearts for his afflicted family, and we can only point you to Him who has said, "Blessed are they that mourn, for they shall be comforted." Hoping that you will bring your wounded, broken heart, with all its burdens and sorrows, to Him who has said He will be the widow's God, and the Father to the fatherless, I subscribe myself,

Yours in affliction,
S. F. LITTLEFIELD,
Captain Co. E.

BENJAMIN LYNDE.

Private in Co. K, Thirty-Eighth Massachusetts Regiment ; died at Baton Rouge, La., Aug. 18, 1863, of disease contracted in the service.

Benjamin Lynde was the oldest son of George and Harriet (Favor) Lynde, and was born in Melrose, Aug. 14, 1831.

At the time of his enlistment, August 1862, he was pursuing his occupation as a farmer. He was the brother of George Warren Lynde, who enlisted the year before in the Seventeenth Regiment.

The Thirty-Eighth Regiment was sent into the "Department of the Gulf," where it participated in the "Siege of Port Hudson," and various battles and marches in Louisiana. In the summer of 1863, Lynde was attacked with the chronic diarrhœa, and during the long and wearisome march through the "Teche" country, he was hardly able to keep his place in the ranks, and was often advised to go to the hospital ; but he would not listen to such advice, and persevered much longer than he ought, performing every duty incumbent upon a well man. After a rest at Alexandria, he recovered somewhat, but after passing through the "Siege of Port Hudson," he became worse, and on the 18th of August, while the regiment was lying at Baton Rouge, he died. His comrades placed a head board at his grave, giving his name, age, residence, regiment, company, and date of death, and he sleeps in a soldier's grave on the distant banks of the "Father of Waters." He left behind a wife to mourn his loss.

GEORGE JAMES MORSE.

Private in Co. A, Thirteenth Massachusetts Regiment; 2d Lieutenant in Second U. S. Colored Troops; 1st Lieutenant in Co. G, Fifty-Ninth Massachusetts Regiment; killed at the "Battle of Spottsylvania," May 12, 1864.

> "With sword on thigh, 'to do or die,'
> I march to meet the foe."

> "A nation's tears will greet the dead,
> Whose blood for Freedom's cause was shed."

George James Morse — brother of Sidney Bradford Morse — was the oldest son of George H. and Sarah (Bird) Morse, and was born in New York, Dec. 7, 1842.

He was one of the earliest of our citizens to enlist. On the 19th of April, — with his brother Sidney, — he joined the Fourth Battalion of Rifles, which offered its services to the government for three months' service, but being refused for that period of time, was soon afterwards recruited to the Thirteenth Regiment of three years' troops.

During the fall and winter of 1861-2, he experienced the fortunes of the Thirteenth on the upper waters of the Potomac, engaged in many severe skirmishes, hard marches and arduous picket duties; followed by the campaign of General Pope, ending with the battles of "Groveton," "Second Bull Run," and "Chantilly."

While at Warrenton, Va., before the hard fighting of this campaign commenced, he says, in a letter to his mother:

To-day ends our first year in " Uncle Sam's " service. Two years more at the farthest, and our troubles and privations will be over, and we can return to our homes with the proud consciousness of having done our duty, and spent the best years of our lives in our country's service.

At the "Second Bull Run Battle" he narrowly escaped with his life. Two bullets pierced his knapsack; his canteen and rifle-sling were both shot away; and his right hand was shattered by a musket ball, on account of which he was sent to the hospital at Philadelphia. Amputation of his hand was at first thought necessary; but it was saved, and he soon afterward received the appointment of a clerkship in the hospital where he was confined. It was while here that his much loved brother, Sidney, died. Poignant was his grief at the sad tidings, as will be seen by the following letter to his mother, written with his left hand:

PHILADELPHIA, Sept. 19, 1862.

My dear mother: — Last evening I received your letter, announcing the departure of my beloved brother to the spirit world. May God give us strength to bear with our affliction, and make us better because of it. I feel it deeply, — more so than I can express; but I find comfort in the reflection that he is in a better world, where we shall all meet again. He "has fought the good fight," *and died in the service of his country!*

Although so young in years, he was old in experience, and has given up his young life to the best cause that has engaged the attention of our countrymen since the days of the American Revolution. He was beloved by all who knew him. No one knows the pain and anguish I suffer; but it is softened by the remembrance that what I could do for him was cheerfully and gladly done. He little knew that many a time I had given him the last cracker, and knew not where to get more. But I am thankful it was in my power to do so. For fifteen months we were together, — and, so far as I was able, I feel that I have done my duty by him. This comforts me; and now I only look forward to that time when I shall meet him in that life where there are no wars, " nor rumors of war," but wheie all is peace and love. And, oh, what a joyful meeting it will be! Father, mother, brothers and sisters, all united in one happy family, — never more to part!

After recovering from this wounded hand, and having been discharged from the Thirteenth Regiment, he was commissioned, for valor displayed and meritorious services rendered, 2d Lieutenant in the Second United States Volunteers, — colored troops, — in the "Department of the Gulf." Here he participated in the sieges of "Vicksburg" and "Port Hudson."

On the 5th of July, during the "Siege of Port Hudson," where he was forty-three days in the trenches, he was wounded in the head; and before he could be taken from the field he received a sun-stroke. Soon afterwards a malarial fever seized upon him, and it was the decision of the surgeon, that the only hope of saving his life was for him to leave that region, and return home; and at his positive command, he tendered his resignation, which was accepted, and he was sent North. He arrived at his home in Melrose, in September, in a very dangerous condition; so much so, that no one that saw him at the time supposed it was possible for him to live; but God had other work for him yet to do, and with constant and tender care he began slowly to recover.

In less than two months after arriving home, and while yet convalescent, he learned that J. Parker Gould, his formerly much esteemed and honored Major of the Thirteenth Regiment, had been commissioned Colonel of the Fifty-Ninth Regiment Massachusetts Veteran Volunteers, and at once determined to enlist under him; and, rising from his sick bed, he penned a note to Colonel Gould, soliciting an appointment. Parents and friends, thinking his health not sufficiently established, endeavored to dissuade him from entering the service again so soon.

But his answer was: "I enlisted at first, because I felt it to be my duty; the same cause still exists, and the same necessity for action; and if my life is spared, and I am needed, *five* years from this time will find me in the *field*, for while this war lasts, *that* must be my home."

He received a commission, Oct. 22, 1863, as 2d Lieutenant in Co. G, and, as soon as his health permitted, was ordered on recruiting service for his regiment, and sent to Woburn, Stoneham, and other towns. Dec. 14th, he was ordered to the camp at Readville; and on March 4th, he was promoted to 1st Lieutenant.

During the latter part of April, 1864, the Fifty-Ninth Regiment was hurried off to the seat of war, in order to join in the final campaign under General Grant. It left Readville April 26th, and arrived in Virginia just in season to cross the Rappahannock with the grand army, and entered into the "Battle of the Wilderness," without rest, only ten days after leaving the State. Here Lieutenant Morse was wounded in the head by a falling tree; but he remained from his regiment only a very short time, returning with bandaged head to take command of his company, the Captain of which had retired.

During the battles of the succeeding days he was often cautioned and warned from going ahead of his men during action. His answer was: "If you want your men to go anywhere, you must lead them."

He seems to have had a presentiment before leaving home, and more especially before entering his last battle, that he should be killed, as was manifested by messages left behind, and from the fact that just before the "Battle of Spottsylvania," or as it is sometimes called the "Battle of the Angle," he took a paper from his pocket, directed it to his mother, and requested Sergeant Bearce, of his company, to see that she received it, as he felt that he should not survive the coming battle.

He led his company into that battle, and a ball pierced his right side, shattering at the same time a pistol in his belt. Placing him upon a stretcher, two of his men started with him for the hospital four miles in the rear. When about half way there, he became faint, said that he was dying, and requested them to stop: after leaving with them messages for the wife, mother, and other dear ones at home, he said: "Tell the boys I die like a soldier"; after which his spirit took its flight to that other and better world. And thus did he die the "proudest of all deaths," as he termed the death of a comrade in arms, killed in the battles before Richmond in 1862; saying of him, in a letter to his mother:

Poor fellow! he is at rest, with the proudest of all names; and he died the proudest of all deaths, a soldier fighting for his country.

His body was taken to the hospital, and buried under the direction of his Colonel, who was then at the hospital on account of a sun-stroke, received during the "Battle of the Wilderness"; and there, in the blood-stained soil of Virginia, lies one who was, in the words of Colonel Gould, who wrote his parents a few days afterwards, "a very brave soldier." His remains were afterwards removed by the Government to the National Cemetery in Fredericksburg, Va., Grave No. 201, Division A, Section C.

Lieutenant Morse was a member of Guiding Star Lodge, No. 28, Independent Order of Good Templars, in Melrose, and at a meeting, held May 26th, 1864, a series of resolutions was offered and adopted, one of which was as follows:

Resolved, That we tender our deepest sympathy to his bereaved wife, parents and relatives, in this our mutual affliction, and we unite with them in mourning the loss of a worthy brother, an affectionate son, husband and father ; and we also seek to participate with them in the only consolation to be derived from the circumstances of his decease ; that his life having illustrated his unbending courage, he merits the martyr's crown by being able, amid the allurements of wife, child and home, to lay down his life upon the battle-field, exclaiming with other dying heroes:

"It is sweet to die for one's country."

The following incident is told of Lieutenant Morse while in the trenches before "Port Hudson": One day he was ordered to have his men build some breastworks on a certain portion of the line, very much exposed to the enemy's fire. While overseeing this labor, a colonel rode out to the spot, saying that he had been told that there was a coward out there ; the bullets flew by, and close to the colonel, and off he started for a more retired position. Very soon after a major rode out, and made the same assertion. Lieutenant Morse said nothing ; but the flying bullets spoke for him, whistling such a melody about the major's ears, that he soon turned his horse, and followed the course of the colonel before him. Nothing more was heard about cowardice.

Remarks made by those who go from us and return again are seldom remembered ; but let them be made by one that is taken from us, and they are recalled and treasured. A remark made by Lieutenant Morse to his mother, just before leaving home for the last time, was: "If I am worthy to go and wear a soldier's uniform, I am worthy to fill a soldier's grave."

We close this sketch with a stanza from a poem entitled "The Dying Soldier," suggested by the death of the two brothers,—George and Sidney,—and written by a resident of Melrose:

> Thou Southern clime! e'en thou must be
> " His Chancel, Nave and Sacristy";
> Death ended many a bright career
> Whose noble forms lie buried here;
> Ye winds and rains, a requiem raise,
> And chant it o'er these warriors' graves.
> They've ended here all dreams of fame,
> But leave behind an honored name.

AUGUSTUS GREEN.

Private in Co. G, Twenty-Second Massachusetts Regiment; killed at the "Battle of Bethesda Church," June 3, 1864.

> "He sleeps where he fell, 'mid the battle's roar,
> With his comrades true and brave;
> And his noble form we shall see no more, —
> It rests in a hero's grave."

Augustus Green, the oldest son of Levi and Sarah (Davis) Green, was born in Malden on the 28th of May, 1841.

He enlisted in Co. G, Twenty-Second Massachusetts Regiment, in September 1861. The Twenty-Second Regiment was organized by Hon. Henry Wilson, and left the State in October 1861. It was encamped a number of months at Hall's Hill, Va., after which it was engaged in the battles of the Peninsular campaign, under General McClellan, followed by "Antietam," "Fredericksburg," "Chancellorsville" and "Gettysburg," and then in the final campaign under General Grant. For a month previous to the "Battle of Bethesda Church," it was engaged in constant fights and skirmishes. Up to this time, Green had followed the fortunes of his regiment without receiving a wound. On the second day of the fight at this place, — which besides the church, a small, one-story, unpainted building, consisted of only three or four houses, — the Twenty-Second had been in line of battle, behind its breastworks, all day, and Green had occupied a position behind a large oak-tree during this and the previous day. Just before night he ventured to put his head out from behind the tree, to take a look at the enemy's line, when a sharpshooter shot him through the forehead, and he expired almost instantly. He was buried by his comrades on the field of battle, and there his body now rests. He is spoken of by his comrades in arms as a bold soldier, and one that fought well, never shrinking from his duty.

> "He fought and died. A nameless grave
> Where no sad willows o'er him wave,
> Or sculptured stone extóls the brave
>   In chiselled numbers,
> Was his. The bird's shrill symphonies,
> The restless murmur of the trees,
> The sighing of the evening breeze,
>   Mar not his slumbers."

ALBERT WATERSTON CROCKETT.

Private in Co. K, Seventeenth Regiment; died in "Andersonville Prison," Ga., Aug. 1, 1864.

Albert Waterston Crockett, — brother of George F. Crockett, who served in the Third Battery, — was the son of George B. and Adeline D. Crockett, and was born in Boston, Jan. 3, 1843.

At the time of his enlistment, August 1861, he was employed in French's daguerrotype and photographic material establishment on Washington Street, Boston. His regiment was sent to and served its time in the "Department of North Carolina," and Crockett was one of the best of soldiers, performing his duties well and faithfully up to the time of his captivity, which was at the "Battle of Batchelder's Creek," Feb. 1, 1864. On that day, at four o'clock, A. M., the rebels made an attack on the pickets and camp of the One Hundred and Thirty-Second New York Regiment, near Batchelder's Creek, nine miles from New Berne. Lieutenant-Colonel John F. Fellows, with portions of the five companies stationed near Fort Totten — D, E, H, I and K, — the other five being in New Berne, went to assist in repelling the attack. The Seventeenth arrived just as the enemy, numbering fifteen thousand men, had succeeded in carrying the bridge, and, under cover of woods and fog, it succeeded in flanking our small force; and, finding resistance useless against such overwhelming numbers, orders were given to fall back to the crossing of the railroad and Trent road, there to make another stand. At this time, the remainder of the Union force had retreated, leaving the Seventeenth alone to check the advance of the enemy. Soon after, Lieutenant-Colonel Fellows, together with seven other officers and fifty-eight enlisted men, were taken prisoners. Three were killed, and three severely wounded. Lieutenant-Colonel Fellows was one of the Union officers who were placed by the rebel authorities in the city of Charleston, they thinking to prevent our gunboats and batteries from shelling it. He was afterwards exchanged, and returned to his regiment. Crockett, with others, was taken first to "Belle Isle," and thence to "Andersonville"; and while performing these marches became very foot-sore. Before his imprisonment he was one of the most cleanly and careful of soldiers as regarded his bodily health; but afterwards, while being slowly starved to death, he became disheartened, and was careless of himself; in consequence of which, dirt and vermin, ever abounding in those Southern prisons, aggravated his troubles, — and chronic diarrhœa and scurvy seizing upon him, soon ended his life. He died a very hard death, suffering terribly from his disease, and for want of proper care and nourishment. At the time of his death, he had bartered everything he had for food, excepting an old pair of drawers and a blouse; the latter given him by his fellow prisoner and sufferer, John E. Quinn, who first went out from our town, in 1861, in the Thirty-Second Regiment, but was discharged for disability, and afterwards re-enlisted in the Seventeenth Regiment, and was taken prisoner at the same time with Crockett, but who survived all the horrors of "Andersonville" and "Belle Isle," and returned to tell the tale.

Crockett was buried outside the "prison pen," where so many thousands of our brave boys are now sleeping, and the number of his grave is 4,483; and there he will sleep with his comrades "till a clarion, louder than that which marshalled them to the combat, shall awake their slumbers."

JAMES ROWLAND HOWARD.

Private in Co. K, Thirty-Eighth Massachusetts Regiment; died Aug. 16, 1864, of disease contracted in the service.

"The least in rank, but not in honor."

James Rowland Howard, the fourth son of James and Mary (Holt) Howard, was born in Melrose, Feb. 15, 1841. His father and grandfather were also natives of Melrose, or, as it was then called, North Malden. When the Rebellion broke out, James was in Charlestown, Mass., learning the harness-maker's trade, and he expressed a very strong desire to enlist in the service of his country at once; but, as he was not then of age, yielded to the remonstrances of his widowed mother.

In July 1862, when the renewed and earnest call came for more men, he could no longer withstand the appeal. The spirit and desire to serve his country, which actuated so many thousands of our young men at this time, was his; and listening to the lines of Oliver Wendell Holmes,

> Listen, young heroes! your country is calling!
> Time strikes the hour for the brave and the true!
> Now, while the foremost are fighting and falling,
> Fill up the ranks that have opened for you!

and the mother telling him to act as he thought best, as he was then free, he enlisted during the latter part of July, with several other Melrose men, in Co. K, Thirty-Eighth Regiment, and was mustered in at "Camp Stanton," Lynnfield, Aug. 12, 1862, and left the State Aug. 26th.

The Thirty-Eighth was ordered to join the "Banks'

Expedition," and was sent into the "Department of the Gulf," where it experienced hard service; having been engaged, previous to the time that Howard left it, in the "Battle of Bisland," the "Siege of Port Hudson," and many severe marches through the "Teche," and other portions of Louisiana, one of the marches being ninety-six miles in four days. It was during the "Siege of Port Hudson," and while encamped in the woods, that his system became thoroughly impregnated with the poison of the miasmas from the swamps and bayous of the surrounding region; so much so as to deprive him of nearly all sense of feeling in his flesh.

Chronic diarrhœa seized upon him, very much reducing his strength and ability for duty; and yet, although so reduced, he would not listen to appeals to enter the hospital, saying that he "entered the service to work, not to be waited upon." Upon being examined by the surgeon, he saw that it was necessary that he should be sent North; and in August he was granted a furlough, but, owing to detentions, he did not arrive home until October. His furlough expiring in December, he reported himself, with the intention of returning to the field; but the authorities would not receive him, and ordered his discharge, which was given Dec. 5, 1863.

Disease had so firmly seated itself upon him, that consumption was engendered, and he lived but a few months after his discharge, dying Aug. 16, 1864.

Howard is highly spoken of by his companions in arms as a true soldier, and one that performed every duty incumbent upon him. He has gone to his reward. He did not die upon the battle-field, nevertheless he gave his life for his country.

FRANCIS PEABODY.

Private in Co. G, Twenty-Second Massachusetts Regiment; discharged April 21, 1862, for disability; re-enlisted in Co. A, in the Seventeenth Massachusetts Regiment, Aug. 11, 1862; died at New Berne, N. C., Oct. 3, 1864, of yellow fever.

Francis Peabody, son of Torrey and Matilda (Alley) Peabody, was born in Lynn, Mass., Dec. 31, 1845. He enlisted in the Twenty-Second Regiment,—raised by Hon. Henry Wilson,—and was mustered into the service Oct. 5, 1861, but was discharged for disability, April 21, 1862. In the July following, when the exigency of the country demanded a large accession to the ranks in the field, young Peabody, having recovered his health, heard again the cry:

> Our country's calling! Go forth! go forth!
> To danger and glory, ye gallants!

and enlisted in Co. A, Seventeenth Massachusetts Regiment, being sworn into service, Aug. 11, 1862. This regiment experienced severe and honorable service in the "Department of North Carolina." Peabody joined his regiment at New Berne,—two other recruits from our town, Edward W. Kendall and James S. Macey, joining at the same time,—and served his country faithfully and with true soldierly bearing, through the various marches, skirmishes and battles incident to the North Carolina campaigns.

He again re-enlisted, Jan. 4, 1864, as a veteran volunteer, under General Order No. 191 from the War Department. Soon after this re-enlistment, in February 1864, he became Orderly for Brigadier-General I. N. Palmer, and served in that capacity until the time of his death, Oct. 3, 1864. He died of yellow fever, at New Berne, during the prevalence of that epidemic. His body now lies in the "Old Cemetery" of that city. The father and brother of Francis both served in the army, and both are now suffering from the effects of services then rendered.

We close this sketch with the following testimonial from General Palmer, now Lieutenant-Colonel 2d U. S. Cavalry:

Fort Laramie, D. T.,
Jan. 6, 1868.

Mr. E. H. Goss, Melrose, Mass:

Dear Sir: — Your letter of the 1st of August only reached me a short time since, as I was absent for a few months from this Post, and my letters were not forwarded to me.

With regard to the young man, Francis Peabody, late of the Seventeenth Mass. Volunteers, I can only say that he was on duty at my Head-Quarters at New Berne, North Carolina, for some time before his death, which occurred during the terrible season of yellow fever in 1864. He was always a remarkably quiet, well behaved, trustworthy man. Although he did not meet a soldier's death on the battle-field, his name should nevertheless be enrolled with the list of the heroes whose lives were given so freely in the service of their country during the Rebellion.

I am, sir,
Very respectfully, yours,
I. N. Palmer,
Lieut.-Col. 2d Cavalry, Bt. Brig.-General.

GEORGE ELWYN RICHARDSON.

[COMMUNICATED.]

The subject of this notice was born May 11, 1844. He enlisted in Co. K, with other young men from this town, in the Thirty-Eighth Massachusetts Regiment.

At the early age of eighteen, he left a pleasant home and associations to endure the hardships, and meet the dangers of a soldier's life. He went into camp at Lynnfield, Aug. 15, 1862, and left the State, Sept. 24, for Baltimore, and remained there until the 10th of November, when his regiment left for New Orleans; and, after being delayed at Fortress Monroe and Ship Island, arrived safely at that city, Dec. 31. For nearly two years he served under General Banks, in the "Department of the Gulf," sharing with his regiment the dangers and honors of the Western Louisiana and Port Hudson campaigns. He left Louisiana with his regiment, and joined the army of General Sheridan, in the Valley of the Shenandoah, in the fall of 1864.

At the battle of "Cedar Creek" he had the misfortune to be taken prisoner. He was carried first to Richmond and then to Salisbury, N. C., where he died on the 3d of November following, in the rebel prison of that place. Thus he died at the early age of twenty, a martyr in the cause of his country. We have no remarkable incidents of his soldier life to record, but we have the testimony of his comrades, that he was a good soldier, always cheerfully doing his duty; and although he fell thus early, he will not die in the memory and love of his friends. He was a member of the Methodist Episcopal Church and

Sabbath School, and all that knew him had confidence in the purity of his character, and cherish the hope of meeting him in that home above, "where no sorrow shall come," but where the redeemed of the Lord shall enjoy an eternal heaven of joy on high. C. H. U.

GEORGE THOMAS MARTIN.

[COMMUNICATED.]

George Thomas Martin was born in Boston, May 7, 1840. In April, 1846, his parents removed to Melrose, which continued to be his home until his death. He early sought to enter the service of his country, and was commissioned 2d Lieutenant of Co. K, Thirty-Eighth Massachusetts Volunteers, took an active part in recruiting his company, and proceeded with his regiment to Baltimore. While encamped here, he was wounded in the ankle by the accidental discharge of a pistol, and though he soon appeared to recover from it, yet it is probable that it was an indirect cause of his death. The Thirty-Eighth was assigned to General Banks' corps, and sailed soon after for Ship Island. From here it proceeded to Carrollton, La., and thence took part in the first movement on "Port Hudson." At the "Battle of Bisland," young Martin was promoted to be 1st Lieutenant. In the long marches of this campaign, and in the "Siege of Port Hudson," he bore a part. The hardships of this service induced a varicose vein, and he was compelled to ask his discharge, which was given, and he returned to Melrose. Some months' rest followed, when he re-entered the army, and was commissioned Senior 1st Lieutenant of Co. C, Fourth Massachusetts Heavy Artillery, Aug. 16, 1864. He was ordered to the fortifications near Washington. About the 1st of March, 1865, he obtained leave of absence, and entered the Massachusetts General Hospital at Boston, in order to have the varicose vein removed. This was in part successfully accomplished; but pyæmia ensued, causing his sudden death, March 13,

1865. To die, for him, however, "was gain." His dying hours were full of triumphant joy, for he was sustained by a hope in Christ, which did not fail. He united with the Congregational Church in Melrose, in June 1858, and had been active in the Sabbath School and prayer meetings, as well as the more social gatherings of the church. He was also an active member of the Boston Young Men's Christian Association.

Thus in merest outline is the brief life of one of our soldiers sketched! How they loved him and how they miss him at home, in the social gathering, the prayer meeting, the church, the Sabbath School, cannot here be told; we know that his merry laugh, his earnest, cheerful tones are hushed and still here forever! We know, too, that we shall meet him again, where every sound of earthly strife is ended, and where "there shall be no more death, neither sorrow nor crying." C. N. C.

JOHN EASTMAN STILPHEN.

Private in the Second Massachusetts Battery; died June 25, 1865, of disease contracted in the service.

John Eastman Stilphen was born in Dresden, Maine, June 18, 1830. At the breaking out of the Rebellion, and for a few years previous, he was living in Melrose, following his occupation as a carpenter. He enlisted in Nims' Second Battery, which was mustered into the service July 31, 1861, and sent to Baltimore, Md. While here it took part in the "Eastern Shore Virginia Expedition"; and, in April 1862, was ordered to report to Major-General B. F. Butler, commanding "Department of the Gulf," where it saw much and arduous service; taking part in the "Siege of Vicksburg," "Battle of Baton Rouge," "Siege of Port Hudson," "Red River Expedition," and other battles and skirmishes, besides many hard marchings and counter-marchings throughout that Department. Stilphen was one of the best of soldiers, performing every duty incumbent upon him, although suffering from his disease — hemorrhoids — during all the latter part of the period of his service; so much so, that most men under like circumstances would have sought for and obtained a discharge; but Stilphen remained at his post until his time was out; and one who served with him during these many campaigns, says that "he was as true as steel, and never flinched when under fire." He was mustered out of the service, Aug. 11, 1864, after which time he was able to do but little work, gradually failing under the fatal hold of his disease. He died June 25, 1865, leaving a wife and three children to mourn his loss, and was buried in Wyoming Cemetery. A handsome head-stone bears, besides his name and date of death, the following inscriptions :

A SOLDIER'S GRAVE.

HE HAS LEFT US FOR HIS HOME IN HEAVEN.

GEORGE WARREN LYNDE.

Private in Co. A, Seventeenth Massachusetts Regiment; commissioned Brevet 1st Lieutenant, Dec. 31, 1864; died Jan. 30, 1866, of disease contracted in the service.

George Warren Lynde was the youngest son of George and Harriet (Favor) Lynde and was born in Melrose, Sept. 2, 1846.

This was another of our boy-soldiers, he being but fifteen years of age at the time of his enlistment. He was then attending school, and, on the morning of the 23d of August, 1861, as had been his custom, he drove his father's cows to pasture; but instead of returning home, he kept on his way to "Camp Schouler," at Lynnfield, and at once enlisted in Co. A, Seventeenth Regiment, giving his age as eighteen. For some time previous to this he had been in the habit of asking his father and mother, nearly every day, for their consent to his entering the service of his country. A negative answer was invariably given, until the day before he started for Lynnfield, when, in answer to the question, his father, half sportively and half in earnest, said "yes." This was enough, and George took the first opportunity that offered and started off on foot for the camp, eight miles distant. He was at this time captain of a boy's military company, organized a month or two previous, in which he took a great interest; and undoubtedly his taste for military matters was enhanced by his experience in this company.

He left the State with his regiment, which was assigned to the "Department of North Carolina," and served throughout its period of service with much honor to himself and his country. He was in the battles of "Kinston," "Whitehall" and "Goldsborough," besides many skirmishes and long marches over the wretched and swampy roads, and almost impenetrable jungles of North Carolina.

His comrades bear evidence that during his absence as a soldier he did not become addicted to any of the habits and vices which cursed so many; but so straightforward and soldierly had been his career, that his colonel frequently recommended him for promotion.

While at New Berne, he suffered severely at times with the fever and ague, and was also otherwise unwell; but he remained at his post, fighting the good fight well, and performing every duty satisfactorily until his period of service expired, when he returned home, and was mustered out on the 3d of August, 1864; but he was never well. Comsumption had marked him for its victim. From the day of his muster-out he was never warm, suffering almost constantly from feeling cold until his death, which took place on the 30th of January, 1866.

He was brevetted 1st Lieutenant, Dec. 31, 1864, for gallant conduct and bravery displayed at the "Battle of Blount's Mills, "when, with a few others, he rushed out from the ranks and rescued Belger's Fifth Rhode Island Battery, which had become disabled and been left in the field between the two forces, Captain Belger himself having lost an arm, the horses being killed, and the battery abandoned.

XIV.

In Rebel Prisons.

" 'The world's ear is full of cries from the land of rebel barbarism, where starvation walked at the side of every captive, and suffering, despair and death sat at every prison door."

"Andersonville"! "Belle Isle"! "Florence"! "Millen"! Salisbury"! Who that has had friends or relatives starved in these hideous "prison-pens," or that has read the story of those who have experienced and survived the systematic cruelty there practised by the rebel authorities,—the "horrible and predetermined scheme, contrived for the purpose of depleting our armies and discouraging our soldiers," "to destroy them, or to disable them for further military service, or to compel our Government to an exchange on other than the terms to which it is in honor and by necessity committed,"—does not shudder at mention of these names, so suggestive are they of brutality, sickness, disease, starvation, death, and almost every conceivable inhumanity? It is impossible for any one to realize the amount of suffering and misery endured by Union men in these terrible places.

After hearing the recital, or reading the account of one who has experienced this severe treatment, suffered its horrors, and has returned and told his story, the wonder is that any one of the many thousands that have been there incarcerated[1] ever survived the fearful ordeal. But there are those, — and we have a few in our midst, — who lived through all and returned, and have related their sufferings, giving the world a picture of the misery and torture endured by our men at the instigation of rebel leaders, whose names and memories will ever be accursed and stigmatized, be they wandering up and down the face of the earth, or be they in their graves.

Not many of our own citizens were destined to experience these fearful sufferings, although at one time, Jan. 1, 1863, twenty-five (25) Melrose men, belonging to the Forty-Second Massachusetts Regiment, were taken prisoners at Galveston, Texas ; but this was before the extreme cruelty and barbarity toward our men, — the systematic determination to let them perish from neglect, — was fully exercised, — although great suffering had then been endured by our men in more eastern prisons, — and they were treated comparatively well, being cared for, and as good and as much food given them as it was in the rebels' power to give ; and, after passing through Texas and Louisiana to the Mississippi River, by railroad and steamboat, with one foot-march of one hundred and twenty-five miles in five days, they were paroled, having been in the rebel authorities' hands only about two months.

---

[1] The number of Union prisoners held in the South during the Rebellion was 126,940. Of this number 22,576 died, or were starved to death. The first Union prisoner held by the rebels was John L. Worden, — who afterwards commanded the "Monitor" in its encounter with the "Merrimack," — who was kept in the common jail at Montgomery from April 15, 1861, until Nov. 11, and then exchanged.

Besides these twenty-five (25) men, the following of our citizens have been prisoners of war:

Henry H. Jones,	George W. Batchelder,
Archibald Bogle,	Benjamin F. York,
George E. Richardson,	Frederick W. Krantz,
Albert W. Crockett,	George W. Elliot,
William H. Eastman,	John E. Quinn,
Edmund W. Davis,	Henry Stone.

Ten of these lived to return to their homes. Richardson and Crockett were starved to death at "Salisbury" and "Andersonville." Sketches of them have appeared on a previous page. We now give short notices of the imprisonment of some of those who survived the fierce conflict with sickness and starvation.

HENRY H. JONES,

of Co. A, Thirteenth Massachusetts Regiment, was taken prisoner during the first day's fighting of the "Battle of Gettysburg," July 1, 1863, and, after suffering eight months the horrors of rebel prisons, was exchanged, and rejoined his regiment in May 1864, just before the "Battle of Cool Arbor," during the final campaign under General Grant.

From Gettysburg young Jones was taken to Staunton, Va., where, with between four and five thousand other prisoners, he remained six weeks, waiting transportation to Richmond ; to which place prisoners were finally carried on cattle cars.

His first night in Richmond was spent in the famous — and *in*famous — "Libby Prison"; after which he was sent to "Belle Isle," where commenced his sufferings, and where he remained until exchanged.[1]

Here he suffered the horrors and torments incident to this overcrowded, ill-fed and ill-treated body of prisoners. There were at times from ten to twelve thousand men congregated in this small space, — turned in like so many cattle, — to find what resting-place and comfort they could. When the least crowded, they could not have had a space for each man larger than three feet by nine. Here disease and death held high carnival. Thousands without tent or shelter of any kind; through summer, fall and winter; through torrid sun, rains and floods; malarial fogs and sharp, cutting winds; covered with dirt and vermin; "stripped of blankets and overcoats, hatless often, shoeless often, in ragged coats and rotting shirts, they were obliged to take the weather as it came. Here and there a tent had a fire, and the inmates gathered round it, but the thousands outside shivered as the cold cut them to the bone, and huddled together for warmth and sympathy"; "the cold froze them because they were hungry, — the

---

[1] Belle Island is a small island in the James River, opposite the Tredegar Iron-works, and in full sight from the Libby windows. It has pretensions enough to beauty at a distant view to justify its name, as part of it is a bluff covered with trees. But the portion on which the prisoners are confined is low, sandy and barren, without a tree to cast a shadow, and poured upon by the burning rays of a Southern sun. Here is an enclosure, variously estimated to be from three to six acres in extent, surrounded by an earthwork about three feet high, with a ditch on either side. On the edge of the outer ditch, all round the enclosure, guards are stationed about forty feet apart, and keep watch there day and night. The interior has something of the look of an encampment, a number of Sibley tents being set in rows, with "streets" between. These tents, rotten, torn full of holes, — poor shelter at any rate, — accommodated only a small portion of the number who were confined within these low earth walls. — *Report of Committee to U. S. Sanitary Commission.*

hunger consumed them because they were cold." So severe was the treatment, that, according to the Confederate Surgeon-General's quarterly report for the months of January, February and March, 1864, out of nearly twenty-eight hundred patients in the hospital, about fourteen hundred — half the number — died! This is but a slight picture of the sufferings experienced in this and other rebel prisons.

Jones was released from this scene of misery in April 1864, and after his exchange was sent to Annapolis, Md., — then a rendezvous for exchanged prisoners, — where he remained, recuperating his nearly exhausted system, for six weeks; after which he joined his regiment, went with it through the remaining period of its service, returned, and was mustered out, Aug. 1, 1864. Some idea of the suffering he experienced can be imagined, not realized, when it is stated that when taken prisoner he weighed one hundred and fifty-eight pounds; when he arrived at Annapolis he weighed ninety-five pounds. He still suffers from deafness and rheumatism, engendered by the cruel treatment received while in the hands of " our erring sisters."

ARCHIBALD BOGLE

Went into the service in 1861 as 2d Lieutenant of Co. I, Seventeenth Massachusetts Regiment, was promoted 1st Lieutenant, May 28, 1862, and discharged May 20, 1863, to become Major of the Thirty-Fifth U. S. Colored Troops in General Wild's Brigade, then stationed in North Carolina. At the " Battle of Olustee," in Florida, Feb. 20, 1864,[1] he was left on the field, supposed to be dead, being severely wounded in bowels and leg. His colonel being absent, and the lieutenant-colonel being wounded, the command of the regiment devolved upon Major Bogle for five hours, during the hottest part of the strife. For distinguished gallantry at this battle Major Bogle was published in General Orders, and in March following was brevetted Lieutenant-Colonel. As the "Olustee" battle-ground remained in the possession of the Confederates, Major Bogle fell into their hands and was taken, — notwithstanding he was an officer, and should have been taken to "Macon" or some other officer's prison, — to "Andersonville," where he experienced the horrors of that "prison-pen" for nine months.

"Andersonville" was an open space, of twenty-five acres, in the shape of a parallelogram, sloping on both sides, without trees or shelter of any kind, and with a sandy soil over a bottom of clay. The fence was made of upright trunks of trees, about twenty feet high, near the top of which were small platforms, where the guards were stationed. Twenty feet inside and parallel to the fence was a light railing, forming the "dead-line," beyond which the projection of a foot or finger was sure to bring the deadly bullet of the sentinel. Here were crowded at times as many as twenty-eight thousand fellow-soldiers,[2] — so

---

[1] The "Battle of Olustee," or "Ocean Pond" was fought between 5,000 Union Soldiers under General Seymour, and 10,000 Rebels under General Finnegan. Unionists compelled to retreat, leaving five guns, nearly six hundred stand of small arms, all its battery horses, and about one thousand two hundred killed and wounded on the field. Rebel loss nine hundred and thirty-five killed and wounded.

[2] The Macon Journal and Messenger of the summer of 1864 said that there were over 27,000 prisoners in Andersonville, and the deaths from fifty to sixty per day. By sworn testimony before the Commissioners of the "Sanitary Committee," it was proved that the average number of deaths in August, 1864, was over one hundred and thirty a day. Warren Lee Goss,

crowded that it was difficult to move in any direction without jostling or being jostled. We cannot spare the space to give details of the condition of this prison; of the utter disregard to all cleanliness and health of the prisoners; of the perfectly horrid state to which the swampy portion of the inside became. So wretched an appearance did it present that new comers on reaching it would exclaim, " Is this hell?" yet they soon would become callous, and enter unmoved the horrible rottenness.

From this living death at "Andersonville," Major Bogle was successively removed to Millen, Savannah, Charleston, and Columbia, and was finally paroled at Wilmington, N. C., March 1, 1865. He received the rank of Brevet-Colonel March 13, 1865.

Colonel Bogle is honorably mentioned and interestingly spoken of, while at " Andersonville," in " The Soldier's Story of his captivity at Andersonville, Belle Isle, and other Rebel Prisons," by Warren Lee Goss of the Second Massachusetts Regiment of Heavy Artillery. Mr. Goss was twice a prisoner in the hands of the rebels, witnessing and experiencing the things of which he speaks; and if one desires to learn something of the sufferings through which our men passed, — although he says in conversation with the writer, that were he to tell the story with all its fiendish cruelties and barbarities, it would not be believed, — we advise them to read his volume, in which he " proposes to relate the tale of horrors experi-

---

in his book, — hereafter referred to, — says that " July and August of this year were the most terrible experienced by the general prisoners. In one day in August, no less than one hundred and sixty died. From the 1st of February to the 16th of September, 12,000 Federal Soldiers, prisoners of war, were carried from the prison to the dead man's trench and the felon's burial."

enced in these prisons, without exaggeration." An extract from this sadly interesting book, relating to Col. Bogle, is here introduced.

Understanding that there was a major of colored troops in prison, I hunted him up, and found Major Archibald Bogle, who was formerly, I believe, a Lieutenant in the Seventeenth Massachusetts Infantry. He was captured at Olustee, after being severely wounded in several places. He informed me that he formerly lived in Melrose, Massachusetts. Since he came into the pen, he had been refused all medical and surgical treatment, though the prisoners detailed as hospital stewards had covertly afforded him aid, and dressed his wounds. He wore his uniform, and freely declared himself an officer of negro troops, — a fact which all officers of negroes were not willing to own, by reason of the hard treatment received therefor from the rebels. His was an instance of the fact that a true gentleman remains the same amidst the most squalid misery and accumulated misfortunes. His intercourse with others was dignified, courteous, and urbane, as if in command of his regiment. There were many in prison, as there always have been in our army, who professed to despise negro troops, and have a contempt for their officers. Major Bogle was at one time, I was informed, compelled to mess with his negroes; yet he always maintained his gentlemanly bearing and his self-respect, and commanded the respect of others amid all the accumulated misery of the "prison-pen." Such were my impressions of Major Bogle.

Many loose statements have been made in print indicating that officers were as common among prisoners at Andersonville, as enlisted men. With the exception of Major Bogle, there were no commissioned officers intentionally placed in Andersonville. Others were there by their own act; but the prison was intended for enlisted men only. At any time an officer of white troops could be sent to Macon, or some other officers' prison, by merely making a plain statement of facts which looked plausible. So much is required to be said, as there seems to be a great misunderstanding in relation to this matter; and it is my desire to write such a description of the prison that those who were prisoners at the time with myself will be the ones most ready to testify to the truth of these pictures, crudely drawn with pen and ink. Major Bogle at one time was engaged in a tunnelling operation, in which he plotted to release all the prisoners of the stockade. It failed through the treason of some one in the secret, though it came near being a success. About the time I became acquainted with him, an extensive plot was formed to break the stockade. Over two thousand men were pledged to risk their lives upon an effort to liberate the prisoners of the stockade. Here seemed the choice before us, to die without an effort, amid all the misery of the "prison-pen," or to die with our hands uplifted to strike one blow at our enemies, before death, in an attempt to liberate ourselves and starving comrades. To no reasonable man did there appear at that time to be any hope for life but in that manner. I went into the project, I am willing to confess at this day, having full confidence in our ability to achieve the desired result, and with a feeling that it was better to die in such an attempt than to die a miserable, loathsome death by gradual starvation.

Acting in concert, we set ourselves at work, and dug tunnels up to the stockade; then the tunnel branched off at right angles, running parallel with the stockade, a shoulder of earth being left as a temporary support, so that when a rush was made against the wall from the outside, it would be thrown down in the places thus mined. In this manner three portions of the stockade walls were undermined, — at least, I have reason to suppose so, although I was engaged in digging and engineering on but one of them. Our plans were as follows: One detachment of prisoners was to break through on the south side, near the gate, and capture the reserve of the guard; another to break through on the north side, and, making a circuit of the stockade, capture the guard thereon; another party, breaking through on the south-west side, near the gate, was to capture the rebel artillery near headquarters, and use it according to circumstances, and make such capture of rebel officers as was possible ; while prisoners outside, under detail, were to cut the telegraph wires. This achieved, prisoners were to be liberated, rations equally distributed, the cars seized, ammunition and arms placed in the hands of the "organization," and then, raiding through the rebel country, seize upon horses and other modes of transportation, and effect an escape to the Gulf. Such were our plans generally.

All was pronounced ready for the grand assault, and we were waiting with trembling expectancy, when a proclamation was read in prison, and posted in conspicuous places, stating that such a plan was known to be organized, and the commandant of the prison had full knowledge of all its details, even to the names of those concerned; and that, if we persisted in carrying it out, there would be great bloodshed, which he wished to avert Such, in substance, was a proclamation signed by Henry Wirz. We had been betrayed by one who, we supposed, from every motive of interest, would keep the secret. Artillery was posted at various points, with men in position to use it: twice shots were fired over the heads of prisoners in crowds, while white flags were placed all over the prison, as ranges for the artillerists. Thus ended the best-conceived plan for liberating the prisoners *en masse* during my imprisonment, and proved the assertion frequently made among the Kentucky boys, that, " Everything in the Confederacy was drefful onsartain, and liable to bust."

WILLIAM H. EASTMAN,

of Nims' Second Battery was taken prisoner at Bayou Bœuf, June 18, 1863, while the army was on the march to "Port Hudson,"— he, with others, having been left behind in charge of sick horses belonging to the battery. As our army moved forward, the rebel army followed, taking what spoils and prisoners it could. Eastman was taken to Brashear City, where he was held only about a fortnight, and then paroled and sent within the Union lines, where he arrived just before the fall of "Port Hudson." He was not exchanged until the following November, and during the intermediate time he acted as clerk for the Provost Marshal of one of the Louisiana Districts. During the short time he was in the hands of the Rebels, his treatment was comparatively good, and he escaped without suffering the tortures of an "Andersonville" or a "Salisbury."

JOHN L. CHAMBERS.

Acting Master's Mate, John L. Chambers, although living in East Boston at the time he entered the service, was a citizen of Melrose before the war, and has been since his return; therefore, a short sketch of his imprisonment is here introduced, notwithstanding his name did not count on our quotas. It was, by far, the longest imprisonment suffered by any of our citizens, being over two years in duration.

Mr. Chambers was appointed Acting Master's Mate, August 15, 1862, and ordered on board the gunboat "Albatross." In September, while at Ship Island, he was transferred to the ship "Morning Light,"—Acting Master John Dillingham in command,—which was on blockading duty on the coast of Louisiana and Texas. She had an armament of eight long 32-pound guns and a rifled Butler gun, with a crew of eighty-four men, all told. In November, 1862, she was ordered on duty off Sabine Pass. On the morning of the 21st of January, 1863,—a consort, the schooner "Velocity," which carried two twelve-pound howitzers, being also then on duty,—when four miles from shore, and in a perfect calm, these vessels were attacked by two river boats, which had been converted into cotton-clad Rebel gunboats; they were the "John Bell" which carried a 64-pound rifled cannon, and the "Uncle Ben," with two twelve-pounders, and with five hundred sharp-shooters on board, all under the command of Major O. M. Watkins. Although the "Morning Light" had the heaviest armament, yet she failed to keep the Rebel steamers at a distance, and, approaching within a thousand yards they poured in a terrific and constant fire; and after a fight which lasted about two hours and a half, both vessels surrendered, with a loss of five killed and fifteen wounded. The prisoners were first taken to Sabine City, thence to Houston, where they were imprisoned in a large warehouse. About ninety men were confined in the room with Chambers, which was about one hundred feet square. But the treatment here was not severe, the men being allowed two hours each day for walking, under a guard of twelve men.

About the last of April, the officers of the "Morning Light," together with those of the "Harriet Lane" and the "Forty-Second Massachusetts Regiment," taken prisoners at the "Battle of Galveston," Jan. 1, 1863,—twenty-two in all,—were sent to Huntsville, where for three days, by order of the rebel authorities, they were confined in the cells of its State Prison. These cells were anything but inviting places of abode, being about eight feet by five, and overrun with cockroaches and overbrooded with mosquitoes. But by the kindness of Colonel Caruthers, the Superintendent, they were released from these close quarters and given a large upper room, which was fitted up and made comfortable for them.

Here Chambers remained until the 27th of June, when he, with the rest of the officers, was ordered to "Camp

Groce," seventy miles southwest from Huntsville, on the "Houston and Navasota Railroad," to which place the crews of the "Morning Light" and the "Velocity" had been previously sent. "Camp Groce" was first a camp of instruction for the Rebels, but afterwards was turned into a "prison-pen" or "corral." It consisted of four stacks of barracks surrounding an area, beyond which a tract of wild country, wood, swamp and prairie, stretched for miles around. It was under a guard of from sixty to eighty men, commanded by a fat officer known as "Captain Buster." Among the officers now congregated at "Camp Groce" were Colonel Isaac S. Burrill and Surgeon A. I. Cummings of the "Forty-Second Massachusetts," Colonel A. J. H. Duganne,[1] of the "One Hundred and Seventy-Sixth New York," and many others taken at Galveston, Sabine Pass, and other points in Texas. In "Camp Groce" Chambers remained until the 9th of December following, and during this time much sickness had prevailed, and many deaths had taken place, one of which was that of Surgeon Cummings. Nov. 20th, Chambers and three hundred other prisoners were paroled, and ordered to dispose of all superfluous clothing, bedding and baggage, and prepare for a march to Shrevesport, Louisiana, about three hundred miles distant, for the purpose of being exchanged. Up to this time the Rebel authorities had transported for the prisoners all bedding, baggage, etc., and they had received comfortable care, with good beef and corn-bread rations; but now this kindness ceased and from this time the ill-treatment and sufferings of

---

[1] Author of "A History of Governments," "Footprints of Heroism," "War in Europe," "Battle Ballads," "Twenty Months in the Department of the Gulf," etc.

Chambers increased. This march to Shreveport was about three hundred and thirty miles in length, and occupied twenty-one days; passing through Anderson, Huntsville, Crockett, Palestine, Kickapoo, and Tyler. Near the last town is situated "Camp Ford," now left behind, but which was yet destined to receive these disappointed prisoners. When within ten miles of Shreveport, and near Marshall, La., they were ordered to halt and encamp in the woods near "Four Mile Spring." Here amid rain and snow and very severe weather they suffered great hardships. In the morning orders came not to exchange, and a "camp" was made near by in an open field, where, without shelter, they remained amid much suffering and many privations about three months. In March they were ordered back to "Camp Ford," one hundred miles distant. This march was accomplished in three days, and with terrible suffering, tracks of blood being left in many cases; in such condition were the prisoners, and so severe the treatment. One sad incident of this march deserves mentioning. There were two brothers among the prisoners, one of whom was taken sick during the march, and died just before bivouacking for the night. The officer in command would not allow the brother to remain and bury the body, but compelled him to march on with the rest; but at night, after they had encamped, the guards, more humane than the officer, went back and buried him. Chambers was not in this severe march, but from the camp near "Four Mile Spring" was sent, with twenty other sick prisoners, to Shreveport, where he remained until May 28th, when he was sent back to "Camp Ford," together with a hundred and fifty other prisoners that had been gathered from different sources.

"Camp Ford," the "Andersonville" of Texas, was situated four miles from the town of Tyler, and consisted of a space of six acres, enclosed with a stockade of timbers eight feet high. One-sixth of this area was allotted to the officers, who dwelt in log huts and cabins of various shapes, erected by themselves or purchased of former tenants; while the rest of the area was occupied by the other prisoners, who burrowed under ground, or erected booths of branches, and arranged every conceivable contrivance for a shelter. In April, during the "Red River Expedition," under General Banks, eleven hundred and eighty-six Federal prisoners, captured at the "Battle of Mansfield," April 8, 1864, were brought to "Camp Ford" at one time. Many others were added at subsequent times, so that at the time Chambers entered the "Camp," May 28th, there were congregated as many as forty-seven hundred prisoners, three hundred of whom were officers. The rations for much of the time consisted of corn meal, — cob and all ground up, and generally musty at that; often whole corn, without grinding, was given them. With this kind of food, insufficient clothing, and such general ill-treatment, it is not strange that there were many deaths. From May 1, to Dec. 1, 1864, there were two hundred and thirty-two deaths in the "Camp."[1] It was a constant boast with the guard, as they went on duty, that they would "shoot a

---

[1] A very good picture of life at "Camp Ford," as then experienced, is given in the following letter written by the Confederate Post-Surgeon.

TYLER, TEXAS, June 14, 1864.

Surgeon J. M. Hayden, Chf. Med. Bureau, T. M. D.

Sir: — In obedience to orders, I reported to the officer in command of the camp of Federal prisoners at this place (Colonel Anderson), who immediately placed me on duty, as surgeon in charge. I at once set about examining the sanitary condition of the stockade, and although my mind was prepared by representations to meet with abundant materials for disease, it fell far short of the reality. The enclosed ground is entirely too small for the number

Yank to-day," and often, without any provocation whatever, would a prisoner be shot down. Many were thus killed during his imprisonment. Notwithstanding all these disheartening circumstances, the Fourth of July, 1864, was duly celebrated by the reading of a poem, of the Declaration of Independence, and the delivery of an oration, interspersed with national airs by a glee club. When the weather permitted, much of the time it being very wet, evening meetings were held, conducted by the chaplains present. During all this time the hope of being exchanged was constantly entertained, fed by rumors, and the fact that occasionally squads of two or three hundred were sent away for that purpose.

Yankee ingenuity developed itself wonderfully at " Camp Ford," and a great variety of articles were manufactured.

---

of men, (over 4,500), and it would be impossible to make them healthy in such a crowded condition. The filth and offal have been deposited in the streets and between the quarters, from which arises horrible stench. A great number of the enlisted men have no quarter nor shelter, and have to sleep out on the ground, without even a blanket to cover them. Some of the sick are thus situated, and I am making preparations to provide for their wants and to make them comfortable. We have a hospital in course of erection, and will need bedding very much. The popular prejudice here is so strong against them that I can get no facilities from the people. I have sent to you for approval the requisition which I would have sent directly to the Medical Purveyor, but I thought your signature would be necessary. I am ready to receive into hospital a few, if we had the articles, and they are not to be had here. No regular register of cases or deaths has been kept, up to a recent period, but I visited the graveyard and counted twenty-five graves, a much smaller number than I was led to believe. * * *
Very respectfully,
Your obedient servant,
F. W. MEAGHER.

The following notice was also found posted one morning :

Hereafter any Federal prisoner, being detected in trying to make his escape from the prison, — either in the act, or after he has made his escape, — will be shot by the one capturing him.
By order of
Lieutenant-Colonel J. P. BORDERS,
Com'd'g Camp Ford Prison.
B. W. McEACHAN,
Lieutenant and Acting Adjutant.

With a half-dozen axes and hatchets, three spades, a dull saw and their jack-knives, the prisoners contrived to multiply tools, and erect machinery, by means of which musical instruments, rakes, hoes, bedsteads, tables, chessmen, pipes, and very many other useful and ornamental articles were manufactured; and in this manner many weary hours of imprisonment were whiled away. While here Chambers contrived to make a very fine and complete model of the ship "Morning Light."[1]

A newspaper was also established, called "The Old Flag," printed with pen and pencil, containing a variety of advertisements and literary emanations, and circulated among the prisoners.

Thus was this long imprisonment passed, amid many privations, much suffering, sickness, and death; but the long looked for and long deferred hour at length arrived. On the 3d of March, with three hundred other prisoners, Chambers was marched to the mouth of the Red River, and on the twenty-sixth day of March, 1865, having been in the hands of the Confederates two years, two months, and five days, he was exchanged and sent to New Orleans; thence up the Mississippi River, home.

EDMUND WALLACE DAVIS.

Enlisted in Co. G, Twenty-Second Massachusetts Regiment, in 1861, and was taken prisoner at the "Battle of Gaines' Farm" or "Gaines' Mills," June 27, 1862. He was

---

[1] Colonel Duganne in his "Twenty Months in the Department of the Gulf," while enumerating the characteristics of some of his co-prisoners, thus refers to Chambers: "The ingenious Chambers whose model of the 'Morning Light' was a trophy of Yankee naval architecture."

first carried to "Libby Prison," and afterwards to "Belle Isle," but was held only about six weeks, when he was exchanged and sent into the union lines; consequently his sufferings, as a prisoner, were of short duration; but the heart disease, with which he had been suffering, was aggravated by the treatment received while in the hands of the Rebels, and he was discharged from the service soon after his exchange. He died at Melrose, July 22, 1864.

Davis was one of five brothers that served in the Union army. Loami G. was in the Thirty-Third and Third Heavy Artillery Regiments; John E. and James L. were in the Forty-Second Regiment; Charles L. in the Eighth Maine Regiment; and Edmund W. in the Twenty-Second Massachusetts Regiment. We had no other instance where one family furnished five persons for the army, but we had two other families that furnished four; Martin and York, as follows: George T. Martin was in the Thirty-Eighth and Fourth Heavy Artillery Regiments; William H. in the Thirty-Eighth Regiment; Charles H. in the Fourth Heavy Artillery; and Jeremiah, Jr., in the Navy. Benjamin F. York was in the Fifty-Sixth Regiment; Josiah R. and William B. were in the Forty-Second; and Arthur, Jr., was in the Twelfth New Hampshire Regiment.

Several families furnished three members for different periods of service, viz: Shelton, Macey, Emerson, — a father and two sons; Peabody, — a father and two sons; Wyman and McLaughlin. Many families gave us two members; viz: Anderson, Barry, Barron, Crockett, Dawes, Fuller, Grover, Howard, Ireson, Lynde; two families two each, — Morse, Marshall, — father and son, — McAllister, Nichols, and Quinn.

FREDERICK W. KRANTZ.

When the Rebellion broke out Krantz was in the U. S. Navy, having enlisted in 1859 for three years; he was discharged at Portsmouth, N. H., Sept. 24, 1861. In July, 1862, he enlisted in Co. C, Thirty-Third Regiment. After the "Battle of Gettysburg" was fought and won, while our army was pursuing General Lee, he became foot-sore, and, with others, was left behind the army to follow as best he could, when he was taken prisoner by Stuart's Cavalry. He was carried to a tobacco warehouse about two miles from Piankatank Point, between the Potomac and Rappahannock Rivers. Here he suffered the usual hard treatment allotted our prisoners, being sick a long while with fever and ague; but, after an imprisonment of seven months, he made his escape in the night and reached Washington, Feb. 3, 1864. He returned to his home in Melrose, and, after recruiting his health during a furlough of two months, was returned to his regiment, then encamped in Lookout Valley, East Tennessee. After taking part in nearly all the engagements of the "great march to the sea," under General Sherman, he was again taken prisoner by Rebel cavalry, while on a foraging expedition. He was taken to the prison at Salisbury, N. C., where he remained suffering the horrors and tortures of that place, until just before the fall of Richmond, when he was removed to "Libby Prison," and after a delay of two weeks was paroled and sent to City Point, where he arrived, once more under the old flag, on the day Richmond was evacuated. He was sent to Annapolis, and soon after discharged and sent home.

The following extract from the "Congregationalist and Recorder" gives a slight idea of some of the experiences passed through by our prisoners while at "Andersonville."

It is from the description of a visit made in April, 1868, by the Rev. C. L. Woodworth, who was Chaplain of the Twenty-Seventh Massachusetts Regiment, two hundred and fifty members of which had been inmates of this "prison-pen."

After speaking of the insufficiency of water allowed our prisoners, received from a small brook running through the enclosure, which in summer "could have been little more than a mere drizzle from the swamps around," and that within bow-shot was "a creek of beautiful, unfailing water, twenty feet wide, and three feet deep, which would have made prison-life almost a joy," of the forests of wood near at hand, and only one stick a day allowed for a squad of fifty men, and of the evidences of the many attempts at "mining out" made by our men, he says:

One can give no account of his feelings as he wanders over these accursed acres, and sees everywhere traces of the unfortunate occupants. The *debris* of cabins, chimneys, fire-places, ovens, holes in the hill-side, are among the painful evidences of the battle they fought for comfort and life. The side-hill on the north, is burrowed all over, and reminds one of a sand bank honey-combed with swallows' holes. Some of these underground excavations were quite spacious, and might hold a score, while others are so small that not more than one could have occupied them at a time. The tops of the larger ones have mostly fallen in, softened by the rain. Indeed, it was no uncommon thing during a rainy night for some one or more of them to cave in and bury the sleepers. Quite a number of lives, it is said, were lost in this way.

But that which most forcibly reminds one of the terrible struggle which the men had for simple comfort, is the wells which they dug in search of water. Forty of these are still in existence, and some of them as fresh as if dug but yesterday. In a number of instances they went down eighty feet, but in nearly every case failed to find the coveted treasure. One marvels how they could have dug them without tools of any sort, using simply their fingers, and bringing up the dirt in the pockets of their blouses, or in their caps, or handkerchiefs. Had I not seen the wells, and waited some moments for a stone, that I dropped in to strike the bottom, I could not have believed it. How consuming the thirst which could impel to such labors! Until near the close of the war there was only one structure inside the stockade, — that was a small, rough building used by the Quartermaster, — where were weighed, and from whence were issued the scanty rations that our men fought over like famished dogs. I saw the platform, and a part of the scales on which this starvartion diet was balanced to the nicety of death.

It was after the attention of the civilized world had been directed to the barbarity practised on our prisoners, that the confederate government put up within the stockade, both at the northern and at the southern end, five large sheds of a hundred feet in length, simply covered at the top; the sides all open like a depot wood-house. These were better than nothing, but in storm and cold, were a poor protection for weak, starving men, and miserably inadequate for all.

South of the main stockade a hundred and fifty yards or so, was the hospital stockade. Within this were twenty-two of these long, low sheds, from which fifteen thousand martyred souls went up to God. The day I visited this ground was hazy and sultry, and I imagined the air was stifling from the boding horrors which every object suggested. Could I forget that only a little time ago these sheds were filled with sick, pale, famished, wasted men, that every hour out of the twenty-four, the dead-cart carried, at least, two, oft times six, lifeless bodies to the trenches!

Seven forts and earthworks commanded the prison, and made all thought of resistance hopeless. Escape, therefore, was a thing which depended entirely on the cunning and craft of the individual man. Mining out was a favorite method; a few scaled the stockade. Some ran the guard, and others, who had passes to cut wood, bring water, or bury a comrade, forgot to return. But this constant attempt to outwit, and elude their keepers, was met on their part with a weapon of warfare known only in the South, and up to this time practised only on negroes, and escaped Yankee prisoners. I refer, of course, to hounds that were kept to track and hunt down the fugitives. There were three block-houses, just west of the stockade, where the hunters and the hounds were quartered. Only one of the houses is now standing, and this will soon disappear, for every relic hunter is sure to carry a piece of it away. The stories told by the colored people of the horrid exploits of the hounds, — human and inhuman, — in running down our boys, is enough to make one's flesh creep. I have no heart to put a single one of them on paper.

We cannot better close these notices of the sufferings of our heroes in these wretched spots, than to give an extract from a letter by a correspondent of the "American Missionary," dated Atlanta, Ga., May 13, 1867, showing, as it does, the great change in the use to which "Andersonville" is now consecrated:

Did they ever imagine, those rebel officers, who used our poor boys to erect those buildings — buildings put up to enable them to hold thirty thousand prisoners in unheard of tortures — did they ever imagine to what use those buildings were to be applied, and so soon? Did they dream that the wail of the captive would scarcely be hushed, and the last victim laid to sleep his last sleep in those awful witness-bearing trenches, before two angels of mercy should take their abode there, transforming that hell upon earth into a little earthly heaven? Yes, "Andersonville" has been cleansed and sanctified; and, thank God, by the purity, the presence, the labor, and the love of woman. Where the rebel soldier's jeer and oath used to be heard, now daily ascends the sweet sound of prayer and praise. For the howl of the hungry hound, eager to chase the perishing Union fugitive, you may now hear the sweet voices of the children blending in song. The jailer has fled, haunted by the memory of his crimes (for Wirz was not alone in the charge), and two gentle women have taken possession of his dwelling ; the persecuted slave has found a shelter in the huts erected by his persecutors, and the Freedman's corn is now growing in the empty stockade.

One of the ladies referred to above, says in the same paper :

You would scarcely know the place were you to come here now. The trees are heavy with the wealth of foliage, the air resonant with the sweet song of birds, and odorous with the breath of flowers. But the stockade with its silent tale of suffering, and the cemetery, with its quiet sleepers, are still here. "Andersonville" will ever be to me a memory of suffering, a home of dead heroes, a planting of freedom's seed. I am glad to have been here, glad of the record we shall leave — I only wish it were more glorious with fruit ; but one soweth, and another reapeth. I am content with sowing, and with the evidence of life in the seed. It is germinating ; already the mellowed soil is breaking from the struggles of the embryo which wants light and air. We have but to lay our ear to the earth, to hear the swelling and the struggling of the new life beneath. A few more rains of love, a few more dews of mercy, a few more suns of grace, and the blade will appear ; after that, the going on from strength to strength, till the harvest time shall come. Oh! it has been good to work here. I thank God for it, and the rich experience it has brought !

XV.

1865.

CLOSE OF THE REBELLION.

Oh, beautiful! my country! ours once more!
Smoothing thy gold of war-dishevelled hair
O'er such sweet brows as never others wore,
    And letting thy set lips
      Freed from wrath's pale eclipse,
The rosy edges of their smile lay bare.
What words divine of lover or of poet
Could tell our love and make thee know it,
Among the nations bright beyond compare?
    What were our lives without thee?
    What all our lives to save thee?
    We reck not what we gave thee;
      We will not dare to doubt thee,
But ask whatever else, and we will dare!
                      James Russell Lowell.

In the "Life of Abraham Lincoln," by Dr. J. G. Holland, — "Timothy Titcomb," — occurs the following vivid passage relative to the fall of Richmond:

The day on which Richmond fell will long be remembered by the people of America, in both sections of the country. When the news was made public on Monday, — April 3, 1865, — the whole North was thrown into a frenzy of joyous excitement. Every bell on every public building, from the Atlantic to the Pacific was rung for hours. Cannon answered to cannon, from mountain to mountain, and from valley to valley. Men grasped one another's hands in the streets, and wept, or embraced each other in the stress of their joyous enthusiasm. Public meetings were called, at which the deeds of the gallant heroes who had won the decisive victories were praised and cheered, and the public exultation found expression in speech and music. Nothing like it was ever seen upon the continent. The war was over. Richmond, that had so long defied the national authority and resisted the national arms, was ours. The rebel President and his associates were fugitives. Lee's army was running away, and Grant was pursuing them. The sun of peace had fairly risen. The incubus of war that had pressed upon the nation's heart for four long, weary years, was lifted; and the nation sprang to its feet, with all possible demonstrations of joyous exultation.

Melrose joined with much enthusiasm in these demonstrations over the joyful termination of this great struggle. Upon the receipt of the telegram,

Richmond and Petersburg are ours. A third part of Lee's army is destroyed. For the remainder there is no escape,

there was great rejoicing; the bells were rung, flags hoisted, houses illuminated in the evening, and a display of fireworks; and a general congratulation over this long wished for event. A concert, given on the same evening by the "Melrose Musical Association," under the direction of Mr. Andrew J. Morse, was closed with patriotic airs, and cheers for General Grant and his noble army.

This great and universal joy was augmented six days later, April 9th, by the news of General Lee's surrender to General Grant, at "Appomattox Court House."

The culmination was now reached, and rebellion crushed.

Henceforth Peace was to take the place of War. The time had come when

"They shall beat their swords into ploughshares, and their spears into pruning hooks."

But this great gladness was very soon turned into the deepest mourning by the death of our beloved president, Abraham Lincoln, who died only six days after Lee's surrender, — April 15, 1865, — by the hand of an assassin.

Governor Andrew communicated this sad intelligence to the Massachusetts Legislature, April 17th, commencing his address as follows:

In the midst of the exultations of repeated victory, in the midst of the highest hopes, of the most auspicious omens, in the hour of universal joy, the nation passed at once, by an inscrutable and mysterious Providence, into the Valley of the Shadow of Death. Assembled while the cloud is yet thick upon our eyes, and the hearts of men are oppressed by the sense of a strange dismay, it has become my mournful duty to record, by formal and official announcement to the Legislative department of the Commonwealth, this calamitous and distressing event.

The day of the funeral, Wednesday, April 19th, was a day of general mourning throughout the land. Business was entirely suspended and funeral ceremonies were everywhere held. Churches were thrown open, and music, prayer, and eulogy testified to the nation's great loss.

In Melrose, a united service was held in the Congregational Church, which was appropriately draped in mourning. This was a deeply interesting occasion, and the exercises were as follows:

1.

CHANT. — "Thy Will Be Done."

II.

INVOCATION AND READING OF THE SCRIPTURES.

BY REV. WILLIAM S. BARNES.

III.

HYMN.

See, gracious God! before thy throne
  Thy mourning people bend;
'T is on thy sovereign grace alone
  Our humble hopes depend.

Dark, frowning judgments from thy hand
  Thy dreadful power display;
Yet mercy spares this guilty land,
  And still we live to pray.

How changed, alas! are truths divine,
  For error, guilt and shame!
What impious numbers, bold in sin,
  Disgrace the Christian name!

Oh, turn us, turn us, mighty Lord,
  By thy resistless grace;
Then shall our hearts obey thy word,
  And humbly seek thy face.

IV.

PRAYER.

BY REV. HENRY BAKER.

V.

HYMN.

God moves in a mysterious way,
  His wonders to perform;
He plants his footsteps in the sea,
  And rides upon the storm.

Deep in unfathomable mines
Of never-failing skill,
He treasures up his bright designs,
And works his sovereign will.

Ye fearful saints, fresh courage take:
The clouds ye so much dread
Are big with mercy, and shall break
In blessings on your head.

Judge not the Lord by feeble sense,
But trust Him for his grace:
Behind a frowning providence
He hides a smiling face.

His purposes will ripen fast,
Unfolding every hour;
The bud may have a bitter taste,
But sweet will be the flower.

Blind unbelief is sure to err,
And scan his work in vain;
God is his own interpreter,
And He will make it plain.

VI.
Address.
BY REV. WILLIAM S. BARNES.

VII.
Address.
BY REV. HENRY BAKER.

VIII.
Anthem.
"REST, SPIRIT, REST."

IX.

Address.

BY REV. HENRY A. STEVENS.

X.

Prayer.

BY REV. WILLIAM S. BARNES.

XI.

Hymn.

My country, 'tis of thee,
Sweet land of Liberty,
  Of thee I sing :
Land where my fathers died,
Land of the pilgrim's pride,
From every mountain side
  Let freedom ring!

My native country, thee —
Land of the noble free —
  Thy name I love :
I love thy rocks and rills,
Thy woods and templed hills ;
My heart with rapture thrills
  Like that above.

Let Music swell the breeze,
And ring from all the trees
  Sweet freedom's song !
Let mortal tongues awake ;
Let all that breathe partake ;
Let rocks their silence break —
  The sound prolong!

Our father's God! to Thee,
Author of liberty,
To Thee we sing:
Long may our land be bright
With freedom's holy light;
Protect us by thy might,
Great God, our King!

XII.

BENEDICTION.

BY REV. HENRY A. STEVENS.

Owing to the length of the programme, the remarks by Messrs. Barnes and Stevens were quite short; the principal address being made by Rev. Mr. Baker, of which the following is an abstract.

I would rather have been a silent listener amid the universal sadness of this hour! The stillness of these draped walls, the sombre flags of a thousand cities at half-mast, and their countless avenues hung with symbols of deepest woe; the silent tread of the *millions* of mourners, and the *universal sadness* unspeakable, welling up from a nation's heart, all speak louder than words the sad consciousness of our terrible bereavement. But not only our own native land, but if angels are interested in the affairs of earth, and carry tidings from continent to continent, and sphere to sphere, the great heart of humanity everywhere bleeds to-day! The down-trodden of every land will shed a tear, for a great, a good man; humanity's universal friend has rudely fallen. A man peculiarly *honest*, for he had earned the enviable name of "Honest Abe." A man *paternal*, for we loved to call him Father Abraham. A *thoughtful, sober, frank, sincere, sagacious, far-seeing, common people's man*, that you and I had learned to love.

A man of *deep religious* faith, that dared to trust in God. A man that recognized the *providence of God*. Leaving Springfield for the great duties which the nation had imposed upon him, how fully he seemed to realize his great responsibilities, as bidding them an affectionate farewell, he says, "pray for me!" And in our sad, dark struggles, with his terse, affectionate proclamations, he summons the afflicted millions to fastings, and then in triumph to thanksgivings and to praise.

Amid all his public *trials* and *anxieties*, affliction hovered around his own home, and his *darling child* is borne to the grave. His soul listened to the voice divine that thus seemed to speak from eternity. On the fields of Gettysburg, weeping over the slaughtered thousands of our fallen heroes, and the deep depravity of human hearts, he there resolved personally to give himself to Christ. From that hour he was a practical Christian.

The first hours of every day, while others slept, he read God's word and bowed in prayer. This was his custom. Who of us so *noble* and so *pure*. Who can offset so many *virtues*, to their *faults* so few?

"Who of us have borne our faculties so meek, as he who has been so clear in his great office, that his *virtues* will plead like angels trumpet-tongued, against the deep damnation of his taking-off?" Oh how foul that malignant spirit that struck at our nation's heart! Do we not now see it, "the sum of all villanies"? Ay, how base this monster evil! How like the hydrophobia it infects with its own vile spirit its own victims. How it butchered at *Lawrence*, and starved at *Andersonville and Libby*. Look upon the already idiotic starvelings of "Anderson Stockade," those brave patriots, and hear the *coward* tyrants declare to them, "If we can't whip you, we can starve you to death!" One million subscription is opened in Alabama to procure assassination! and soon the world is startled at this culminating dastardly act! "Then *you*, and *I*, all of us fell down while bloody *treason* flourished over us."

But there is a Providence still in all this. Truth and error are ever antagonistic, and there will always be *friction* along the line of their contact. Diplomacy had ceased; the clash of arms resounded. Slavery defeated, again appeals to Diplomacy; and here, dear friends, is our present danger.

A sickly, morbid philanthropy is abroad — that dare not recognize treason and rebellion a *crime*; a growing *leniency* that may yet prove the country's doom; the soothing style in which we meet the defeated, but still defiant rebel.

But the *voices* of a half million patriots are to-day crying from the ground for vengeance! "Carleton" writes, the very day of the assassination, "We now witness an impatient longing for 'peace at any price,' which impresses many statesmen with the conviction that Lee's capitulation is but the commencement, rather than the end of our national troubles." Let us not forget the "frozen serpent, the peasant in pity put into his bosom."

God *hates slavery!* And its death-warrant has been read, and it must fall, if the nation goes down with it. Its appointed hour has come! Could any act of this monster have so roused the nation to its danger! God permits Booth for a season to escape, only that the nation may for a season rouse from her slumber, and heed her danger. Oh how this nation is aroused to-day! How the malignant hiss of the copperhead has died away! Shall it ever be heard again? Not if the nation feels as she does to-day! We can't hear a *word* disloyal to-day. The *stars* and stripes must be flung to the breeze from every doubtful door! Our mothers dare to vindicate the death of patriot sons, for there is *freedom* in the very air to-day!

A new era dawns upon us. We are ceasing to be a proslavery nation. God sees a new administration necessary, and does not palsy the loose arm that strikes down the nation's head.

How strangely was our beloved Lincoln nominated; how providentially elected. How like an angel spirit he led the cause of freedom onward, until the land was free. He has done his work, and *so* well. That blow that struck off the executive head of a pro-slavery government, finished that dynasty and inaugurated a world-wide freedom.

God now would use a severer scourge to secure the future of free governments.

How significant the assassin's cry, " Sic semper tyrannis"! It was meet that it should thus destroy itself. Now let us live for freedom and for God.

As it was in Melrose, so was it in every city, town, and village throughout the loyal portion of our land. Eulogies, sermons and addresses were delivered before the assembled multitudes. Resolutions of grief, respect and admiration were offered by various corporated associations, and at the meetings of educational, literary, and historical societies, not only in our own, but in foreign lands.[1]

"As there was never such a funeral as this, so there was never such a procession. That which moved from the White House, on the nineteenth, was but the beginning of a pageant that displayed its marvellous numbers and its every-varying forms, through country, and village, and city, winding across the territories of vast States, along a track of more than fifteen hundred miles. The President was to be borne back to his own people, and to be buried among the scenes of his early life. He had told the people of Springfield, Illinois, when he parted with

---

[1] The Appendix to the " Diplomatic Correspondence of 1865," issued by the United States Government, contained the resolutions, proceedings, articles, and correspondence of 1,139 different bodies and individuals, mostly in foreign countries ; and Mr. Charles H. Hart, of Philadelphia, has made a very complete collection of the printed sermons, addresses, and eulogies called forth by this sad event. It numbers 431. He is soon to issue a work descriptive of the same, with the following title : " Bibliographia Lincolniana. A Catalogue of the Publications occasioned by the Death of Abraham Lincoln, Sixteenth President of the United States of America. With an Introduction and Notes. By Charles H. Hart, Historiographer of the Numismatic and Antiquarian Society of Philadelphia, etc., etc."

them, more than four years before, that he owed to them all he was. It was but right that they should have his dust."

As we commenced this notice of the downfall of the Rebellion by a quotation from Dr. Holland's "Life of Abraham Lincoln," so will we end it with the closing words of the same:

Humble child of the back-woods, — boatman, axe-man, hired laborer, clerk, surveyor, captain, legislator, lawyer, debater, orator, politician, statesman, President, savior of the republic, emancipator of a race, true Christian, true man, — we receive thy life and its immeasurably great results, as the choicest gifts a mortal has ever bestowed upon us; grateful to thee for thy truth to thyself, to us, and to God; and grateful to that ministry of Providence and grace which endowed thee so richly, and bestowed thee upon the nation and mankind.

XVI.

Miscellaneous.

COST OF THE WAR, FOR BOUNTIES AND OTHER NECESSARY EXPENSES.

The amount of indebtedness of the town of Melrose, on the 1st of March, 1861, was twenty-nine thousand two hundred and sixty dollars ($29,260.00). The amount of indebtedness April 1, 1865, was seventy-five thousand, five hundred and thirty-two dollars ($75,532.00);[1] showing an increase for the four years of forty-six thousand, two hundred and seventy-two dollars ($46,272.00). Of this amount thirty-eight thousand, five hundred ninety-two dollars and seventy cents ($38,592.70) was incurred on account of the Rebellion.[2]

A large amount of money was raised and expended during these four years, by the citizens, which of course does not appear in the reports of the financial affairs of the town. In 1862, when our quota was thirty-seven men, and a certain number of citizens agreed to go into the service themselves, or furnish a man in their place, sums ranging from twenty to fifty dollars each, were paid to the substitutes then obtained. The amount thus paid must have been at least eight hundred dollars ($800.00). The

---

[1] The amount of Town Debt, March 1, 1868, was $60,578.11; a decrease in three years of $12,675.20.

[2] In addition to this, $700.00 Bounty money was paid during the years 1866-67, as per votes of the town.

same year a subscription fund was raised by Mr William F. Poole, for the benefit of the families of those then in the service, which amounted to three hundred and forty dollars ($340.00).

In 1863, four of the drafted citizens paid commutation money, three hundred dollars ($300.00) each, amounting to twelve hundred dollars ($1,200.00); and three furnished substitutes, costing nine hundred dollars ($900.00), besides some additional expenses in putting the men into the service.

In 1864, three of our citizens furnished "Representative Recruits" costing three hundred and seventy-five dollars ($375.00); and four furnished "Substitutes for Enrolled Men," costing about twenty-five hundred dollars ($2,500 00); and a fund of five thousand six hundred and fifty dollars ($5,650.00) was raised by the citizens, by subscription, in aid of the recruiting service.

During the war, at least six hundred dollars ($600.00) in money — besides many boxes of hospital and other stores, — were contributed to the "Christian" and "Sanitary Commissions," by the different churches : making a total amount of money, paid by the citizens, of over twelve thousand dollars ($12,000.00). Beside this amount many sums were given to individual soldiers, by their friends, at different times, of which it is impossible to make explicit mention.

LIST OF TOWN OFFICERS.

The town of Melrose was set off from the northern part of the town of Malden and incorporated by Legislative Act, May 3, 1850. It was enlarged by the annexation of a small portion of the eastern part of the town of Stoneham, March 15th, 1853. It contains two thousand nine

LIST OF TOWN OFFICERS.

hundred and twenty-one (2,921) square acres of territory, and is bounded as follows:—on the north by Wakefield, —formerly South Reading,—on the east by Saugus, on the south by Malden, and on the west by Medford and Stoneham. When incorporated it had a population of twelve hundred and sixty (1,260), which had increased to twenty-eight hundred and sixty-five (2,865) at the time of the last census, 1865.

The following is a list of its Selectmen, Town Clerks, Treasurers, Collectors, Assessors, School Committee, and Representatives to the General Court, from the date of its incorporation until the present time:

TOWN OFFICERS.

YEAR.	SELECTMEN.	TOWN CLERK.	TREASURER.	COLLECTOR.
1850.	Jeremiah Martin. Isaac Emerson, Jr. Artemas Barrett.	Elbridge Green.	Isaac Emerson.	Isaac Emerson.
1851.	Jeremiah Martin. Shubael L. Taylor. Jonathan Cochran.	Jonathan Cochran.	Isaac Emerson.	Shubael L. Taylor.
1852.	Jeremiah Martin. Franklin Taylor. Rufus H. Flint.	Jonathan Cochran.	Isaac Emerson.	Freeman Upham.
1853.	Franklin Taylor. Ephraim Avery. Henry Sprague.	Francis Bugbee.	Isaac Emerson.	Asa Slocum.
1854.	George Emerson. John Blake. James M. Thresher.	Francis Bugbee.	John Blake.	Wm. N. Wilkinson.
1855.	John Blake. James M. Thresher. James .M Beckett.	Francis Bugbee.	Caleb Howard.	Caleb Howard.
1856.	George M. Fletcher. Wm. E. Fuller. James M. Beckett.	Francis Bugbee.	Caleb Howard.	Caleb Howard.
1857.	George M. Fletcher. Wm. E. Fuller. Benj. F. Abbott, M.D.	Francis Bugbee.	Caleb Howard.	Caleb Howard.
1858.	Elbridge Gardner. Ephraim Avery. Nelson Cochran.	Chas. H. Shepard.	Caleb Howard.	Caleb Howard.
1859.	Elbridge Gardner. Wm. J. Farnsworth. George M. Fletcher.	Edward R. Knights.	Caleb Howard.	Stephen J. Phinney.
1860.	George Emerson. Nelson Cochran. Wm. J. Farnsworth.	Edward R. Knights.	Caleb Howard.	George Newhall.

[1] The new Representative system went into operation this year. The towns, Stoneham, South Reading, — now Wakefield, — and Melrose, forming the Twentieth Middlesex Representative

TOWN OFFICERS.

ASSESSORS.	SCHOOL COMMITTEE.	REPRESENTATIVES TO GENERAL COURT.
Aaron Green. Shubael L. Taylor. Wm. J. Farnsworth.	Henry A. Norris. Caleb Howard. Elbridge Green.	
Shubael L. Taylor. Aaron Green. Rufus H. Flint.	Erastus O. Phinney, M.D. Rev. Wilson R. Parsons. Rev. Josiah W. Talbot.	John T. Paine.
Aaron Green. German S. Phippen. Henry Sprague.	Rev. Wilson R. Parsons. Erastus O. Phinney, M.D. George E. White.	Daniel W. Gooch.
Rev. John C. Ingalls. German S. Phippen. Joshua Upham.	Daniel W. Gooch. George P. Burnham. John Shelton.	Samuel O. Dearborn.
Jonathan Cochran. German S. Phippen. Asa Upham.	Elbridge Green. Erastus O. Phinney, M.D. Charles H. Simonds.	Voted not to send.
Geo. M. Fletcher. Jonathan Cochran. Edward P. Nevens.	Erastus O. Phinney, M.D. Rev. Alex'r. J. Sessions. Rev. J. A. Coolidge.	John Vial.
Jonathan Cochran. Benjamin Linikin. Geo. M. Fletcher.	Rev. Alex'r. J. Sessions. Walter Littlefield. Caleb Howard.	Voted not to send.
Jonathan Cochran. Geo. M. Fletcher. Joseph Holbrook.	Rev. Alex'r. J. Sessions. Rev. Wm. H. Munroe. Rev. J. S. Dennis.	Guy Lamkin.
Jonathan Cochran. Joseph Holbrook. Henry Robinson.	Moses Parker, M.D. Rev. Wm. H. Munroe. George N. Noyes.	[1] Walter Littlefield, Jr. J. Sullivan Eaton, *South Reading*.
Jonathan Cochran. Henry Robinson. Wm. E. Fuller.	Erastus O. Phinney, M.D. Rev. Wm. H. Munroe. Rev. James Cooper.	J. Parker Gould, *Stoneham*. Loren L. Fuller.
Jonathan Cochran. Wm. B. Burgess. Geo. M. Fletcher.	Erastus O. Phinney, M.D. Aaron Green. Elbridge Gardner.	John Wiley, 2d, *South Reading*. Lyman Dyke, *Stoneham*.

District, sending two Representatives to the General Court each year. Changed to the Twenty-Third District in 1866.

YEAR.	SELECTMEN.	TOWN CLERK.	TREASURER.	COLLECTOR.
1861.	Wm. B. Burgess. George M. Fletcher. Col. John H. Clark.	Edward R. Knights.	Caleb Howard.	George Newhall.
1862.	Col. John H. Clark. Wm. B. Burgess. George M. Fletcher.	Edward R. Knights.	Caleb Howard.	George Newhall.
1863.	Col. John H. Clark. Wm. B. Burgess. George M. Fletcher.	Edward R. Knights.	Caleb Howard.	George Newhall.
1864.	Col. John H. Clark. Wm. B. Burgess. Wm. E. Fuller.	Edward R. Knights.	Caleb Howard.	John Smith.
1865.	Wingate P. Sargent. George M. Fletcher. Isaac Emerson, Jr.	Stinson Sewall.	David Fairbanks.	David Fairbanks.
1866.	Wingate P. Sargent. George M. Fletcher. Isaac Emerson, Jr.	Stinson Sewall.	David Fairbanks.	David Fairbanks.
1867.	Wingate P. Sargent. Isaac Emerson, Jr. George M. Fletcher.	Stinson Sewall.	David Fairbanks.	Aaron Green.
1868.	Wingate P. Sargent. James C. Currier. George Newhall.	Stinson Sewall.	David Fairbanks.	Geo. F. Boardman.

LIST OF TOWN OFFICERS

ASSESSORS.	SCHOOL COMMITTEE.	REPRESENTATIVES TO GENERAL COURT.
Edward P. Nevens.	Erastus O. Phinney, M.D.	Artemas Barrett.
Joseph R. Simonds.	Luther Robinson.	William H. Pierce, *South Reading*.
Theo. B. Merrick.	Charles H. Isburgh.	
Edward P. Nevens.	Luther Robinson.	Captain John H. Dyke, *Stoneham*.
Geo. M. Fletcher.	Charles H. Isburgh.	William H. Atwell, *So. Reading*.
Stephen Shelton.	Henry E. Trowbridge.	
Edward P. Nevens.	Charles H. Isburgh.	Isaac Emerson, Jr.
Geo. M. Fletcher.	George A. Mansfield.	Leander F. Lynde, *Stoneham*.
Stephen Shelton.		
Edward P. Nevens.	Joseph B. Sanford.	Daniel Allen, *South Reading*.
Stephen Shelton.	Rev. John B. Richmond.	Isaac Emerson, Jr.
Geo. M. Fletcher.	Thomas W. Chadbourne.	
George Emerson.	Hon. Samuel E. Sewall.	
Joel Snow.	Thomas W. Chadbourne.	
Geo. M. Fletcher.	Rev. John B. Richmond.	Leander F. Lynde, *Stoneham*.
	George N. Noyes.	Daniel Allen, *South Reading*.
	George A. Mansfield.	
	George Emerson, 2d.	
George Emerson.	Charles H. Isburgh.	
Joel Snow.	Thomas W. Chadbourne.	Rufus Smith.
Geo. M. Fletcher.	George N. Noyes.	John Kingman, *Stoneham*.
	George Emerson, 2d.	
	George A Mansfield.	
Joel Snow.	Charles H. Isburgh.	
Geo. M. Fletcher.	Thomas W. Chadbourne.	John Botume, Jr., *Stoneham*.
George Emerson.	Moses Parker, M.D.	James F. Mansfield, *So. Reading*.
	Rev. Nathan P. Selee.	
Erastus O. Phinney, M.D.	Rev. Wm. S. Barnes.	Levi S. Gould.
Aaron Green.	Nelson Cochran.	James F. Mansfield, *So. Reading*.
Elbridge Green.	Gilbert Nash.	

VALUATION OF MELROSE.

Year.	Real Estate.	Personal Estate.	Total.
1861.	$1,288,066	$134,754	$1,422,820
1862.	1,320,280	125,867	1,446,147
1863.	1,334,643	161,186	1,495,829
1864.	1,329,685	126,057	1,455,742
1865.	1,366,485	311,369	1,677,854

The increase of valuation in the real estate of our town, during the Rebellion, was seventy-eight thousand four hundred and nineteen ($78,419.00) dollars; in the personal estate the increase was one hundred and seventy-six thousand, six hundred and fifteen ($176,615.00) dollars; an aggregate of two hundred fifty-five thousand and thirty-four ($255,034.00) dollars; an average of fifty-one thousand and seven ($51,007.00) dollars a year.

It should be stated that the great increase in personal property for the year 1865, over previous years, was owing to the fact that income from business was taxed that year, and not the years preceding.

TABLE OF DEBT.

[1] United States Debt.		[2] Massachusetts Debt.		[3] Melrose Town Debt.	
July 1, 1860.	$64,769,703 08	Dec. 31, 1860.	$7,175,977 94	March 16, 1861.	$29,260 00
" 1, 1861.	90,867,828 68	" 31, 1861.	10,988,919 65	" 24, 1862.	35,560 00
" 1, 1862.	514,211,371 92	" 31, 1862.	11,129,578 71	" 2, 1863.	57,560 00
" 1, 1863.	1,098,793,181 37	" 31, 1863.	12,794,862 42	" 1, 1864.	53,900 00
" 1, 1864.	1,740,690,489 49	" 31, 1864.	22,529,015 34	" 1, 1865.	73,253 31
" 1, 1865.	2,682,593,026 53	" 31, 1865.	23,233,631 75	" 1, 1866.	69,819 67
" 1, 1866.	2,783,425,879 21	" 31, 1866.	25,555,747 51		

[4] *Tabular statement showing the bounties paid by the United States during the war.*

Amount.	By what authority paid.	To whom paid.	Between what dates paid.
$100	Act of July 22, 1861.	All volunteers.	From com. of war to July 18, 1864.
400	G. O. 191, of June 25, 1863, A. G. O.	Veterans.	From June 25, '63, to April 1, 1864.
300	Circular, Oct. 24, 1863, P. M. G. O.	New recruits enlisting in old organizations.	From Oct. 24, '63, to April 1, 1864.
300	Telegram, Dec. 24, 1863, from A. G. O.	New recruits enlisting in any three year organization authorized by the War Department.	From Dec. 24, '63, to April 1. 1864.
100 200 300	Act approved July 4, '64, and circular No. 27, of 1864, from P. M. G. O.	Volunteers enlisting for one, two, and three years.	From July 19, '64, to July 1, 1865.
300	G. O. 287, A. G. O., Nov. 28, 1864.	Men enlisting in 1st Army Corps.	From Nov. 28, '64, to July 1, 1865.
10	Letters of War Department, Nov. 29, 1863, and Dec. 22, 1863, to Gens. Butler and Gilmore.	Colored recruits.	

[1] Obtained through the kindness of Mr. William B. Willson, of Southboro', Mass.

[2] The real debt for these years was some $6,000,000 less than these figures, that amount being loaned to different Railroads in the State and secured by mortgages. The State Debt for Jan. 1, 1868, was $26,573,560.12, and it was classified in the report of the Finance Committee as follows :

Railroad Debt $6,751,196 00
Ante-War Debt 1,340,000 00
War Debt 16,573,244 00
Temporary Debt 1,909,120 12
$26,573,560 12

The war cost Massachusetts nearly $28,000,000.

[3] For net amount of expenses incurred on account of the war, see page 219.

[4] This table, and the one following is from the final report of the Provost-Marshal General of the United States, James B. Fry.

Estimate of the number of men to whom United States Bounty has been paid, the amount paid each man, and the total amount paid, from May 3, 1861, to the end of the war.

Periods embraced.	Class of men.	Periods of service.	Number of men.	Amt. per man.	Total amount paid.	Aggregate for each period.
From May 3, 1861, to Oct. 17, 1863.	Volunteers.	3 years.	905,869	$100	$90,586,900	$90,586,900
From Oct. 17, 1863, to July 18, 1864.	Veteran volunteers.	"	158,507	400	63,402,800	
	[1] Recruits.	"	257,028	300	77,108,400	146,417,500
	[2] "	"	11,025	100	1,102,500	
	Drafted men and substitutes.	"	48,038	100	4,803,800	
From July 18, 1864, to the end of the war.	Volunteers.	1 year.	191,936	100	19,193,600	
	"	2 years.	10,606	200	2,121,200	63,219,100
	"	3 years.	139,681	300	41,904,300	
Total			1,722,690	. .	$300,223,500	$300,223,500

DESTRUCTION OF A REBEL BLOCKADE RUNNER.

The following is an account of the burning of the schooner "Isabel" while under the guns of Fort Morgan, in May, 1863, by Lieutenant N. Mayo Dyer, — then Acting Master's Mate, — written by him the next day after the transaction. It was a daring and brilliant achievement; and Captain Jouett, in recommending him very strongly for promotion as Ensign, spoke of it as "one of the boldest of the war, and was conducted with matchless coolness from beginning to end."

U. S. S. "R. R. CUYLER,"
Off Mobile Bar, May 18, 1863.

* * * I had asked and obtained permission of Captain Jouett, to allow me to take an armed boat into Swash Channel, by which most of the blockade runners ran out and in, in order to board them if possible; if not, to signalize the direction they

---

[1] Enlisted between Oct. 17, 1863, and April 1, 1864.
[2] Enlisted between April 1, 1864, and July 18, 1864

took, so as to be taken by the steamers. Last night being a favorable night for some schooners that we knew were inside to run out, I had everything prepared, and at 6.20 left the ship and pulled in shore. The position I wished to get in was about a quarter of a mile from "Fort Morgan," where the channel is not above a half-mile wide, and I could readily see anything coming out or in. The tide was running very strong and I did not reach the position I desired until 10.30. Coming to an anchor, I watched; I could plainly see a man on the beach, we were so close. About 11 I discovered, as it lit up a little, a vessel ahead of me and nigher the Fort. I at once took it to be a steamer from the inside, come out to look after just such fellows as myself; so taking a position a little nearer him so as to observe any movement he might make, I kept shady. He was apparently at anchor. About a quarter to 12, behold what I supposed was a steamer, hoisted her mainsail, and I made her out to be a schooner looking quite rakish; but still thought, as she lay so quietly at anchor, that it was a picket boat; however I pulled up to her, going so nigh as to hear noises distinctly. She lay about two hundred yards from the beach of "Fort Morgan," and I could plainly see the guns frowning over the parapets of the Fort. I wanted to board her at once, and proposed it to the men. But three of them seemed to take the idea favorably; and as she lay so nigh the Fort, I did not like the idea of boarding her with a crew of unwilling men. So pulling up again and reconnoitring her closely, on the in-shore side, I saw a boat pull off to her from the shore, and discovered she had a hawser out to the Fort also. I then got on the off-shore side of her and dropped my anchor quietly, near her. I was provoked to find any disposition to back out on the part of the men; but finally, asking them individually, seven of the thirteen expressed their desire to board her, and the others said they would go into "Fort Morgan" if I *said* so, but considered it a little imprudent, as I had orders *not* to board anything until out of the range of the Fort. You see I was hardly justified in ordering my men to follow me unwillingly. However I now concluded to do it, and pulling right astern of her, giving my directions to the men as I took my place in the bow, to pull steadily, and the moment she touched the schooner, to trail oars and get on her decks as soon as possible, using only the cold steel, as fire-arms would have brought a hornet's nest about our heads. Fully expecting to find her armed, I was surprised on getting close to her to see that she had a deck-load of cotton. Whispering my men to give way, in another stroke we were alongside and aboard of her. We took them completely by surprise. The whole crew, seven men, were on deck and awake, and the first intimation they had of what was up, they beheld us coming on to the deck-load, with drawn cutlasses, and there was a sharp pointed instrument at each man's breast before he knew what the matter was; and commanding the utmost silence, I ordered them all into the boat under a guard. They were as docile as lambs. I went at one poor fellow with my cutlass, the first man I saw as I reached the deck, and thinking his days were numbered, he gave a scream, and leaped overboard like a frog; however I managed to get him aboard again. I soon found that she was hard ashore, having run aground in attempting to run out. Finding it impossible to save her, that is get her off, I at once determined to burn her; so securing all her papers, some of them valuable, I spread cotton all over the cabin floor and saturated it with turpentine, of which she had seventy or eighty barrels on deck. I also emptied a barrel of the same on deck all over her cotton, and then took a bucketful of it, and seeing every man in the boat, set fire to the cabin and threw my bucketful into the galley on the stove, where there was a fire. Like a flash she was completely covered with flames fore and aft, nearly blinding me with smoke and heat as I jumped into the boat and shoved off, just as a Rebel gun-boat came round Mobile Point, about a thousand yards off, to her assistance. The boat I had seen board the schooner was from this steamer, and had returned for the steamer to tow her off. I arrived on board the "Cuyler" at 3.30, with my seven prisoners, and was warmly congratulated by Captain Jouett and my fellow officers. She was the rebel schooner "Isabel" with two hundred bales of cotton and about one hundred barrels turpentine, quite a valuable cargo if it could have been saved.

FARRAGUT'S GREAT NAVAL VICTORY AT MOBILE — PASSAGE OF FORTS "MORGAN" AND "GAINES."

The following is Lieutenant Dyer's interesting account of the terrific fight and complete victory of our navy, in passing Forts "Morgan" and "Gaines." Dyer was, at the time of this writing, Acting Master; and for some months previous to this action, had been in command of the steamer "Eugenie."

U. S. S. "METACOMET,"
Inside Mobile Bay,
Aug. 5, 1864.

* * * Our fleet, consisting of fourteen wooden vessels and four iron-clads, successfully passed Forts "Morgan" and "Gaines" this morning at 8 o'clock, whipping the Rebel fleet, and is at this moment in complete possession of Mobile Bay. I wish you could just be on board this, or any other vessel here for a few minutes and witness the scene. We are all now lying quietly at anchor in the Bay, with the Star Spangled Banner floating from every gaff and mast-head in the fleet, and in our midst the famous ram "Tennessee," Admiral Buchanan, and the Confederate gunboat "Selma," both of which struck their colors to our victorious flag. Our loss has been the heaviest of any naval fight of the war by far. This ship was struck about twenty times, but strange to say we have lost but one killed and two wounded. In all we have about fifty killed and seventy-five wounded, not including the monitor "Tecumseh," which was blown up by a

torpedo, and all hands sank with her except twelve or fourteen — ten of whom were picked up by a boat from this ship. But to give you something of an idea of the fight, I will inclose a diagram of our position at the time the "Tecumseh" blew up. I have placed the ships in the position they were at the decisive moment of the fight, the time that the "Tecumseh" blew up. As you will see, the line was formed as follows: — "Brooklyn," with the "Octorora" alongside; "Hartford" — Flag-Ship, — with the "Metacomet"; "Richmond" and "Port Royal"; "Lackawanna" and "Kennebec"; "Ossipee" and "Seminole"; "Monongahela" and "Itasca," and the "Oneida" and "Galena"; the "Tecumseh" was to the right of the "Brooklyn," the "Manhattan" to the right of the "Hartford," the "Winnebago" to the right of the "Richmond," and the "Chickasaw" to the right of the "Lackawanna," the four last being monitors.

At 6.30 our line was formed, and we advanced to the conflict, — with an ensign at every mast-head and gaff in the fleet. And in the light of an August morning's sun the bright hues of our banners seemed to inspire every one with courage and hope, notwithstanding many, no doubt, with myself, felt the momentous importance of the moment; and with an inward prayer for victory, nerved themselves for the fight. At seven o'clock "Fort Morgan" opened fire, which was at once returned from the "Brooklyn's" forecastle gun, and soon after, by a broadside from the "Brooklyn" and "Hartford," when the fight became general with the leading ships. From this time until 7.45 the firing was rapid. The rebel fleet had come out from behind the point and lay directly ahead of our line delivering a raking fire upon us, which we could not return. About this time the "Brooklyn" discovered a torpedo ahead, and backing to clear it, the "Hartford" and this ship took the lead, and at eight o'clock were in the position described by the diagram. At 8.05 the "Tecumseh" blew up, close on our starboard beam — and the firing now was terrific. To attempt a description is impossi-

NAVAL FIGHT IN MOBILE BAY. 233

ble. Forts "Morgan" and "Gaines" upon either side — four gunboats ahead raking us, and the "Tecumseh" going down before our eyes. We sent a boat to pick up the floating. The Admiral then steamed with the "Hartford" close in to the Fort, within two hundred yards of the beach, closely followed by the "Brooklyn," and poured broadside after broadside of grape and canister into them, steaming slowly ahead all the time. As soon as we had passed out of range of their *grape*, we cut loose from the "Hartford" and steamed off on our own hook for the three gun-boats ahead; they at once headed up the bay, fighting us at the same time. We engaged the whole of them, leaving the "Tennessee" to the tender mercies of the fleet. We soon succeeded in crippling the "Gaines," and we then had the "Morgan" on one bow and the "Selma" on the other. Soon the "Morgan" turned her tail, and after a running fight of fifty minutes the "Selma" struck her colors and I was ordered on board to take charge. I did so, and found five men killed and ten wounded, three of whom have since died. Transferred prisoners to our ship, buried the dead, hoisted the Stars and Stripes and steamed down to the Admiral. We were about seven miles from our fleet when she surrendered. As the "Metacomet" is to go to Pensacola with the wounded, myself with my prize crew have just returned to our ship, having been relieved, and the wounded on both sides are now coming on board. The "Tennessee" surrendered to the fleet after a desperate fight. She did not fulfil the boast of Admiral Buchanan, C. S. Navy, of "whipping the whole Yankee fleet in one hour" *quite!* though she is a most formidable vessel; and nothing but a determination to destroy her, or be destroyed, effected her capture. Admiral Buchanan, commanding the rebel fleet, is now on board wounded in the leg. The officers of the "Selma" and "Tennessee," so far as I have seen, take it quite coolly, though evidently much chagrined at the result; they are gentlemen, and I think have no fault to find with their treatment so far. I am deeply thankful for my escape thus far and I hope I may be equally fortunate still.

PENSACOLA, Aug. 6.

At daylight this morning got under weigh from our anchorage and ran down to "Fort Morgan" with all the wounded on board. I was sent to communicate with the Fort, under a flag of truce, and delivered the bodies of two officers, killed on board the "Selma," and received permission to take the wounded to this place, where we arrived at 2 P. M. We have delivered the wounded to the hospital, and to-morrow morning start again for Mobile Bay, having come out with the express understanding that we were to return and report to the Fort as soon as possible. The only outlet is by the same way we entered, and therefore, until we effect the capture of one of the three forts, we are virtually blockaded, our communications cut off, etc. "Fort Powell" is the smallest and weakest fort, and without doubt we shall have that within a day or two, when we can work at our leisure, as their communications are as effectually cut off as ours. With five thousand troops all three forts would be in our possession in less than a fortnight, in my opinion, and I think we shall have that number soon. Already our forces occupy a portion of Dauphin Island, on which "Fort Gaines" is situated, and are operating against it, under command of General Granger.

A short extract from another of Lieutenant Dyer's letters, written five days later, is interesting as giving an idea of the sentiments of the people in and about Mobile at that time.

. . . . You are doubtless looking for the fall of Mobile City daily, but be not impatient; when we get ready then the thing will be accomplished. "Fort Powell," commanding "Grant's Pass," has been blown up and abandoned, and "Fort Gaines" has surrendered to the Navy, with its garrison of eight hundred and fifty men, and our flag now waves over both forts. "Fort Morgan" still holds out, but its surrender is but a question of time. Our fleet is all around it, that is, have complete control of its water approaches, and the army is within four hundred yards of its walls on the land. .... To-day we have been up the Bay on a reconnoissance, to within five miles of the city, and have had a grand view of the town and its water defences. About three and a half miles below the town is what is called Dog River Bar, where they have made extensive preparations to receive us. The channel is sealed up by sunken vessels, piles, etc.; and then above them they have three rams and two iron-clad floating batteries, besides batteries upon the shore both sides up to the city. .... About eight miles below the city I landed with a party, and visited several houses in the vicinity. Saw one woman who left the city this morning; she says the greatest excitement exists in Mobile, but that there are very few troops there. There is not an able-bodied man, nor boy over twelve years of age, on either side of the Bay; every one is conscripted, or fled to the woods to escape it. Those that I saw, most of them, are manifestly glad to see us, but dare not say all they wish till they are sure that we will remain. One very pretty young lady remarked to me, in answer to my question, as to whether there were any Union people about, "If we only were certain of your stopping here, you could find nothing but Union people, and *real* Union people, too; but if it should be known that we gave you any information, they would take us to town and put us in the common jail." Consequently when we wanted to purchase some chickens or peaches, they would take no money, but told us to take them, and then they could say we took them by force. They seemed anxious to hurry us off, for they momentarily expected a company of cavalry from town. I established a code of signals with one woman there, by which I can tell hereafter whether there are any troops in the vicinity, before landing.

INCIDENTS.

The following incidents are here introduced from "Carleton's" "Four Years of Fighting," because they happened in connection with the Thirteenth Massachusetts Regiment, in which we had a goodly number of "boys in blue," and relate so closely to him who was our friend and neighbor, the brave and lamented Colonel — then Major — J. Parker Gould, of Stoneham.[1] Colonel Gould represented our district in the Legislature during the winter of 1858-9. He led his Regiment, — the Fifty-Ninth Massachusetts, — into the last campaign, and was then assigned to the command of First Brigade, First Division, Ninth Army Corps ; and when before Petersburg, he was severely wounded. While at Philadelphia, on his way home, he died. He was a noble man, loved and respected for his heroic qualities and Christian virtues, by all who knew him ; and by none more so than by those who served under him during the war.[2]

---

[1] The Thirteenth Regiment furnished many officers for other organizations. Our Lieutenant Dyer, now in the U. S. Navy, Captain Simonds of the Third Massachusetts Cavalry, and Lieutenant Morse, killed at "Battle of Spottsylvania," all rose from its ranks. In recommending men in the service for appointments, Governor Andrew said of the Thirteenth : — "Batchelder is *not* needed there. *That* regiment could furnish officers for a *whole* regiment outside of itself, and be no more weakened than is a bird by laying its eggs. It is remarkable for its excellence of material."

Several poems were written complimentary to this regiment. One entitled "Song of the Thirteenth Regiment, Massachusetts Rifles." Another "The Gallant Thirteenth," written just after the fights of "Bolivar Heights" and "Harper's Ferry," two stanzas of which are as follows :

Tried, and found not wanting ! valiant, firm, and true,
Boston fathers' flowing hearts send greeting back to you ;
Tears were dried in loving pride, when first you marched away,
How proudly now lifts every brow, that you have *won* the day !
* * * * * * * * *
And now, all question put aside, they know you as you are,
The heroes who set at nought at *Heights of Bolivar !*
And *Harper's Ferry*, names which hence, long as Potomac roll,
Emblazoned, shine along the line, on the gallant Thirteenth's scroll !

[2] The following extract from a letter to one of our citizens, written just before the Peninsula campaign of 1862, shows his hopeful spirit : "I think I have seen most all the varieties in the bill of *war*fare, from the common duties to

These incidents happened while a detachment of the Thirteenth Regiment, under Major Gould, was stationed at Hancock, Md., and in the winter of 1861-2. And it must be remembered that at that time slaves were returned to their so-called loyal masters, and the Hutchinsons had been expelled, by order of General McClellan, from the camps of our soldier boys, where they had been singing, because they sang abolition songs, and it was feared the soldiers' minds would be poisoned thereby. But a change was gradually taking place in public opinion, on these matters.

A negro slave, belonging in Winchester, came into the lines. He was intelligent, cautious, shrewd, and loyal. Major Gould did not return him to his master, but asked him if he would go back and ascertain the whereabouts of Stonewall Jackson; the negro readily assented. He was supplied with packages of medicine, needles, thread, and other light articles greatly needed in the South. With these he easily passed the Rebel pickets: "Been out to get 'em for massa," was his answer, when questioned by the rebels.

---

the smart skirmish. Yet I wish to see it out, for no man can see the service that I have seen, without leaning to warlike feelings. The rebels must be taught one everlasting lesson. I predict that the Union forces will succeed, and if so, slavery is a dead letter. Though slavery is not the question in the contest, it will die away naturally, and perforce Union is *the* question, and it is the only necessary question now, and it is going to be decided in the affirmative. I thought some time ago that most of the fighting would be over by June, so that perhaps we should be ordered home by July — but now I think it may possibly take longer. If the coming battles at Yorktown and Corinth must decide the hard fate of the war so far as large battles are concerned, — still, from the character of the people, there will probably be much guerilla fighting. But the Southern people have become singularly educated, and they are singularly ignorant." In the spring of 1864, when Colonel of the 59th Regiment, and just before the final campaign, the same cheerful and hopeful spirit animated him, he then predicting, in conversation, certain successes, and that by the following Christmas.

Thus he passed repeatedly into the rebel lines, obtaining information which was transmitted to Washington. He had great influence with the slaves.

"They are becoming restless," said he, "but I tells 'em that they must be quiet. I says to 'em keep yer eyes wide open and pray for de good time comin'. I tells 'em if de Souf whip, it is all night wid yer; but if de Norf whip it is all day wid yer." "Do they believe it?" Major Gould asked. "Yes, massa, all believe it. The black men am all wid yer, only some of 'em isn't bery well informed; but dey is all wid yer. Massa tinks dey isn't wid yer, but dey is."

How sublime the picture! — a slave counselling his fellow-bondmen to keep quiet and wait till God should give them deliverance.

Among the many rebel ministers who had done what they could to precipitate the Rebellion, was a Presbyterian minister in the vicinity of Charlestown, Va. It was his custom, after closing his sermon, to invite the young men to enlist in the regiments then forming. On one of these occasions he made an address in which he gave utterance to the following sentiment:

"If it is necessary to defend Southern institutions and Southern rights, I will wade up to my shoulders in blood!"

This was brave; but the time came when the chivalry of the parson was put to the test. When the rebels were routed at Bolivar, he, not being mounted on so fleet a horse as those of his flock who had given heed to his counsels and joined the cavalry, found himself left behind. A bullet lodged in the body of his horse prevented escape. He then tried his own legs, but soon found himself in the hands of the soldiers, who brought him to head-quarters.

He at once claimed protection of Major Gould on the most extraordinary grounds. He had read the poems of Hannah Gould, and presumed that Major Gould, hailing from Massachusetts, must be her kinsman. When confronted with the Major he promptly exclaimed,

"Major, I have read the poems of Miss Hannah Gould, and admire them; presuming that she is a relative of yours, I claim your protection and consideration."

The Major replied that he had not the honor to be a relative of that gifted lady, but that he should accord him all the consideration due to those who had rebelled against the peace and dignity of the United States, and had been taken with arms in their hands. He was marched off with the others, and placed under guard.

ARTICLES EXCHANGED.

In a letter to the writer, from Lieutenant George C. Kaulback, of the Tenth Massachusetts Regiment, written after the battle of "Fredericksburg," while lying on the banks of the Rappahannock, is described the manner in which articles of daily use were frequently exchanged between the rebels and our troops. This was done by means of slips of wood, two or three feet long, cut into the form of boats, and sent across with little sails. The following letter came over in this way, tied to the mast of one of these boats:

OUTPOST, Feb. 9, 1863.

Gents. on U. S. Duty: We have received the small cargo of coffee. Accept our sincere thanks. In return we send you a small quantity of tobacco. We regret it is so small. In regard to Abe's negro proclamation — we suppose you all cordially endorse this last great act. Abe says " he cannot escape history." But he need not be alarmed. He is not known outside of his own dominions as anybody but Abe Lincoln, a perjured villain. How does he and you reconcile to your vile consciences his oath he took on the 4th of March, 1861, when he pledged his honor as a dog, that he had no intention to interfere with the institution of slavery where it existed, and to support the Constitution of the United States, as made by our forefathers.

We are, gents,
Yours truly,
REBELS.

P. S. How long before your army of observation will make another " On to Richmond ! "

XVII.

LIST OF COMMISSIONED OFFICERS FROM MELROSE.

Names. Date of commission.

BREVET COLONEL.

ARCHIBALD BOGLE. Seventeenth Massachusetts Regiment Infantry and Thirty-Fifth U. S. C. Troops. Second Lieutenant, Aug. 21, 1861; First Lieutenant, May 28, 1862. Major, May 20, 1863; Brevet Lieutenant-Colonel, March 13, 1864; Brevet Colonel, March 13, 1865; Commissioned First Lieutenant in United States Army, and assigned to Thirty-Ninth U. S. Infantry at New Orleans, March, 1868.

MAJOR.

J. SPENCER DRAYTON.[1] Thirty-Fifth U. S. Colored Troops. First Lieutenant and Quartermaster, April 28, 1863; Captain, July 14, 1863; on General Wild's Staff, from July 14, 1863, until June 28, 1864, when discharged for disability; Commissioned Paymaster for State of Massachusetts, with rank of Major, July 23, 1864, and ordered to New Berne, N. C. Remained until April, 1865. Discharged Dec. 31, 1866.

---

[1] When Rebellion broke out was resident in Dedham, and enlisted in Second Massachusetts Battery; discharged for disability; re-enlisted Feb.

CAPTAINS.

JOSEPH R. SIMONDS. Seventeenth Massachusetts Regiment Infantry, Aug. 21, 1861.

JOSEPH F. SIMONDS. Third Massachusetts Cavalry. Second Lieutenant, Sept. 20, 1864; First Lieutenant, May 28, 1865; Captain, Oct. 5, 1865.

FIRST LIEUTENANTS.

GEORGE W. BATCHELDER. Thirty-Second Massachusetts Regiment Infantry. Second Lieutenant, Dec. 4, 1864; First Lieutenant, April 1, 1865.

J. WESLEY JONES. Twelfth U. S. Infantry. May 14, 1861.

GEORGE T. MARTIN. Thirty-Eighth Massachusetts Regiment Infantry and Fourth Heavy Artillery. Second Lieutenant, Aug. 16, 1862; First Lieutenant, April 14, 1863; Senior First Lieutenant, Aug. 16, 1864.

GEORGE J. MORSE. Second U. S. Colored Troops and Fifty-Ninth Massachusetts Regiment Infantry. Second Lieutenant, March 2, 1863; Second Lieutenant Fifty-Ninth Regiment, Oct. 22, 1863; First Lieutenant, March 4, 1864.

GEORGE G. NICHOLS. Seventh Unattached Company Infantry. First Lieutenant, May 6, 1864. Fourth Heavy Artillery. First Lieutenant, Aug. 18, 1864.

21, 1862, in Co. A, First Heavy Artillery; appointed Quartermaster-Sergeant March 1, 1862; detached in August, and ordered to report to Colonel J. Dimmock, commanding First U. S. Artillery at Fort Warren, as Commissary-Sergeant.

LIST OF OFFICERS. 243

SECOND LIEUTENANTS.

GEORGE A. CHIPMAN. Sixth Massachusetts. July 20, 1864.
JACOB M. ELLIS. Second Massachusetts Battery. Jan. 8, 1865.
GURDON MCKAY. Twenty - Second Massachusetts Regiment Infantry. Oct. 1, 1861.
CHARLES H. STEVENS. First Massachusetts Cavalry. Jan. 2, 1864.

BREVET LIEUTENANTS.

EDWARD W. KENDALL. Seventeenth Massachusetts Regiment. Brevet First Lieutenant, Sept. 2, 1864.
GEORGE W. LYNDE. Seventeenth Massachusetts Regiment. Brevet Second Lieutenant, Dec. 31, 1864.

ASSISTANT SURGEON.

SAMUEL INGALLS, M. D. Fifth Massachusetts Cavalry. Jan. 11, 1864.[1]

OFFICERS IN THE NAVY.

N. MAYO DYER. Acting Master's Mate. May 2, 1862 ; Acting Ensign, May 20, 1863 ; Acting Master, Jan. 12, 1864; Acting Lieutenant, April 22, 1865 ; Lieutenant in Regular Navy, March 12, 1868.
EDWARD A. SMALL. Acting Ensign, June 16, 1862; Acting Master, Feb. 22, 1865.
JAMES F. PERKINS. Acting Ensign, Nov. 14, 1862.
WILLIAM A. FULLER. Third Assistant Engineer, March 23, 1864.

---

[1] Was Acting Assistant-Surgeon U. S. A. in Lincoln General Hospital, Washington, D. C., and U. S. General Hospital, at Portsmouth Grove, R. I., from Dec. 1862 to Jan. 1, 1864.

THE MELROSE MEMORIAL.

ALPHABETICAL ROLL OF

Names.	Regiment.	Company.	Rank.
A.			
Aldridge, William H. .	59	F	Private.
Anderson, John H. L.	8	E	"
Anderson, Leonard B. .	44	I	"
Andrews, Edwin A. .	2d Bat.		Corporal.
Arnold, Charles H. .	15	A	Private.
B.			
Barnard, John M., Jr. .	42	G	Private.
Barrett, Charles . .	42	G	"
Barrett, Charles L. .	42	G	"
Barron, Elliot F. . .	50	E	"
Barron, Henry . . .	22	G	Wagon'r.
Barry, Garrette . . .	28	A	Private.
Barry, John	59	A	"
Barry, Royal P. . . .	45	D	Serge'nt.
Barry, William F. . .	13	A	Private.
Beaman, William .	Navy		Seaman.
Bickford, Nelson W. .	38	I	Private.
Batchelder, George W.	5	B	"
	22	G	Serge'nt.
	32	C	1st Lieut.
Boardman, Charles . .	42	G	Private.
Bodwell, Henry A. .	22	G	"
Bogle, Archibald	Navy		Seaman.
	17	I	2d Lieut.
	35 U. S. C. T.		Bvt. Col.
Bosson, Samuel .	Navy		Seaman.
Boyd, Robert .	19	A	Private.

SOLDIERS FROM MELROSE.

Term of Enlistment.	Discharged.	Remarks.
Three years.	Expiration of service.	Non-resident.
One hundred days.	With Regiment.	
Nine months.	"	
Three years.	Expiration of service.	
"	"	Non-resident.
Nine months.	With Regiment.	Prisoner, Texas.
"	"	"
"	"	"
"	"	
Three years.	Expiration of service.	
"	"	Non-resident.
"	"	"
Nine months.	With Regiment.	
Three years.		Killed, Antietam Sept. 17, 1862.
"	Expiration of service.	Substitute for Geo. W. Heath.
"	Disability.	
Three months.	With Regiment.	Re-enlisted.
Three years.		Prisoner, Libby.
	Close of war.	Re-enlisted.
Nine months.	With Regiment.	Prisoner, Texas.
Three years.		Re-enlisted.
"	Expiration of service.	
"	For promotion.	Wd.Pris.,Andersonville. Now in U. S. Army.
"	Close of war.	
Three years.	Expiration of service.	Non-resident.
"	"	"

Names.	Regiment.	Company.	Rank.
Brand, Nathan H. . . .	9th Bat.		Private.
Brandon, Edward A. .	2d Cav.	I	"
Bridges, Henry . . .	42	G	"
Brierly, James . . .	5th U.S. Cav.	B	"
Brimmer, Daniel . .	11th U. S. I.		"
Brown, George . . .			"
Brown, Jonas G. . .	50	E	"
Brown, Robert . . .	11		"
Brown, Thomas . . .	5th U.S. Cav.	I	"
Bryant, Thomas O. .	42	G	"
Buckley, James . . .	Vet. R. C.		"
Buffum, Adelbert A. .	24	B	Corporal.
Burke, Patrick . . .	2d Cav.	D	Private.
Burnham, Oliver R. .	6	A	"
Burnham, Paschal E. .	42	G	"
Burns, Francis . . .	39	I	"
Burtwell, Thomas . .	19		"
Bush, Henry	54		"
Buttrick, John W. . .	42	G	Corporal.
C.			
Carlisle, John. . . .	18	E	Private.
Chambers John. . . .	28		"
Chandler, Roswell W. .	1st Cav.	G	"
Chapin, Joseph A. . .	9th Bat.		"
Chase, Ede K. . . .	5	A	"
Cheever, Augustus L. .	3d H. Art.	C	"
Cherain, Charles . .	5th U.S. Cav.		"
Chipman, George A. . {	45	D	"
	6	A	2d Lieut.

ROLL OF SOLDIERS.

Term of Enlistment.	Discharged.	Remarks.
Three years.		Died at Washington, D. C., March 6, 1864.
"	Expiration of service.	Non-resident.
Nine months.		Non-res. des'tr.
Three years.	Expiration of service.	Non-resident.
"	"	"
"	"	Sub. J.C. Howes.
Nine months.		Died at Baton Rouge, La., June 18, 1863.
Three years.	Expiration of service.	Non-resident.
"	"	"
Nine months.	With Regiment.	Prisoner, Texas.
Three years.	Expiration of service.	Non-resident.
"	"	
"	"	Non-res. des'tr.
One hundred days.	With Regiment.	
Nine months.	Disability.	
Three years.	Expiration of service.	Non-resident.
"	"	"
"	"	"
Nine months.	With Regiment.	Died Feb. 23,'63. Prisoner, Texas.
Three years.	Expiration of service.	Non-resident.
"	"	"
"	Disability.	
"	For promotion.	Hos. Steward, U. S. Army.
Nine months.	With Regiment.	
Three years.	Disability.	
"	Expiration of service.	Non-resident.
Nine months.	With Regiment.	
One hundred days.	"	

Names.	Regiment.	Company.	Rank.
Clark, Frederick F.	42	G	Private.
Clark, James	2d Cav.	C	"
Clark, Symonds	4th U.S. Art.	A	"
Colbert, Thomas	5th U.S.Cav.		"
Condon, James	5th U.S.Cav.		Drum'er.
Conway, Thomas	Vet. R. C.		Private.
Corson, Frederick U.	42	G	"
Cowan, Thomas	12th U. S. I.	I	"
Cox, James P.	50	E	"
Crane, William P., Jr.	48	D	"
Creeley, William	9	E	"
Crocker, John H.	13	A	"
Crocker, Joseph C.	44	I	Private.
Crockett, Albert W.	17	K	"
Crockett, George F.	3d Bat.		"
Cronk, Sydnia	19	C	"
Currier, Henry	3d U. S. Art.	I	"
Currier, John H.	17	A	"
Cutting, William H. Jr.	45	D	"

D.

Names.	Regiment.	Company.	Rank.
Darley, Caspar	3d U. S. Art.		Private.
Davis, Edmund W.	22	G	Corporal.
Davis, James L.	{ 42 7th Un.Co. I.	G	Private. "
Davis, John E.	42	G	"
Davis, John W.	3d H. Art.	E	"
Davis, Loami G.	{ 33 3d H. Art.	C F	" "
Dawes, Ambrose	13	A	"

ROLL OF SOLDIERS.   249

Term of Enlistment.	Discharged.	Remarks.
Nine months.	With Regiment.	Prisoner, Texas.
Three years.	Expiration of service.	Non-resident.
"	"	"
"	"	"
Three years.	Expiration of service.	Non-resident.
"	"	"
Nine months.	With Regiment.	Prisoner, Texas.
Three years.	Expiration of service.	Non-resident.
Nine months.	With Regiment.	
"	"	Non-resident.
Three years,	Expiration of service.	"
"	Disability.	
Nine months.	With Regiment.	
Three years.		Re-enlisted.
		Prisoner. Starv'd at Andersonville Aug. 1, 1864.
"	Disability.	Re-enlisted on Mansfield quota.
"	Expiration of service.	Non-resident.
"	"	
"	Disability.	
Nine months.	With Regiment.	
Three years.	Expiration of service.	Non-resident.
"	Disability.	Pris., Belle Isle. Died July 22' '64.
Nine months.	With Regiment.	Prisoner, Texas.
Ninety days.	"	
Nine months.	"	Prisoner, Texas.
Three years.		Non-res., des'tr.
"	Disability.	Re-enlisted.
"	Expiration of service.	
"	"	Wd. Antietam, Sept. 17, 1862.

Names.	Regiment.	Company.	Rank.
Dawes, Richard C.	44	H	Private.
Deshon, Francis	38	K	"
Devine, John	3d U. S. Cav.	I	"
Dix, Joseph O.	50	E	"
Domenico, Bilotto	5th U.S. Cav.		"
Donagan, Maurice	23	K	"
Dorring, John	45	I	"
Double, Edmund B.	42	G	"
Drayton, J. Spencer	35 U. S. C. T.		Captain.
Drew, William H.	29	F	Private.
Duffy, Bernard	Vet. R. C.		"
Dunn, Dennis	5th U.S. Cav.	D	"
Dyer, N. Mayo	13	A	"
	Navy.		Lieut.

E.

	Navy.	Sabine.	Seaman.
Earl, William H.	39	G	Private.
	Navy.	Mendota.	Seaman.
Eastman, William H.	2d Bat.		Private.
Eddy, Orrin	3d H. Art.		"
Ellis, Alvan T.	13th Bat.		Corp'l.
Ellis, Jacob M.	2d Bat.		2d Lieut.
Emerson, James G.	42	G.	Private.
	7th Un.Co. I.		"
Emerson, James W.	38	K	"
Emerson, Joseph S.	7th Un.Co. I.		"
Esbeck, Charles	3d H. Art.		"
Evans, Thomas C.	45	D.	"

F.

Fargo, Charles O.	3d H. Art.	F	Private.
Farrell, Michael	50	E	"

Term of Enlistment.	Discharged.	Remarks.
Nine months.	With Regiment.	
Three years.	"	
"	Expiration of service.	Non-resident.
Nine months.	With Regiment.	
Three years.	Expiration of service.	Non-resident.
"	"	Non-res., des'tr.
Nine months.	With Regiment.	Non-resident.
"	"	Wd. Pris., Texas.
Three years.	Disability.	Afterwards Paymaster, Rank of
"		Major.
"	Expiration of service.	Non-resident.
"	"	"
"	"	"
"	To enter Navy.	Now in Regular Service.
One year.	Expiration of service.	Re-enlisted. Wd.
Three years.	Transferred.	at Hagerstown,
	Expiration of service.	Md.
"	"	Prisoner, Texas.
"		Non-resident.
"		Non-res., des'tr.
"	"	Re-enlisted.
Nine months.	With Regiment.	Prisoner, Texas.
Ninety days.	"	
Three years.	"	
Ninety days.	"	
Three years.		Non-resident.
Nine months.	Disability.	Wd. Kinston, Dec. 14, 1862.
Three years.	Disability.	
Nine months.	With Regiment,	

Names.	Regiment.	Company.	Rank.
Ferguson, John	39	I	Private.
Fimeyer, Philip	8th U. S.I.	K	"
Fisher, George W.	17	A	"
Foss, George A.	45	I	"
Foss, James T.	45	D	"
Frank, William	5th U.S.Cav.	F	"
Freeland, Joseph V.	45	A	Music'n.
Frisby, John	59	A	Private.
Fuller, George P.	50	E.	"
Fuller, Henry F.	17	A	"
Fuller, William A.	Navy.	Ft. Donelson.	3d Ass't Eng'r.
Ferguson, John	45	I	Private.

G.

Names.	Regiment.	Company.	Rank.
Gallagher, Edward	5th U.S. Cav.	D.	Private.
Gallagher, John	50	F	"
Gallagher, Richard	99 N.Y. Reg.	G	"
Gillispie, John	2d Cav.	D	"
Goericke, Frederic	U. S. Cav.		"
Goffeney, Robert	8th U. S. I.	K	"
Green, Augustus	22	G	"
Greene, Martin	2	G	"
Grover, Andrew J.	22	G	"
	3d H. Art.	C	"
Grover, George W., Jr.	3d H. Art.	C	"
Grover, John C.	17	K	"
Grover, William W.	5	K	"

Term of Enlistment.	Discharged.	Remarks.
Three years.	Expiration of service.	Non-resident.
"	"	"
"	Disability.	
Nine months.	With Regiment.	Non-resident.
"	"	Wd. Kinston, Dec. 14, 1862.
Three years.	Expiration of service.	Non-resident.
Nine months.	With Regiment.	"
Three years.	Expiration of service.	"
Nine months.	With Regiment.	
Three years.		Died at Baltimore, Md., Oct. 6, 1861.
One year.	Expiration of service.	
Nine months.	With Regiment.	Non-resident.
Three years.	Expiration of service.	Non-resident.
Nine months.		Non-res., des'tr.
Three years.	"	
"		Non-res., died from wounds, July 20, 1864.
"	"	Non-resident.
"	"	"
"		Killed, Bethesda Ch.Va., June 3, '64.
"		Died from w'nds, Aug. 16, 1862.
"	Disability.	Re-enlisted.
"	With Regiment.	"
"	"	
"	Expiration of service.	"
One hundred days.	With Regiment.	

Names.	Regiment.	Company.	Rank.

H.

Names.	Regiment.	Company.	Rank.
Hagan, John J.	Vet. R. C.		Private.
Haggerty, Daniel	59	A	"
Halpine, Bartholomew	59	B	"
Hamilton, Robert	50	E	"
Hammond, George	3d H. Art.	C	"
	Navy.	Juniata.	Seaman.
Hanigan, John	32	C	Private.
Hare, Andrew	48	G	Serg't.
Harrington, Charles T.	50	E	Private.
Harris, John	45	I	"
Harris, Samuel	71 U.S.C.T.		"
Harris, William	2d Cav.	H	"
Hart, Abner B.	44	G	"
Harvey, Franklin	Navy.	Miami.	Seaman.
Hawkes, John	50	E	Private.
Hayes, James	U. S. Cav.		"
Haynes, Joseph W.	17	K	"
Hecker, Charles F.	5th U.S. Cav.		Music'n.
Heton, John	42	G	Private.
Hinckley, George H.	20	A	"
Hollis, Henry P.	2d Cav.	H	"
Howard, Avery B.	3d Bat.		Corp'l.
Howard, James R.	38	K	Private.
Howe, Francis E.	2d Bat.		Serg't.
Hughes, James	3d Cav.	G	Private.
Hyde, George S.	42	G	"

I.

Names.	Regiment.	Company.	Rank.
Ireson, Alonzo D.	42	G	Private.
Ireson, David A.	42	G	Music'n.
Ingalls, Samuel	5th Cav.		Ass't Surgeon.

ROLL OF SOLDIERS. 255

Term of Enlistment.	Discharged.	Remarks.
Three years.	Expiration of service.	Non-resident.
"	Disability.	"
"	Expiration of service.	"
Nine months.	With Regiment.	"
Three years.	Transferred.	
	Expiration of service.	
"	"	"
Nine months.	With Regiment.	
"	"	Non-resident.
"	"	"
Three years.	Expiration of service.	Rep. Recruit for David Fairbanks.
"		Non-res., des'tr.
Nine months.	With Regiment.	
Two years.	Expiration of service.	
Nine months.	With Regiment.	Non-resident.
Three years.	Expiration of service.	"
"	"	Re-enlisted.
"	"	Non-resident.
Nine months.	With Regiment.	Prisoner, Texas.
Three years.	Expiration of service.	Non-resident.
"	"	
"	"	
"	Disability.	Died at Melrose, Aug. 16, 1864.
"	"	
"		Non-res., des'tr.
Nine months.	With Regiment.	Prisoner, Texas.
Nine months.	With Regiment.	Prisoner, Texas.
"	"	"
	Resigned.	

Names.	Regiment.	Company.	Rank.

J.

Names.	Regiment.	Company.	Rank.
Jackson, Henry M.	59	B	Private.
Jackson, Jacob F.	16	F	"
Jackson, William H.	39	G	"
Jackson, William P.	13	A	"
Jenkins, George	59	A	"
Johnson, William A.	59	B	"
Johnson, William H.	54		"
Jones, Charles S.	39	G	"
Jones, Davis	58 U. S. C. T.		"
Jones, Henry H.	13	A	Corp'l.
Judkins, Roland C.	42	G	Wag'nr.
Junkins, Edwin W.	45	D	Private.

K.

Names.	Regiment.	Company.	Rank.
Kelley, Patrick	38	I	Private.
Kendall, Edward W.	17	A	Bvt. 1 Lt.
Kennelly, James A.	38	I	Corp'l.
Kennerk, John	5th U.S. Cav.	B	Private.
Kenniston, Charles	38	I	Music'n.
Kilby, Theophilus	13	A	Private.
King, David H.	2d Cav.	K	"
King, George L.	13	A	"
King, John S.	5th U.S. Cav.	F	"
Kingdom, John	Navy.	Tioga.	Seaman.
Kingman, William W.	50	E	Private.
Knights, Henry C.	50	E	"
Kober, Charles	5th U.S. Cav.		"
Koeppen, John	2d U. S. I.	K	"
Kohler, Charles	Navy.		Seaman.
Krantz, Frederick W.	33	C	Private.

ROLL OF SOLDIERS. 257

Term of Enlistment.	Discharged.	Remarks.
Three years.	Expiration of service.	Non-resident.
"	Disability.	
"	"	
"	"	
"	Expiration of service.	Non-resident.
"	"	"
"	"	"
"	"	Vet. Res. Corps.
"	"	Rep. Recruit for Daniel Russell.
"	"	Pris., Belle Isle.
Nine months.	With Regiment.	Prisoner, Texas.
"	"	
Three years.	With Regiment.	Non-resident.
"	Expiration of service.	
"	Disability.	"
"	Expiration of service.	"
"	With Regiment.	Wounded, Port Hudson, June 14, 1863.
"	Disability.	
"	Expiration of service.	Non-resident.
"	"	
"	"	Non-resident.
Three years.	Expiration of service.	"
Nine months.	With Regiment.	"
Nine months.	"	"
Three years.	Expiration of service.	"
"	"	"
"	"	"
"	"	Prisoner, twice.

33

L.

Names.	Regiment.	Company.	Rank.
Lafferty, James	Navy.		Seaman.
Lahey, John	Vet. R. C.		Private.
Lalley, Thomas J.	Navy.		Seaman.
Lamb, John R.	"		"
Lane, Francis W.	30	B	Private.
Lane, John	Navy.		Seaman.
Lange, Andrew	"		"
Launzen, Christian	"		"
Lee, George E.	"		"
Leeds, Samuel	16	C	Serg't.
Leighton, William F.	45	D	Private.
Lemont, Henry	Navy.	Maratanza.	Seaman.
Lever, Richard	59	A	Private.
Lewis, Thomas	Navy.	Mahaska.	Seaman.
Lewis, Walter H.	59	B	Private.
Liffin, James	29	F	Drum'r.
Lindsey, Joseph			Private.
Littlefield, Cushing W.	24	B	"
Lombard, Charles E.	Navy.		Seaman.
Long, John	11	K	Private.
Longwood, John	19		"
Ludirzen, George S.	Navy.		Seaman.
Lutz, William	12th U. S. I.	B	Bugler.
Lyall, David S.	8	E	Private.
Lyman, Henry H.	50	E	"
Lynde, Amos W.	42	G	"
	7th Un.Co. I.		Corp'l.
Lynde, Benjamin	38	K	Private.
Lynde, Charles B.	42	G	"
Lynde, George W.	17	A	Bvt. 2 Lt.

Term of Enlistment.	Discharged.	Remarks.
Three years.	Expiration of service.	Non-resident.
"	"	"
"	"	"
"	"	"
"	"	"
"	"	"
"	"	"
"	"	"
"	"	Re-enlisted.
Nine months.	With Regiment.	
Three years.	Expiration of service.	Non-resident.
"		K'ld., Spottsylvania, May 12, 1864.
"	Expiration of service.	Non-resident.
"	"	"
"	"	"
"	"	Sub. for Henry W. Barrett.
"	Disability.	Wounded.
"	Expiration of service.	Non-resident.
"	"	"
"	"	"
"	"	"
One hundred days.	With Regiment.	
Nine months.	"	
"	"	Prisoner, Texas.
Ninety days.	"	
Three years.		Died at Baton Rouge, La., Aug. 18, 1863.
Nine months.	With Regiment.	Prisoner, Texas.
Three years.	Expiration of service.	Died at Melrose, Jan. 30, 1866.

Names.	Regiment.	Company.	Rank.
Lynde, Sherman	1st Cav.	G	Corp'l.

M.

Names.	Regiment.	Company.	Rank.
Macey, James	13	E	Private.
Macey, John S.	17	A.	"
	Navy.	Philippi.	Seaman.
Marra, James	59	D	Private.
Marshall, James	45	D	"
Marshall, Samuel	42	G	"
Marston, James M.	42	G	"
Martin, George T.	38	K	1st Lieut.
	4th H. Art.	C	"
Martin, Jeremiah Jr.	Navy.	Tritonia.	Paymasters' Cl'k.
Martin, William H.	38	K	Serg't.
McAllister, Daniel W.	22	G	Private.
McAllister, George H.	50	E	"
McDonald Angus	20	A	"
McKay, Gurdon	5	B	"
	22	G	2d Lieut.
McLaughlin, Frank M.	Navy.	Kearsarge.	Yeoman.
McLaughlin, Hiram	6	A	Private.
McLaughlin, George W.	45	D	"
McMahan, Philip	17	I	"
Mitchell, George	Navy.	Tioga.	Seaman.
Moran, Bernard	5th U.S. Cav.		Private.
Moran, Thomas	Vet. R. C.		"
Morrison, Charles H.	22	G	"
	38	I	Serg't.
Morrison, Seth	4	F	Private.
Morse, George J.	13	A	"
	2d U.S.C.T.		2d Lieut.
	59	G	1st Lieut.

ROLL OF SOLDIERS.   261

Term of Enlistment.	Discharged.	Remarks.
Three years.	Expiration of service.	
Three years.	Expiration of service.	
"	Disability.	Re-enlisted.
One year.	Expiration of service.	
Three years.	"	Non-resident.
Nine months.	With Regiment.	
"	"	Prisoner, Texas.
"		Non-res., des'tr.
Three years.	Disability.	Died at Boston,
One year.		March 13, 1865.
"	Expiration of service.	
Three years.	"	
"	Disability.	
Nine months.	With Regiment.	
Three years.	Disability.	
Three months.	With Regiment.	Re-enlisted.
Three years.	Dismissed.	
"	Expiration of service.	
One hundred days.	With Regiment.	
Nine months.	"	
Three years.	Expiration of service.	Re-enlisted.
"	"	
"	"	Non-resident.
"	"	"
"	Disability.	Re-enlisted.
"		Deserter.
Three months.	With Regiment.	
Three years.	Disability.	Wd. Sec'nd Bull Run, Aug. 30, '62. Wd, Port Hudson, July 5, '63. Killed Spottsylvania, May 12, 1864.
"	"	

Names.	Regiment.	Company.	Rank.
Morse, Sydney B. 2d .	13	D	Corp'l.
Mullcott, Adolphus .	59	A	Private.
Munn, Thomas J. . .	13	A	"
Murphy, Patrick . .	Vet. R. C.		"
Myars, John	45	I	"
N.			
Nichols, George G. .	42	G	Serg't.
	7th U. Co. Inf.		1st Lieut.
	4th H. Art.		"
Nichols, Smith W., Jr.	Navy.	Shenandoah	Lieut.
Nichols, William R. .	50	D	Music'n.
Nolan, Thomas . . .	4th U.S. Art.	A	Private.
Noonan, Edward . .	5th U.S. Cav.		"
Noyes, George O. .	38	K	Corp'l.
O.			
O'Donaghue John . .	50	E	Private.
O'Leary, Timothy . .	U. S. Marines.		"
O'Regan, Michael . .	59	A	"
Otslott, Frederick . .	8th U. S. I.	K	"
P.			
Page, Moses S. . . .	6	E	Private.
Parsons, William . .	50 U. S. C. T.		"
Peabody, Francis	22	G	"
	17	K	Orderly.
Peabody, Torrey .	22	G	Private.
Peabody, Torrey, Jr.	17	K	"

Term of Enlistment.	Discharged.	Remarks.
Three years.		Died at Washington, Sept. 16, '62.
"	Expiration of service.	Non-resident.
"	"	Wd. Gettysburg, July 1, 1863. Vet. Res. Corps.
"	"	Non-resident.
"	"	"
Nine months.	With Regiment.	As Acting Lieut. Co. E.
Ninety days.	"	On Col. King's Staff.
One year.	"	U. S. Navy.
Nine months.	With Regiment.	Non-resident.
Three years.	Expiration of service.	"
"	"	"
"	"	Wounded, Port Hudson, June 14, 1863.
Nine months.		Non-res., des'tr.
Four years.	Expiration of service.	Non-resident.
Three years.	Disability.	"
"	Expiration of service.	"
One hundred days.	With Regiment.	
Three years.	Expiration of service	Rep. Recruit for Dexter Bryant.
"	Disability.	Re-enlisted.
"		Re-enlisted. Died at New Berne, N. C., Oct. 3, 1864.
"	Disability.	
"	Expiration of service.	

Names.	Regiment.	Company.	Rank.
Pearson, William H. .	3d U. S. Art.		Private.
Peaseley, Charles D. .	59	D	"
Pemberton, Lewis E. .	61	F	"
Penn, Isaac	4th U.S. Art.	A	"
Perkins, Benjamin W.	59	B	"
Perkins, James F. . .	Navy.		Act. Ensign.
Perkins, John, Jr. .	45	D	Private.
Perse, William A. . .	8th U. S. I.	F	Private.
Pike, Jacob F. . . .	39	G	"
Pilling, James L. . .	60	G	"
Pratt, Daniel S . .	1st Cav.	G	"
Pratt, Henry W. . .	8	E	"
Prentice, Charles . .	50	E	"
Prescott, Horace . .	9th Bat.		"
Prince, Albert G. . .	18	E	"

Q.

Quinn, John E. .	32	A	Private.
Quinn, John H. . . .	99th N. Y.	B.	Private.
Quinn, Patrick . . .	8	E	"

R.

Rain, William G. . .	8th U. S. I.	D	Corp'l.
Reardon, Lawrence .	3d H. Art.	K	Private.
Reynard John H. .	Navy.		Seaman.
Rice, George .	38	F	Private.
Richardson, Alfred C.	48	D	Music'n.
Richardson, George E.	38	K	Private.
Richardson, John P. .	17	K	"

Term of Enlistment.	Discharged.	Remarks.
Three years.	Expiration of service.	Non-resident.
"	"	"
One year.	"	
Three years.	"	Non-resident.
"	"	"
"	"	
Nine months.	Disability.	Wd., Kinston, Dec. 14, 1862.
Three years.	Expiration of service.	Non-resident.
"	"	
One hundred days.	With Regiment.	
Three years.	Expiration of service.	
One hundred days.	With Regiment.	
Nine months.	"	
Three years.	Expiration of service.	
"	Disability.	Wd. Second Bull Run, July 30, '62.
Three years.	Disability.	Re-enlisted on quota of Boston.
"	Expiration of service.	
One hundred days.	With Regiment.	
Three years.	Expiration of service.	Non-resident.
"	"	"
"	"	Sub. for James O. Lynde.
"	"	Non-resident.
Nine months.		Non-res. Died at Baton Rouge, La., Aug. 8, 1863.
Three years.		Died at Salisbury, N. C., Nov. 3, '64.
"	Expiration of service.	Re-enlisted.

34

Names.	Regiment.	Company.	Rank.
Richardson, William H.	3d H. Art.	C	Private.
Riley, James	11th U. S. I.		"
Riley, William	11th U. S. I.		"
Roberts, Charles H.	44	E	"
Robertson, William	2d Cav.	D	"
Rowell, Stephen P.	18	H	"
	50	D	Serg't.
Ryan, James	19		Private.
Ryan, Michael	59	F	"
S.			
Sassard, Augustus	13	A	Private.
Sawyer, Obadiah	39	I	"
Scafferman, Henry	5th U.S. Cav.	K	"
Seavey, Leonard C.	2d Bat.		"
Shannon, Martin	23	K	"
Shelton, Albert F.	13	A	"
Shelton, Charles W.	13	A	Serg't.
Shelton, John P.	13	A	Private.
Shelton, Thomas	50	E	Private.
	8	E	"
Shrekler, Frederick	8th U. S. I.	D	"
Shrodenback, Joseph	5th U.S. Cav.		"
Simms, Daniel	"		"
Simonds, Charles H.	50	E	"
Simonds, Joseph F.	13	A	"
	3d Cav.	D	Captain.
Simonds, Joseph R.	17	K	"
Simonds, Joseph W.	44	D	Private.
	8	E	"
Sinclair, Thomas J.	8th U. S. I.	B	"
Singler, Louis	"	B	"
Skinner, Charles E.	5th Bat.		"

ROLL OF SOLDIERS.

Term of Enlistment.	Discharged.	Remarks.
Three years.	Expiration of service.	
"	"	Non-resident.
"	"	"
Nine months.	Disability.	
Three years.		Non-res., des'tr.
"	Disability.	Re-enlisted.
Nine months.	With Regiment.	
Three years.	Expiration of service.	Non-resident.
"	"	"
Three years.	Disability.	
"	Expiration of service.	Non-resident.
"	"	"
"	"	
"	Disability.	
"	"	Wd., Antietam, Sept. 17, 1862.
"	General service.	Wd., Antietam, Sept. 17, 1862.
"		Killed, Antietam, Sept. 17, 1862.
Nine months.	With Regiment.	Re-enlisted.
One hundred days.	"	
Three years.	Expiration of service.	Non-resident.
"	"	"
"	"	"
Nine months.	With Regiment.	"
Three years.	Disability.	Re-enlisted.
"	Expiration of service.	Wd. three times.
"	"	
Nine months.	With Regiment.	Re-enlisted.
One hundred days.	"	
Three years.	Expiration of service.	Non-resident.
"	"	"
"	Disability.	

268 THE MELROSE MEMORIAL.

Names.	Regiment.	Company.	Rank.
Slocumb, Henry W.	30	E	Private.
Small, Edward A.	Navy.	Wabash.	Act. Master.
Smith, Thomas	5 4th Bat.	B	Private.
Smith, Wayland R.	43	A	"
Souggroe, Timothy	Vet. R. C.		"
Spaulding, Henry H.	6	A	"
Spear, William S.	Vet. R. C.		"
Sprague, Samuel Jr.	12	A	Corp'l.
Stantial, Thomas B.	5th Bat.		Artificer.
Starbuck, George M.	26	A	Private.
Stebbens, Thaddeus S.	39	G	"
Stevens, Charles H.	1st Cav.	G	2d Lieut.
Stevens, Thomas H.	16	A	Private.
Stilphen, John E.	2d Bat.		"
Stone, Henry	39	G	Corp'l.
	59	G	Serg't.
Sumner, Stephen	5	H	Private.
Sweetser, Thomas T.	42	G	"

T.

Tainter, George A.	13	A	Private.
Taltersall, Edward	5th U.S. Cav.	F	"
Tobey, Samuel	9th Bat.		"
Todd, Thomas	48	D	Serg't.
Tower, Benjamin	38	K	Corp'l.
Turck, John	3d H. Art.	K	Private.
Tucker, William L.	9th Bat.		Corp'l.
Tyler, William N.	8		Serg't.-Maj.

ROLL OF SOLDIERS.

Term of Enlistment.	Discharged.	Remarks.
Three years.	Expiration of service.	Re-enlisted.
"	"	
Three months.	With Regiment.	Re-enlisted.
Three years.	Expiration of service.	"
Nine months.	With Regiment.	
Three years.	Expiration of service.	Non-resident.
One hundred days.	With Regiment.	
Three years.	Expiration of service.	Non-resident.
"	Disability.	Wd., Antietam, Sept. 17, 1862.
"	Abolishment of office.	
"	Expiration of service.	Non-resident.
"	Disability.	
"	Expiration of service.	Wounded.
"		Died at Boston, March 26, 1863.
"	Expiration of service.	Died at Melrose, June 25, 1865.
"	Disability.	Wounded. Prisoner, Libby.
"	With Regiment.	"
Nine months.	"	
"	"	Wounded. Prisoner, Texas.
Three years.	Disability.	Wd., Antietam, Sept. 17, 1862.
"	Expiration of service.	Non-resident.
"	With Battery.	Wd., Gettysburg, July 2, 1863.
Nine months.	With Regiment.	Non-resident.
Three years.	"	Wounded, Cedar Creek, Oct. 19, 1864.
"	Disability.	Non-resident.
"	With Battery.	
One hundred days.	With Regiment.	Also on S. Reading quota.

Names.	Regiment.	Company.	Rank.
Tyrrill, Andrew . .	Navy.		Seaman.
U.			
Upham, Charles H. .	42	G	Private.
Upham, Henry W. .	60	G	"
V.			
Vinton, Edwin A. .	42	G	Private.
	8	E	"
Vinton, Gray	8	E	"
W.			
Waitt, John R. . . .	6	A	Private.
Wallace, John . . .	19		"
Walsh, Thomas . .	15	B	"
Ward, Reuben D. .	Navy.	George Mayhew.	Seaman.
Warren, Nathaniel . .	"		"
Waters, Henry . . .	"		"
Watts, Simon C. . .	Navy.	Neipsic.	"
Weeks, Seymour . .	"		"
Welden, George E. .	"		"
Wells, Charles A. . .	11	I	Private.
Wharton, Joseph . .	Navy.		Seaman.
White, Charles L. . .	1st H. Art.	E	Private.
Whitney, Edward H. .	13	D	Serg't.
Wilbur, William H.	Navy.	St. Lawrence.	Seaman.
Wilde, Benjamin F. .	42	H	Private.
Wilkins, Charles B. .	Navy.		Seaman.
Wilkinson, Robert . .	"		"
Williams, Charles J. .	Navy.		Seaman.
Williams, George . .	"	St. Lawrence.	"

ROLL OF SOLDIERS. 271

Term of Enlistment.	Discharged.	Remarks.
Three years.	Expiration of service.	Sub. for Daniel W. Wilcox.
Nine months. One hundred days.	With Regiment. "	Prisoner, Texas.
Nine months. One hundred days. "	With Regiment. " "	Prisoner, Texas.
One hundred days. Three years. " "	With Regiment. Expiration of service. " "	Non-resident. " "
" " " " " " " " "	" " " " " " " " "	" " " " " " " Wd., Warrenton Junction.
" "	" "	" Non-resident.
Nine months. Three years. " " "	Expiration of service. " " "	Deserter. Non-resident. " " "

Names.	Regiment.	Company.	Rank.
Williams, Walter	Navy.		Seaman.
Wilson, John	50	F	Private.
Wilson, John	39	I	"
Wilson, Samuel	Navy.		Seaman.
Wilson, Thomas E.	"	Aries.	"
Woodman, Robert	"		"
Wyman, George W.	6	A	Private.
Wyman, Weston	6	A	"
Wyman, William	5	B	"
	24	C	"

Y.

Names.	Regiment.	Company.	Rank.
Yeaton, George	29	A	Drum'er.
York, Benjamin F.	56	B	Private.
York, Josiah R.	42	G	"
	7th Un.Co. I.		"
York, William B.	42	G	"
	7th Un. Co. I.		"
Young, John W.	59	F	"

MELROSE CITIZENS WHO SERVED

Names.	Regiment.	Company.	Rank.
Barrett, David A.	17th Mass.	K	Corp'l.
Chambers, John L.	Navy.	Morning Light.	Master's Mate.
Davis, Charles L.	8th Maine.	E	Private.
Elliott, George W.	"	E	"
Krantz, William F.	33d Mass.	C	"
	Vet. R. C.		"
Macey, William H.	3d Maine.	F	"
Martin, Charles H.	4th Ms. H. A.	C	Corp'l.
Thompson, John	Navy.	Rhode Isl'd.	Seaman.

ROLL OF SOLDIERS.

Term of Enlistment.	Discharged.	Remarks.
Three years.	Expiration of service.	Non-resident.
Nine months.		Non-res., des'tr.
Three years.	Expiration of service.	Non-resident.
"	"	Sub. for George Emerson 2d.
"	"	Non-resident.
"	"	"
One hundred days.	With Regiment.	
"	"	
Three months.	"	Re-enlisted.
Three years.	Expiration of service.	Wounded. Re-enlisted.
Three years.	Expiration of service.	Non-resident.
"	"	Pris., Danville.
Nine months.	With Regiment.	Prisoner, Texas.
Ninety days.	"	
Nine months.	"	Prisoner, Texas.
Ninety days.	"	
Three years.	Expiration of service.	Non-resident.

ON OTHER QUOTAS.

Term of Enlistment.	On what Quota.	Remarks.
Three years.	Malden.	
"	Boston.	Prisoner over two years.
"	Augusta, Me.	
"	"	Pris'r, 4 Months. Re-enlisted.
"	Malden.	Re-enlisted.
"	Douglass.	Died June 13 '66.
"	Skowhegan, Me.	Died at Alexandria, Va., Aug. 30, 1862.
One year.	Franklin.	
"	Boston.	

35

APPENDIX.

APPENDIX.

A.

CERTIFICATE OF A NON-RESIDENT RECRUIT.

BOSTON, Dec. 20, A. D. 1862.

I, William R. Riddle, a 1st Lieutenant Twentieth Mass. Vols. in the military service of the United States, and duly authorized to act as a Recruiting Officer, do hereby certify that I have, on the twentieth day of December, A. D. 1862, caused to be mustered into the military service of the United States, in Co. A, Twentieth Regiment, to serve for three years or during the war, unless sooner discharged, George H. Hinckley, to be applied upon the quota of the town of Melrose; and that, to the best of my knowledge and belief, the said George H. Hinckley has not been previously reported to the Adjutant-General's office, and is not a resident of any other town or city in this Commonwealth.

WM. R. RIDDLE,
1st Lieutenant Twentieth Mass. Vols.,
Recruiting Officer.

B.

FORM FOR PAYMENT OF BOUNTY.

No. 30. MELROSE, Aug. 16, 1862.

MR. CALEB HOWARD, TOWN TREASURER.

Sir: Pay to Joseph A. Chapin of Melrose, a recruit accepted and mustered into the service of the United States by Lieutenant Adams, for the Ninth Battery Massachusetts Volunteers, the sum of One Hundred Dollars bounty, as per order of the

Town, passed July 28, 1862, he being a part of the quota of troops to be furnished by the Town of Melrose, for three years unless sooner discharged by proper authority.

JOHN H. CLARK,
WM. B. BURGESS,
G. M. FLETCHER,
Selectmen of Melrose.

I hereby certify that I enlisted the above named Joseph A. Chapin into the Ninth Battery, and that he was mustered into the service of the United States, on the 29th day of July, 1862, by Lieutenant Adams, of the United States Army.

ALEX. H. WHITAKER,
Lieutenant Ninth Battery.

This was indorsed as follows:

No. 30. MELROSE, Aug. 16, 1862.

I, Joseph A. Chapin, hereby acknowledge to have received of the Town Treasurer of Melrose, One Hundred Dollars as bounty for enlistment in the service of the United States, as within.

JOSEPH A. CHAPIN.
Witness, WILLIAM B. BURGESS.

The form of payment of Bounty for the nine months' men differed from the above only in the date of Town action — Aug. 21, 1862, — and the amount paid, One Hundred and Fifty Dollars.

C.

CERTIFICATE OF CONSENT TO THE ENLISTMENT OF A MINOR.

I, Hiram McLaughlin, do certify, that I am the father of George W. McLaughlin, that he is nineteen years of age; and I do hereby freely give my consent to his enlisting as a soldier in the Massachusetts Volunteer Militia, for the period of nine months in the service of the United States.

HIRAM McLAUGHLIN.
Witness, ROYAL P. BARRY.

Dated at Melrose, this first day of October, A. D. 1862.

D.

The following is a copy of the circular and list of the citizens of Melrose, liable to Draft in 1863, posted in our town by direction of Provost-Marshal Herrick.

ENROLLMENT LIST, SIXTH DISTRICT MASSACHUSETTS.

List of persons enrolled in Sub-District No. Nine, Town of Melrose.

Any person herein enrolled may appear before the Board of Enrollment, at Lawrence, on the   days of December, 1863, from eleven to one o'clock, and two to five o'clock, and have his name stricken off the List, if he can show to the satisfaction of the Board that he is not, and will not be at the time fixed for the next Draft, Jan. 5, 1864, liable to do Military duty on account of

1. Alienage. 2. Non-residence. 3. Unsuitableness of age. 4. Manifest permanent physical disability.

Class I.

A.

Allen, John L.
Allen, William H.
Atwood, Sullivan C.

Alden, David A.
Astle, James
Anderson, John H. L.

B.

Babb, Walter
Banfield, Addison W.
Barrett, Henry W.
Barrett, James A.
Barrett, Jonathan
Bartlett, Nathaniel J.
Biathrow, Franklin
Biffin, James

Bishop, Daniel H.
Blaisdell, Charles H.
Brackett, Gilbert A.
Brown, George E.
Brown, Laroy
Browne, Orrin
Bryant, Dexter

C.

Chase, Daniel L.
Chase, Sanford W.
Cheever, Augustus L.
Coburn, Lucius

Cook, William
Corson, George G.
Crocker, John H.

D.

Davis, Edmund W.
Dodge, James W.

Donalavy, William

E.

Edmonds, Artemas B.
Emerson, George W.
Emerson, Joseph S.

Emerson, Richard W.
Emery, Joshua Jr.

F.

Fairbanks, Joseph A.
Fargo, Charles O.
Farnsworth, George W.
Fernald, James H.
Finnegan, Dennis
Finnegan, Edward

Finnegan, William
Fennerty, Thomas
Freeman, Leander T.
French, Alonzo
Fuller, William A.
Furneaux, Charles

G.

Gilmore, William M.
Goodwin, Joseph
Gordon, Curtis S.
Gordon, William F.
Goss, Elbridge H.

Gould, Levi S.
Greene, Benjamin F.
Grover, Andrew J.
Grover, George W. Jr.
Grundy, William

H.

Hammond, George
Harris, Augustine
Hawkins, John
Hayward, Daniel E.
Hemmenway, William
Henderson, John H. B.
Hill, William L.

Hollahan, Lawrence
Hopkins, James S.
Howard, Caleb G.
Howard, Otis
Howe, Francis E.
Howes, Jonathan C.

APPENDIX.

I.

Irvine, Fayette J.

J.

Jackson, William P.

K.

Keating, Thomas
Keith, Charles E.
Keyes, Silas

Knight, Edwin F.
Knights, Edward R.
Knowles, Theodore L.

L.

Leonard, Henry A.
Littlehale, Henry A.
Lord, Samuel
Lyall, David S.
Lunt, George G.

Lynch, John B.
Lynde, Charles A.
Lynde, Daniel A.
Lynde, James O.
Lynde, Leonard

M.

Magoon, Sylvanus
McCafferty, Michael A.
McLenathan, Charles
Merrick, Theodore B.
Morcomb, Henry P.

Moseley, Randolph L.
Morse, William
Morse, William F.
Murray, John
Munn, Lawrence K.

N.

Newhall, Edward B.
Newhall, Henry B.

Norton, John R.

P.

Parker, Edward
Page, Moses S.
Patterson, Alonzo
Paul, William F.
Peck, Oren H.
Pierce, Ansel B.

Pierce, Robert W.
Pollock, George W.
Porter, Lucius L. D.
. Pratt, Dexter
Prentice, George

Q.

Quinn, Thomas

R.

Rankin, Frederick W. A. Jr.
Richards, Aaron H.
Richardson, Lewis H.
Richardson, William H.

Ripley, Augustus
Roberts, Joseph L.
Robbins, Charles
Robinson, Samuel A.

S.

Sanford, Joseph B.
Sears, Elisha F.
Shelton, Albert F.
Shelton, Richard H.
Shelton, Stephen W.
Skinner, Glover
Small, James M.
Spinney, William K.

Stantial, George C.
Stantial, Thomas B.
Stevens, Henry A.
Stone, George F.
Stone, William H.
Stratton, William D,
Smith, Rufus
Sutton, Joseph P. B.

T.

Tainter, George A.
Tay, Aaron
Taylor, Marcus C.
Taylor, William
Thompson, John

Tower, John W.
Tourtellot, Samuel M.
Towner, Levi C.
Trask, Albert
Trott, Andrew P.

U.

Upham, Albert
Upham, Charles F.
Upham, Osgood W.

Upham, Sylvanus
Upham, Timothy

V.

Vaughn, William W.

W.

Waitt, Charles A.
Warren, William
Watson, Frank
Wells, William H.

Wilcox, Daniel W.
Wilde, Joseph D.
Woodward, George
Wyman, William

APPENDIX.

Class II.

A.
Adams, John Q.

Avery, John Q. A.

B.
Baldwin, John
Barker, Samuel
Barrett, Augustus
Bartlett, George W.
Bickford, Ira H.
Bird, Henry S.
Boardman, George A.
Boardman, William W.

Brooks, Augustus
Brown, Benjamin
Bradford, Erastus F.
Brown, Increase H. Jr.
Brown, John
Bugbee, Samuel S.
Bryant, Napoleon B.
Buffum, Carlon

C.
Chapin, Calvin N.
Clark, William
Cleaveland, Nathan S.
Cobb, John W.
Cobb, Elisha W.
Coburn, Lewis G.
Conway, Daniel

Coolidge, Charles G.
Courriea, Charles M.
Crowley, Jeremiah
Curtis, Samuel
Chase, Daniel G.
Coffin, Galen
Connell, James

D.
Davie, George
Dow, Milo

Dyer, John A.

E.
Edgerly, Obadiah S.
Edgerly, Peter

Emerson, George 2d.
Emerson, Isaac Jr.

F.
Fessenden, George F.

Foster, Daniel W.

G.
Gateley, John
Gilman, Tristram
Gooch, Daniel W.

Goss, Allen C.
Gould, Albert A.
Greeley, William P.

H.

Haley, Reuben F.
Hamblet, James Jr.
Hart, George
Hawkins, Thomas
Hayward, Jabez G.
Heath, George W.
Hemmenway, George

Hicks, Walter
Hill, David
Hodges, James D.
Hoeffner, Lewis G.
Holbrook, Joseph
Horn, James
Hudson, Jarvis P.

I.

Isburgh, Charles H.

J.

Jefferson, Daniel

K.

Kelley, Farnsworth
Kendall, Samuel E.
Kent, Elisha V.

Kimball, Thomas J.
Kirmes, Christopher

L.

Lane, Addison
Lamson, William A.
Leavitt, Rufus
Little, Edmund B.

Littlefield, Walter Jr.
Loring, Martin B.
Lynde, Alonzo V.
Lynde, William O.

M.

Mansfield, George A.
McCoubry, Thomas
McIntyre, Joseph

Messenger, Charles A.
Messenger, Frank A.
Morton, Daniel O.

N.

Newhall, George
Newhall, John

Norton, Daniel Jr.

P.

Parker, Moses
Pemberton, Calvin
Perkins, Albert P.

Perkins, John Jr.
Poole, William F.

APPENDIX.

R.

Robbins, Charles G.
Roberts, John K.

Russell, Daniel

S.

Sales, Ephraim
Sargent, Wingate P.
Severence, Sargent F.
Severy, Solomon
Shepard, Thomas

Sewall, John S.
Simonds, Charles H.
Spaulding, Henry H
Sprague, Alfred W.
Stevens, Edgar M.

T.

Taylor, Fernando C.
Terwillager, Lyell S.

Trowbridge, Henry E
Turner, Henry

U.

Upham, Benjamin R.

Upham, Orne

V.

Varney, Cyrus
Vinton, Aaron Jr.

Vinton, Gray

W.

Warren, Ralph
West, John
Wheeler, Gardner
Wheeler, George G.

Wheeler, Robert
Whowell, John
Whyte, Oliver
Woodward, David R.

Y.

Young, Isaiah A.

H. G. HERRICK,
Captain and Provost-Marshal, Sixth Dist. Mass.

E.

EXEMPTION PAPERS.

Those citizens who had the pleasure of reading their names in the afternoon papers of July 13, 1863, as among the drafted, received soon afterwards a letter from the Provost-Marshal, notifying them of the fact, and to appear before the Board of Enrollment at Lawrence, for examination. If not exempted for any cause, a choice was given the accepted person to furnish a substitute, or pay commutation money. The following is the form of receipt and certificate given in the latter case.

SIXTH MASSACHUSETTS COLLECTION DISTRICT.
No. 121.

Received at Haverhill, on the fourteenth day of August, 1863, from Osgood W. Upham, of Melrose, who was drafted into the service of the United States, on the thirteenth day of July, 1863, from the Sixth Congressional District of the State of Massachusetts, the sum of Three Hundred Dollars ($300), to obtain, under Section 13 of the "Act for enrolling and calling out the national forces, and for other purposes — approved March 3, 1863," a discharge from further liability under the draft.

Signed in triplicate.

GEO. COGGSWELL,
Receiver of Commutation Money.

CERTIFICATE OF NON-LIABILITY TO BE GIVEN BY THE BOARD OF ENROLLMENT.

We, the subscribers, composing the Board of Enrollment of the Sixth District of the State of Massachusetts, provided for in Section 8, Act of Congress "for enrolling and calling out the national forces," approved March 3, 1863, hereby certify that Osgood W. Upham, of Melrose, Middlesex County, State of Massachusetts, having given satisfactory evidence that he is not properly subject to do military duty, as required by said act, by reason of having paid Three Hundred Dollars, is exempt from all liability to military duty for the term of the present draft.

H. G. HERRICK,
Provost-Marshal and Pres. Board of Enrollment.
P. E. DAVIS,
Member of Board of Enrollment.
J. L. SULLIVAN, JR.,
Surgeon of Board of Enrollment.

Dated at Lawrence, this twentieth day of August, 1863.

When a substitute was furnished, or when exemption was granted for the various causes, except disability, the same kind of certificate was used, differing only in the reason given for exemption. For exemption from disability the following was the form.

CERTIFICATE OF EXEMPTION FOR A DRAFTED PERSON ON ACCOUNT OF DISABILITY.

This is to certify, That ――― of Melrose, Middlesex County, State of Massachusetts, having been drafted, and claiming exemption on account of disability, has been carefully examined, and is found to be unfit for military duty by reason of ――― ――― and, in consequence thereof, he is exempt from service under the present draft.

H. G. HERRICK,
Provost-Marshal and Pres. Board of Enrollment.
P. E. DAVIS,
Member of Board of Enrollment.
J. L. SULLIVAN, JR.,
Surgeon of Board of Enrollment.

Dated at Lawrence, this thirty-first of July, 1863.

F.

CERTIFICATE OF NON-LIABILITY TO BE GIVEN BY THE BOARD OF ENROLLMENT.

We, the subscribers, composing the Board of Enrollment of the Sixth District of the State of Massachusetts, provided for in Section 8, Act of Congress, "for enrolling and calling out the national forces," approved March 3, 1863, hereby certify that George Emerson, 2d, of Melrose, of Middlesex County, State of Massachusetts, having given satisfactory evidence that he is not properly subject to do military duty, as required by said Act, and the Act approved Feb. 24, 1864, and July 4, 1864, by reason of having furnished an acceptable substitute, is exempt from all liability to draft, not exceeding the time for which his substitute was enlisted, viz., three years.

H. G. HERRICK,
Provost-Marshal and Pres. Board of Enrollment.
S. W. HOPKINSON,
Member of Board of Enrollment.
JOHN L. SULLIVAN, JR.,
Surgeon of Board of Enrollment.

Dated at Lawrence, Mass., this twenty-third day of July, 1864.

CERTIFICATE OF EXEMPTION OF THE SUBSTITUTE FURNISHED BY THE ABOVE.

I, Samuel Wilson, of Nova Scotia, do hereby certify that I am not legally subject to enrollment or draft, under the Acts of Congress for enrolling and calling out the national forces of the United States, and for the following reasons: That I am an alien and subject to the British Government. That I have never voted in, or declared my intention of becoming a citizen of the United States.

SAMUEL WILSON.

We, the subscribers, do hereby certify that we have such knowledge of said Samuel Wilson as to leave no doubt in our minds of the truth of his statement.

JAMES KUHN, of Boston, 11 *Clark Street.*
W. M. I. BOTHAM, of Boston, 9 *F. H. Square.*

SUFFOLK, SS.

Personally appeared the above named Samuel Wilson, James Kuhn, and W. M. I. Botham, and severally made oath that the above Certificate is correct and true, according to the best of their knowledge and belief.

Dated at Boston, Mass., this twentieth day of July, 1864.

[STAMP.]
THATCHER C. HATCH,
Justice of the Peace.

APPENDIX. 289

G.

RECEIPT AND CERTIFICATE FOR REPRESENTATIVE RECRUIT.

Commonwealth of Massachusetts.

TREASURER'S OFFICE, Boston, Aug. 1, 1864.

Received of Daniel Russell of Melrose, One Hundred and Twenty-Five Dollars, for account of the Provost-Marshal-General of the State of Massachusetts, to be used for recruiting purposes under General Order No. 27, 1864, such recruit to be credited to the quota of Melrose. Representative Recruit.

HENRY K. OLIVER,
Treasurer.

LEVI REED, *Auditor.*

Commonwealth of Massachusetts.

This is to certify that Daniel Russell of Melrose, in said Commonwealth, a citizen not liable to be drafted into the military service of the United States, has paid the sum of One Hundred and Twenty-Five Dollars into the State Treasury, under General Order of Commonwealth, No. 27, dated July 14, A. D. 1864, to assist in recruiting the national armies, and has had assigned to him as his Representative Recruit, Private Davis Jones, Fifty-Eighth U. S. Colored Infantry. Enlisted under the Act of Congress providing for the recruitment of volunteers in the Rebellious States, approved July 4, A.D. 1864.

Given under my hand, at the Head-Quarters of said Commonwealth at Boston, this fourth day of January, one thousand eight hundred and sixty-five.

JOHN A. ANDREW,
Governor of Commonwealth of Massachusetts.

J. M. DAY,
Colonel and Provost-Marshal of Commonwealth of Massachusetts.

H.

PROVOST-MARSHAL'S OFFICE,
6TH DISTRICT, MASS.,
LAWRENCE, May 6, 1864.

You are hereby informed that the Board of Enrollment of the Sixth District Massachusetts has appointed you an Enrolling Officer for the Sub-District, as follows, viz : No. 9, being the town of Melrose, at a compensation of three dollars per diem, for the time actually employed.

You will immediately enter upon your duties, and complete the enrollment required under the amended Enrollment Act of Feb. 24, 1864, without the least delay.

You will enroll,

1st. All persons liable to draft whose names have been omitted in the former enrollment. These omissions you will learn by reference to the accompanying printed lists.

2d. All persons who, since the former enrollment, and prior to this, shall have arrived at the age of twenty years.

3d. All aliens who have declared their intention of becoming citizens, and not heretofore enrolled.

4th. All persons discharged from the military or naval service of the United States, who have not been in such service two years during the present war, whether heretofore enrolled or not; except those borne upon the printed lists.

5th. You will enroll, upon separate sheets, the names of any and all persons whose names are borne on the printed lists, who shall have arrived at the age of forty-five at the time of the completion of your enrollment.

6th. You will return, on a separate sheet, the names of all persons borne on the printed list, who are now in the service, stating as far as you are able, their regiment and company, and all who have died.

H. G. HERRICK, *Capt. and Pro.-Mar.*,   *Board*
S. W. HOPKINSON, *Com'r*,   *of*
JOHN L. SULLIVAN, JR., *Surgeon*,   *Enrollment.*

To Mr. STEPHEN SHELTON, Melrose, Mass.

APPENDIX.

I.

DISCHARGE PAPERS.

ARMY.

To all whom it may concern.

[Vignette : Eagle standing on shield, surrounded with flags and stars.]

KNOW YE, That Moses S. Page, a Private of Captain Frank H. Whitcomb's Company (E) Sixth Regiment of Infantry, Massachusetts Volunteers, who was enrolled on the fifteenth day of July, 1864, to serve one hundred days, is hereby discharged from the service of the United States, this twenty-seventh day of October, 1864, at Readville, Massachusetts, by reason of term of enlistment having expired. (No objection to his being re-enlisted is known to exist.)

Said Moses S. Page was born in Haverhill, in the State of New Hampshire, is twenty-six years of age, five feet eight and one-half inches high, light complexion, blue eyes, brown hair, and by occupation, when enrolled, a Broker.

Given at Readville, this twenty-seventh day of October, 1864.

J. W. MEANS,
First Lieutenant Eighth Infantry, U. S. M. O.

FRANK H. WHITCOMB,
Captain Comd'g. Co. E, Sixth Mass. Reg't.

NAVY.

UNITED STATES OF AMERICA.

[Vignette : War vessels at sea.]

Navy Department.

The war for the preservation of the Union having, under the beneficent guidance of Almighty God, been brought to a successful termination, a reduction of the naval force becomes necessary.

Having served with fidelity in the United States Navy from the fourteenth day of November, 1862, to the present date, you are hereby honorably discharged with the thanks of the Department.

Given under my hand and seal of the Navy Department, at the City of Washington, this twentieth day of September, 1865.

GIDEON WELLES,
Secretary of the Navy.

{ SEAL OF THE NAVY }
{ DEPARTMENT. }

JAMES F. PERKINS,
Acting Ensign U. S. Navy,
Melrose, Mass.

J.

ACTION OF THE TOWN,

NOV. 3, 1868.

Hon. Samuel E Sewall offered the following resolution, which was unanimously adopted :

That the Selectmen be authorized to subscribe and pay for a sufficient number of copies of Mr. Elbridge H. Goss' work, entitled "The Melrose Memorial: The Annals of Melrose, County of Middlesex, Massachusetts, during the Great Rebellion of 1861-5," to furnish a copy to every inhabitant of this town who served as a soldier or sailor in the Rebellion, now living, and a copy for the family of each of said soldiers and sailors as have deceased; also for twenty-five additional copies for the town, any of which may be given to public libraries at the discretion of the Selectmen.

And on motion of Hon. Daniel W. Gooch, it was voted that the following inscription be embossed in gilt letters on the cover of each copy thus given :

Presented to — (name of soldier or sailor) — by the Town of Melrose, in recognition of his services during the Great Rebellion of 1861-5.

ERRATA.

Page 100 — For Bodwell, *Daniel* A., read *Henry* A.

" 175 — For *James* S. Macey, read *John* S. Macey.

" 243 — Omitted in List of Officers in the Navy:

SMITH W. NICHOLS, Jr. Midshipman, Sept. 27, 1858; Lieutenant, Feb. 21, 1863; Lieutenant Commander, July 25, 1866.

Page 256 — Omitted in Alphabetical Roll:

Jones, J. Wesley, 12th U. S. Inf. 1st Lieut.

www.ingramcontent.com/pod-product-compliance
Lightning Source LLC
Chambersburg PA
CBHW030750230426
43667CB00007B/910